References for the Rest of Us

COMPUTER BOOK SERIES FROM IDG

Are you baffled and bewildered by programming? Does it seem like an impenetrable puzzle? Do you find that traditional manuals are overloaded with technical terms you don't understand? Do you want to know how to get your PC to do what you want? Then the *...For Dummies* programming book series from IDG is for you.

...For Dummies programming books are written for frustrated computer users who know they really aren't dumb but find that programming, with its unique vocabulary and logic, makes them feel helpless. *...For Dummies* programming books use a humorous approach and a down-to-earth style to diffuse fears and build confidence. Lighthearted but not lightweight, these books are a perfect survival guide for first-time programmers or anyone learning a new environment.

"Simple, clear, and concise. Just what I needed."
—Steve P., Greenville, SC

"Finally, someone made learning to program easy and entertaining. Thanks!"
—Diane W., Chicago, IL

"When I saw this book I decided to give programming one last try. And I'm glad I did!"
—Paul G., St. Louis, MO

Millions of satisfied readers have made *...For Dummies* books the #1 introductory-level computer book series and have written asking for more. So if you're looking for a fun and easy way to learn about computers, look to *...For Dummies* books to give you a helping hand.

POWERBUILDER 4 PROGRAMMING FOR DUMMIES™

POWERBUILDER 4 PROGRAMMING FOR DUMMIES™

Jason Coombs

and

Ted Coombs

IDG Books Worldwide, Inc.
An International Data Group Company

Foster City, CA • Chicago, IL • Indianapolis, IN • Braintree, MA • Dallas, TX

PowerBuilder 4 Programming For Dummies

Published by
IDG Books Worldwide, Inc.
An International Data Group Company
919 East Hillsdale Boulevard, Suite 400
Foster City, CA 94404

Library of Congress Catalog Card No.: 94-73171

ISBN 1-56884-325-9

Printed in the United States of America

First Printing, March, 1995

10 9 8 7 6 5 4 3 2 1

Distributed in the United States by IDG Books Worldwide, Inc.

For More Information...

For general information on IDG Books in the U.S., including information on discounts and premiums, contact IDG Books at 800-434-3422.

For information on where to purchase IDG's books outside the U.S., contact Christina Turner at 415-655-3022.

For information on translations, contact Marc Jeffrey Mikulich, Foreign Rights Manager, at IDG Books Worldwide; fax number: 415-655-3295.

For sales inquires and special prices for bulk quantities, contact Tony Real at 800-434-3422 or 415-655-3048.

For information on using IDG's books in the classroom and ordering examination copies, contact Jim Kelly at 800-434-2086.

The ...*For Dummies* book series is distributed in Canada by Macmillan of Canada, a Division of Canada Publishing Corporation; by Computer and Technical Books in Miami, Florida, for South America and the Caribbean; by Longman Singapore in Singapore, Malaysia, Thailand, and Korea; by Toppan Co. Ltd. in Japan; by Asia Computerworld in Hong Kong; by Woodslane Pty. Ltd. in Australia and New Zealand; and by Transword Publishers Ltd. in the U.K. and Europe.

Welcome to the world of IDG Books Worldwide.

IDG Books Worldwide, Inc. is a subsidiary of International Data Group, the world's largest publisher of computer-related information and the leading global provider of information services on information technology. IDG was founded more than 25 years ago and now employs more than 7,000 people worldwide. IDG publishes more than 220 computer publications in 65 countries (see listing below). More than fifty million people read one or more IDG publications each month.

Launched in 1990, IDG Books Worldwide is today the #1 publisher of best-selling computer books in the United States. We are proud to have received 3 awards from the Computer Press Association in recognition of editorial excellence, and our best-selling *...For Dummies*™ series has more than 15 million copies in print with translations in 25 languages. IDG Books, through a recent joint venture with IDG's Hi-Tech Beijing, became the first U.S. publisher to publish a computer book in the People's Republic of China. In record time, IDG Books has become the first choice for millions of readers around the world who want to learn how to better manage their businesses.

Our mission is simple: Every IDG book is designed to bring extra value and skill-building instructions to the reader. Our books are written by experts who understand and care about our readers. The knowledge base of our editorial staff comes from years of experience in publishing, education, and journalism — experience which we use to produce books for the '90s. In short, we care about books, so we attract the best people. We devote special attention to details such as audience, interior design, use of icons, and illustrations. And because we use an efficient process of authoring, editing, and desktop publishing our books electronically, we can spend more time ensuring superior content and spend less time on the technicalities of making books.

You can count on our commitment to deliver high-quality books at competitive prices on topics consumers want to read about. At IDG, we value quality, and we have been delivering quality for more than 25 years. You'll find no better book on a subject than an IDG book.

John Kilcullen
President and CEO
IDG Books Worldwide, Inc.

IDG Books Worldwide, Inc. is a subsidiary of International Data Group, the world's largest publisher of computer-related information and the leading global provider of information services on information technology. International Data Group publishes over 220 computer publications in 65 countries. More than fifty million people read one or more International Data Group publications each month. The officers are Patrick J. McGovern, Founder and Board Chairman; Kelly Conlin, President; Jim Casella, Chief Operating Officer. International Data Group's publications include: **ARGENTINA'S** Computerworld Argentina, Infoworld Argentina; **AUSTRALIA'S** Computerworld Australia, Computer Living, Australian PC World, Australian Macworld, Network World, Mobile Business Australia, Publish!, Reseller, IDG Sources; **AUSTRIA'S** Computerwelt Oesterreich, PC Test; **BELGIUM'S** Data News (CW); **BOLIVIA'S** Computerworld; **BRAZIL'S** Computerworld, Connections, Game Power, Mundo Unix, PC World, Publish, Super Game; **BULGARIA'S** Computerworld Bulgaria, PC & Mac World Bulgaria, Network World Bulgaria; **CANADA'S** CIO Canada, Computerworld Canada, InfoCanada, Network World Canada, Reseller; **CHILE'S** Computerworld Chile, Informatica; **COLOMBIA'S** Computerworld Colombia, PC World; **COSTA RICA'S** PC World; **CZECH REPUBLIC'S** Computerworld, Elektronika, PC World; **DENMARK'S** Communications World, Computerworld Danmark, Computerworld Focus, Macintosh Produktkatalog, Macworld Danmark, PC World Danmark, PC Produktguide, Tech World, Windows World; **ECUADOR'S** PC World Ecuador; **EGYPT'S** Computerworld (CW) Middle East, PC World Middle East; **FINLAND'S** MikroPC, Tietoviikko, Tietoverkko; **FRANCE'S** Distributique, GOLDEN MAC, InfoPC, Le Guide du Monde Informatique, Le Monde Informatique, Telecoms & Reseaux; **GERMANY'S** Computerwoche, Computerwoche Focus, Computerwoche Extra, Electronic Entertainment, Gamepro, Information Management, Macwelt, Netzwelt, PC Welt, Publish, Publish; **GREECE'S** Publish & Macworld; **HONG KONG'S** Computerworld Hong Kong, PC World Hong Kong; **HUNGARY'S** Computerworld SZT, PC World; **INDIA'S** Computers & Communications; **INDONESIA'S** Info Komputer; **IRELAND'S** ComputerScope; **ISRAEL'S** Beyond Windows, Computerworld Israel, Multimedia, PC World Israel; **ITALY'S** Computerworld Italia, Lotus Magazine, Macworld Italia, Networking Italia, PC Shopping Italy, PC World Italia; **JAPAN'S** Computerworld Today, Information Systems World, Macworld Japan, Nikkei Personal Computing, SunWorld Japan, Windows World; **KENYA'S** East African Computer News; **KOREA'S** Computerworld Korea, Macworld Korea, PC World Korea; **LATIN AMERICA'S** GamePro; **MALAYSIA'S** Computerworld Malaysia, PC World Malaysia; **MEXICO'S** Compu Edicion, Compu Manufactura, Computacion/Punto de Venta, Computerworld Mexico, MacWorld, Mundo Unix, PC World, Windows; **THE NETHERLANDS'** Computer! Totaal, Computable (CW), LAN Magazine, Lotus Magazine, MacWorld; **NEW ZEALAND'S** Computer Buyer, Computerworld New Zealand, Network World, New Zealand PC World; **NIGERIA'S** PC World Africa; **NORWAY'S** Computerworld Norge, Lotusworld Norge, Macworld Norge, Maxi Data, Networld, PC World Ekspress, PC World Nettverk, PC World Norge, PC World's Produktguide, Publish& Multimedia World, Student Data, Unix World, Windowsworld; **PAKISTAN'S** PC World Pakistan; **PANAMA'S** PC World Panama; **PERU'S** Computerworld Peru, PC World; **PEOPLE'S REPUBLIC OF CHINA'S** China Computerworld, China Infoworld, China PC Info Magazine, Computer Fan, PC World China, Electronics International, Electronics Today/Multimedia World, Electronic Product World, China Network World, Software World Magazine, Telecom Product World; **PHILIPPINES'** Computerworld Philippines, PC Digest (PCW); **POLAND'S** Computerworld Poland, Computerworld Special Report, Networld, PC World/Komputer, Sunworld; **PORTUGAL'S** Cerebro/PC World, Correio Informatico/Computerworld, MacIn; **ROMANIA'S** Computerworld, PC World, Telecom Romania; **RUSSIA'S** Computerworld-Moscow, Mir - PK (PCW), Sety (Networks); **SINGAPORE'S** Computerworld Southeast Asia, PC World Singapore; **SLOVENIA'S** Monitor Magazine; **SOUTH AFRICA'S** Computer Mail (CIO),Computing S.A.,Network World S.A., Software World; **SPAIN'S** Advanced Systems, Amiga World, Computerworld Espana, Communicaciones World, Macworld Espana, NeXTWORLD, Super Juegos Magazine (GamePro), PC World Espana, Publish; **SWEDEN'S** Attack, ComputerSweden, Corporate Computing, Macworld, Mikrodatorn, Natverk & Kommunikation, PC World, CAP & Design, Datalngenjoren, Maxi Data,Windows World; **SWITZERLAND'S** Computerworld Schweiz, Macworld Schweiz, PC Tip; **TAIWAN'S** Computerworld Taiwan, PC World Taiwan; **THAILAND'S** Thai Computerworld; **TURKEY'S** Computerworld Monitor, Macworld Turkiye, PC World Turkiye; **UKRAINE'S** Computerworld, Computers+Software Magazine; **UNITED KINGDOM'S** Computing /Computerworld, Connexion/Network World, Lotus Magazine, Macworld, Open Computing/Sunworld; **UNITED STATES'** Advanced Systems, AmigaWorld, Cable in the Classroom, CD Review, CIO, Computerworld, Computerworld Client/Server Journal, Digital Video, DOS World, Electronic Entertainment Magazine (E2), Federal Computer Week, Game Hits, GamePro, IDG Books, Infoworld, Laser Event, Macworld, Maximize, Multimedia World, Network World, PC Letter, PC World, Publish, SWATPro, Video Event; **URUGUAY'S** PC World Uruguay; **VENEZUELA'S** Computerworld Venezuela, PC World; **VIETNAM'S** PC World Vietnam.

About the Authors

Since 1972 **Ted Coombs** has stayed at the forefront of technology in the areas of electronics, lasers, robotics, computer networking, telecommunications, database technology, and software development. His education is in biological anthropology, and he follows a deep interest in ocean sciences. For the last several years Ted has been actively involved with the Internet. As President of Pacific Knowledge, a science and engineering think tank, he saw how this technology would begin reshaping the way people communicate. He began following the development of technologies such as multimedia, VR, wireless packet data communications, and GPS.

Ted has authored several large PowerBuilder applications for organizations such as the State of California, Nielsen Media Research, and many other businesses. He began developing applications using PowerBuilder 2.0 and has continued using PowerBuilder 3.0 Enterprise and Desktop editions.

He currently lives and works on his sailboat in San Diego. He can be reached at tedc@pk.com.

Jason Coombs has worked in the computer and telecommunications industries since 1991 when he co-founded Pacific Knowledge. Since then Jason has conducted research in many areas of science and technology including aspects of computer science such as software engineering and computer networking.

Jason's software engineering experience includes work on large cellular communications systems, business management and automation tools, and cable television analysis applications. He has developed software in many languages and under several operating systems including UNIX, Macintosh, and MSDOS/Windows. His Internet e-mail address is jasonc@pk.com.

Credits

Vice President
Christopher J. Williams

Publishing Director
Amorette Pedersen

Project Editor
Anne Marie Walker

Manuscript Editor
Vicki L. Hochstedler

Technical Reviewer
Mark Jordan

Managing Editor
Beth A. Roberts

Proofreader
Mildred Rosenzweig

Indexer
Liz Cunningham

Composition and Layout
Ronnie K. Bucci
Reuben Kantor

Book Design
University Graphics

Cover Design
Kavish + Kavish

Dedication

"Iron rusts from disuse, stagnant water loses its purity and in cold weather becomes frozen; even so does inaction sap the vigors of the mind."

— *Leonardo da Vinci*

This book is dedicated to the memory of Leonardo da Vinci, the World's most famous Application Painter.

Acknowledgements

We would like to thank all of the people who helped make this book possible. Thanks to Anne Marie Walker, who made it through her first ...*For Dummies* project without killing us or sending Navy Seals to sink our boat. We want to thank Vicki Hochstedler for doing a really thorough '"editing"' job. Mark Jordan, who technically edited this book; thanks for your insight and for hanging in there. We want to thank everyone at Powersoft for both creating such an excellent product, and for helping us with this book. A very special thanks goes to Amy Pedersen for believing in us. We have your number programmed in our speed dialer under Emergency. Kate Tolini, you really are wonderful. We want to thank all of the people at Waterside Productions for putting up with us. Mr. Patrick McGovern, we don't know you, but thanks for making all our *Dummies* books possible.

Contents at a Glance

Cartoons at a Glance

by Rich Tennant

"HOW SHOULD I KNOW WHY THEY TOOK IT OFF THE LIST? MAYBE THERE JUST WEREN'T ENOUGH MEMBERS TO SUPPORT AN 'AIREDALES FOR ELVIS' BULLETIN BOARD."

page 1

"A CONSULTANT TOLD US THAT POLYESTER CAN CAUSE SHORTS IN THE SYSTEM, SO WE'RE TRYING AN ALL LEATHER AND LATEX DATA ENTRY DEPARTMENT."

page 83

"WHY A 4GL TOASTER? I DON'T THINK YOU'D ASK THAT QUESTION IF YOU THOUGHT A MINUTE ABOUT HOW TO BALANCE THE MAXIMIZATION OF TOAST DEVELOPMENT PRODUCTIVITY AGAINST TOASTER RESOURCE UTILIZATION IN A MULTI-DINER ENVIRONMENT."

page 29

"A STORY ABOUT A SOFTWARE COMPANY THAT SHIPS BUG-FREE PROGRAMS ON TIME, WITH TOLL-FREE SUPPORT, AND FREE UPGRADES? NAAAH - TOO WEIRD."

page xxv

"YOU KNOW THAT GUY WHO BOUGHT ALL THAT SOFTWARE? HIS CHECK HAS A WARRANTY THAT SAYS IT'S TENDERED AS IS AND HAS NO FITNESS FOR ANY PARTICULAR PURPOSE INCLUDING, BUT NOT LIMITED TO, CASHING."

page 308

"I SAAAID WHAT COMPANY DO YOU REPRESENT?"

page 259

"Here at MIC, leaders in OEM, it's SOP to wish a happy retirement to a great MIS like Douglas U. Hodges, or, DUH as we came to know him."

page 279

"'MORNING MR. DREYEL. I HEARD YOU SAY YOUR COMPUTERS ALL HAD BUGS. WELL, I FIGURE THEY'RE CRAWLING IN THROUGH THOSE SLOTS THEY HAVE, SO I JAMMED A COUPLE OF ROACH-DISKS IN EACH ONE. LET ME KNOW IF YOU HAVE ANY MORE PROBLEMS."

page 20

SO POORLY DOCUMENTED IS THE SOFTWARE THAT ROY IS BETA TESTING THAT HE FAILS TO NOTICE THAT THE GAME RULES TO "TWISTER" HAVE ACCIDENTALLY BEEN INCLUDED.

page 169

"OH THOSE? THEY'RE THE SEAT-CUSHION-MOUSE. BOUNCE ONCE TO ACCESS A FILE, TWICE TO FILE AWAY - KEEPS THE HANDS FREE AND THE BUTTOCKS FIRM."

page 319

Table of Contents

Introduction

PowerBuilder is the number one cross-platform, client-server software development tool, and *PowerBuilder 4.0 Programming For Dummies* shows you how to take advantage of its power with simple-to-follow explanations. This light and humorous guide to developing applications in PowerBuilder will get you started writing applications quickly and painlessly. Combining the strength of PowerBuilder and the clear style of the ...*For Dummies* series, *PowerBuilder 4.0 Programming For Dummies* is your guide to object-based development and client-server database application programming. With this book you will be developing PowerBuilder applications in no time.

"A STORY ABOUT A SOFTWARE COMPANY THAT SHIPS BUG-FREE PROGRAMS ON TIME, WITH TOLL-FREE SUPPORT, AND FREE UPGRADES? NAAAH – TOO WEIRD."

Who This Book Is For

This book is for entry-level to seasoned application developers who want to learn PowerBuilder 4.0 programming quickly and easily. This book is ideal for anyone who wants to get right to the heart of developing client-server applications with PowerBuilder 4.0.

About This Book

This book is your guide to developing applications with PowerBuilder 4.0. This fun and easy-to-read book covers some of the most important topics in desktop computing, such as:

- Developing graphic user interfaces
- Writing client-server database applications
- The ins and outs of cross-platform development

While working with this book you will master the PowerBuilder Painters that help you create windows, objects, functions, expressions, and SQL. By using these tools you can create complete applications with very little code writing.

This book teaches you to develop applications using the PowerBuilder PowerScript language. You will learn how easy it is to write event-driven programs, use the principles of object-orientation, and write programs that run in the Windows, Macintosh, and Xwindows environments.

How This Book Is Organized

This book has seven parts that take you through the steps of developing an application in PowerBuilder 4.0. The book begins right away with creating an application object, the foundation of all PowerBuilder applications. It then takes you through communicating with your database using PowerBuilder's Database Painter. From there, you'll learn how to create windows, add PowerScript code, and create your own objects.

If this is your first time using PowerBuilder, it's a good idea to start at the beginning and work your way through the book. Each chapter successively builds on principles and explanations from the chapter before. If you are a veteran PowerBuilder programmer and want to learn the finer points of PowerBuilder 4.0, you may want to go right to your favorite part:

- *Part I* gets you started building your application with the right foundation.
- *Part II* teaches you a fun and easy way to administer and work with your database.
- *Part III* covers what you need to know to create excellent graphic user interfaces.
- *Part IV* guides you through one of the most powerful data management tools, the DataWindow.
- *Part V* helps you learn how to create your executable program and deploy your application.
- *Part VI* provides more information on creating dynamic and versatile PowerBuilder applications
- *Part VII* is the Part of Tens, a treasure trove of information on objects, optimizing your application, and cross-platform development.

Icons Used in This Book

There are several icons used in this book to identify important points and things to watch out for.

This points out one of two things: First, it may alert you to important things that you should try to remember. Or, it may remind you of things you're already supposed to be remembering. ■

This one identifies technical discussions that aren't essential to the material being covered, but that offer insight into why something is the way it is. You can skip these if you'd like. ■

The tip icon looks like a crop circle. Crop circles may be aliens trying to give you tips on better PowerBuilder programming. ■

Watch out! There are some things you should be careful to avoid. This icon points these out for you. ■

Keep your eye on these icons as they guide you through the fun and interesting adventure of PowerBuilder Programming. Be the first on your block to create client-server applications that will run on multiple platforms. Create applications in a distributed environment so you can mix them, match them, and trade them with your friends. Use the mother-approved non-toxic PowerBuilder Painters to assemble powerful applications right before your eyes. These applications are "As seen on TV." No sales reps will call you. No operators are standing by. It's all up to you. PowerBuilder is within your grasp. Don't reach for the stars, reach for your keyboard, and remember, only you can prevent forest fires.

Part I

Taking Care of Business with PowerBuilder

"HOW SHOULD I KNOW WHY THEY TOOK IT OFF THE LIST? MAYBE THERE JUST WEREN'T ENOUGH MEMBERS TO SUPPORT AN 'AIREDALES FOR ELVIS' BULLETIN BOARD."

In This Part...

Imagine if programming were as simple as coloring in a coloring book. Some blue here, some red there, and poof, your network-ready cross-platform client-server database application would be finished. With Power-Builder as your application development tool and with this book to guide you, it's almost that easy.

In Part 1, you'll learn how applications are crafted in PowerBuilder. We'll show you how PowerBuilder supports the entire software engineering process — planning, design, development, debugging, and documentation. When you're finished with Part 1, you'll be ready to start programming in PowerBuilder.

Chapter 1

Building a PowerBuilder Application

In This Chapter

- Creating new applications with the Application Painter
- Visually managing the files in your application with the Library Painter

PowerBuilder applications are crafted with programming tools called *painters*. Painters simplify application development by doing some of the work for you so you can concentrate on the more interesting programming challenges in your application. Painters are a bit like work centers — each one allows you to perform a different type of programming task.

Two of PowerBuilder's painters are covered in this chapter; we'll introduce more of them in later chapters. Notice that these tools are called painters, not artists. You're the artist in PowerBuilder programming — the painters are simply your assistants.

Don't Do It Yourself, Hire a Painter

The people who designed and wrote PowerBuilder put a lot of thought into making your job as a programmer easier. "Why," they must have reasoned, "should programmers waste their time fiddling with database interface peculiarities and operating system quirks when they could be designing and building exceptional applications?" Thus they created painters to handle these things for you.

Table 1-1 lists the major PowerBuilder painters and briefly describes their purposes. Some painters, like the Database Painter, contain additional painters that we describe later.

Table 1-1: PowerBuilder Painters

Painter	*Purpose*
Application Painter	Helps you create new applications
Window Painter	Makes it easy to build complete windows
Menu Painter	Creates the basics of a menu and allows you to customize the menu for your needs
DataWindow Painter	Allows you to create special data entry and reporting formats called DataWindows
Structure Painter	Builds custom PowerBuilder variable types
Database Painter	Lets you create and manage databases graphically
Query Painter	Allows you to define database queries visually
Function Painter	Builds custom PowerBuilder functions
Project Painter	Manages information about ongoing development projects
Library Painter	Allows you to visually manage the files in your application
User Object Painter	Defines new PowerBuilder objects

...And an electrician

Like many other applications, PowerBuilder provides special icon menus called *toolbars* that are easier to use than standard menus. To select an item from a toolbar, simply click on one of the icons with your mouse.

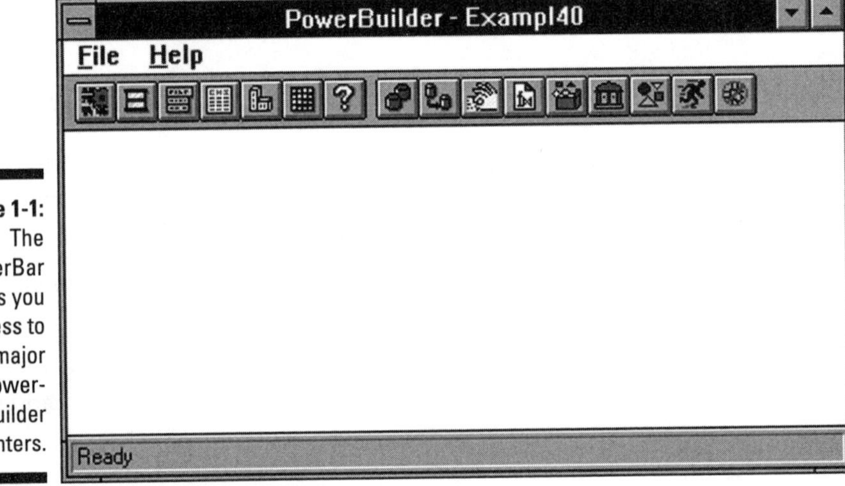

Figure 1-1: The PowerBar gives you access to the major Power-Builder painters.

Figure 1-1 shows the main PowerBuilder toolbar, called the *PowerBar*. The PowerBar appears when you start PowerBuilder; use it to access the painters listed in Table 1-1.

Each PowerBar icon runs a different part of the PowerBuilder development environment. Table 1-2 describes each of these icons.

The PowerBar doesn't have to stay at the top of the screen. You can move it to the left, right, or bottom of the screen — it can even float around aimlessly. To change the location of the PowerBar, do the following:

1. Choose the Toolbars... option from the File menu to open the Toolbars window shown in Figure 1-2.
2. Click on the Move radio button to change the location of the PowerBar.
3. Click on the Done button to accept your changes.

If you want to hide the PowerBar, click on the Hide button. The Hide button then changes to a Show button. Click on the Show button to see the PowerBar again. When you're tired of playing Hide and Show, click on the Done button. ■

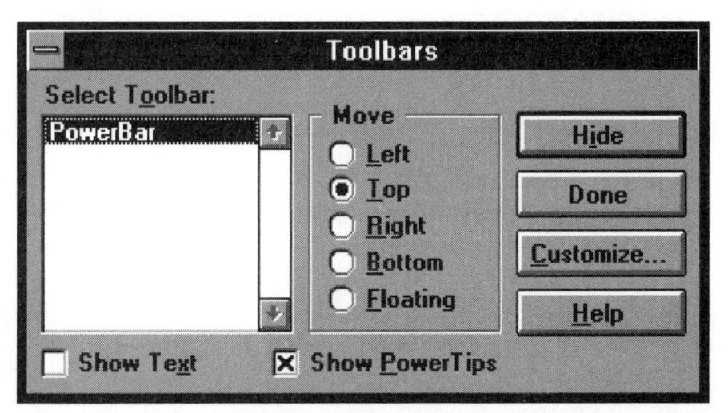

Figure 1-2: Use the Toolbars window to configure the PowerBuilder toolbars.

The PowerPanel is shocking

While the PowerBar is simple to use, it displays only a subset of the icons available in PowerBuilder. To select from a complete list of icons, use the *PowerPanel*. The PowerPanel is a popup window that can be opened from anywhere in PowerBuilder by pressing Ctrl+P. You can also open the PowerPanel by choosing PowerPanel... from the File menu.

When the PowerPanel appears on the screen, click on the icon for the painter or tool you want to access. To see a description of an icon, press and hold the left mouse button while the mouse pointer is on top of the icon. A description will be displayed in the Description section of the PowerPanel.

Table 1-2: The PowerBar icons

Icon	*Description*
	The Application Painter
	The Window Painter
	The Menu Painter
	The DataWindow Painter
	The Structure Painter
	System Preferences setup
	On-line Help
	The Database Painter
	The Query Painter
	The Function Painter
	The Project Painter
	The Library Painter
	The User Object Painter
	Run current application
	Debug current application

...And professional decorators

When you install and run PowerBuilder for the first time, the PowerBar is set up as shown in Figure 1-1. This is the default configuration for the PowerBar. You can customize the PowerBar by doing the following:

1. Choose the Toolbars... option from the File menu to open the Toolbars window.
2. Click on the Customize... button to open the Customize window shown in Figure 1-3.
3. To add an icon to the PowerBar, click and drag an icon from the Selected palette to the Current toolbar.
4. To remove an icon from the PowerBar, click and drag an icon from the Current toolbar to the Selected palette.
5. To add custom icons to the PowerBar, click on the Custom radio button then click and drag an icon from the Selected palette to the Current toolbar. This will open the Toolbar Item Command window, as shown in Figure 1-4.
6. Type a command in the Command Line: field or press the Browse... button to find the program you want to run when the icon is clicked.
7. If you want a query or a report to be executed when you click the custom icon, you can click on one of the Special Command buttons.
8. Click on the OK button when you're done setting up the custom icon.
9. When you've finished making changes to the PowerBar, click on the OK button in the Customize window.

Simple icon menus and painters are the foundations of PowerBuilder programming. When you're comfortable using painters and familiar with the PowerBuilder toolbars, you'll know enough about PowerBuilder programming to do just about anything you need to do.

Give Me a Home

You won't hear any discouraging words from us if you create a new directory to hold the files for your application. Using a separate directory, sometimes known as a folder, for each application makes file management much simpler. We've even heard that it keeps antelope from bothering you while you work.

If you don't create a new directory or folder for your application, you'll have to choose an existing one. Once you have a place for your files to live, use the Application Painter to create a new application.

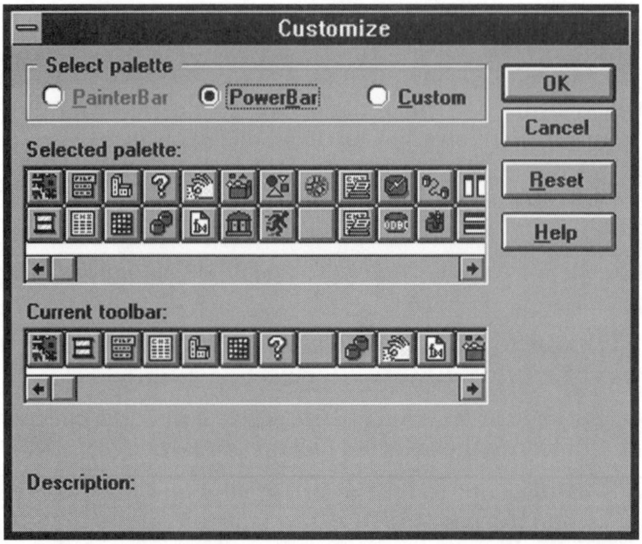

Figure 1-3: The Customize window lets you configure the toolbars in PowerBuilder.

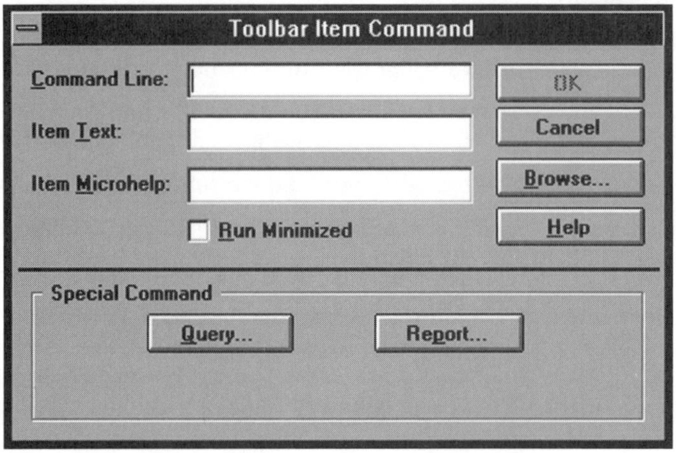

Figure 1-4: Use the Toolbar Item Command window to define custom icons on a toolbar.

Leonardo da Vinci was an application painter

To start the Application Painter, click on the application icon in the PowerBar (see Table 1-2). Figure 1-5 shows the Application Painter. By default, the current application is the PowerBuilder sample application called Exampl40. If you've previously selected a different application or created one of your own, then that application will be the current application.

The vertical toolbar in Figure 1-5 is the *PainterBar*. The PainterBar is a painter-specific toolbar that contains different icons depending on which painter you're in. In the Application Painter's PainterBar, the bottom icon exits the Application Painter.

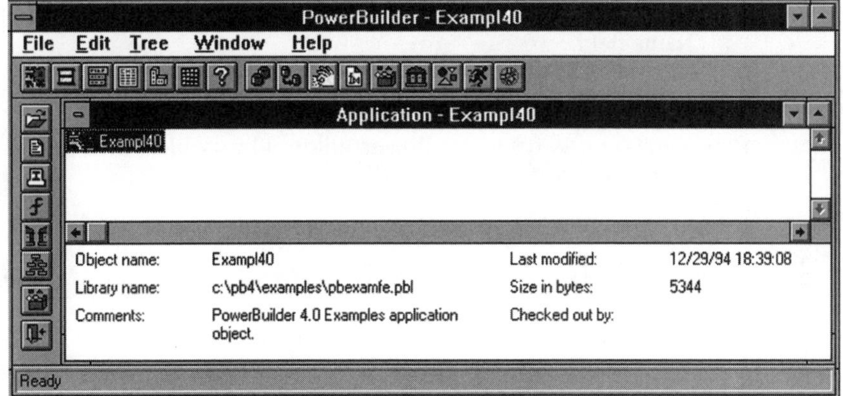

Figure 1-5: The Application Painter lets you create new PowerBuilder applications.

Just like the PowerBar, all PainterBars are customizable. Click on either toolbar with the right mouse button and choose Customize... from the popup menu. Then follow the instructions given in the previous section to customize the PainterBar. ■

To create a new application, choose New... from the File menu. The Select New Application Library window shown in Figure 1-6 appears on the screen. You'll select a *PowerBuilder library* file for your application from this window. PowerBuilder library files (.PBL files) store the components of an application such as its windows, menus, and custom functions. Every part of a PowerBuilder application except the database itself resides in one .PBL file or another.

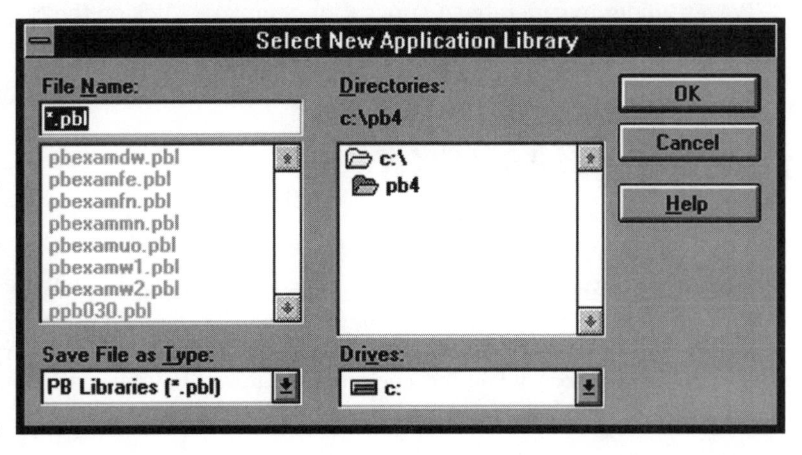

Figure 1-6: Use the Select New Application Library window to select a library for your new application.

To create a new PowerBuilder library file, do the following in the Select New Application Library window:

1. Use the Directories list box to choose the directory in which you'd like to create a new PowerBuilder library.
2. Next, pick a name for the new PowerBuilder library and type it in the File Name field.
3. Click on the OK button to accept your name and directory selections.

PowerBuilder creates a new PowerBuilder library file with a .PBL file extension in the directory you selected.

No talking in the PowerBuilder Library

Now that you have a PowerBuilder library, you can choose a name and let PowerBuilder get on with the business of creating a new *application object.* An application object is a lot like the big X on a pirate's treasure map. It lets you know which library the application is buried in. If you're like us, you love libraries and visit them every chance you get. The application object helps you remember which library you buried your application in, so you don't need to dig up all of them to find it later.

The Save Application window appears next, allowing you to give your application object a name. You may also type a description of your application in the Comments section. See Figure 1-7 for an example. When you're done, click on the OK button to save the application object in the PowerBuilder library file.

Once the application object is saved, the Application Painter will display your new application object. A message then appears that asks if you'd like PowerBuilder to generate an application template. Click on the No button. Otherwise, see Chapter 23 if you'd like to know more about this feature.

Managing Files with the Library Painter

The Library Painter manages the contents of PowerBuilder library files (.PBL files). It's like an electronic librarian that keeps everything tidy and organized and will never charge you overdue fees. Figure 1-8 shows the Library Painter. To access the Library Painter, click on the Library Painter icon in the PowerBar. (See Table 1-2.)

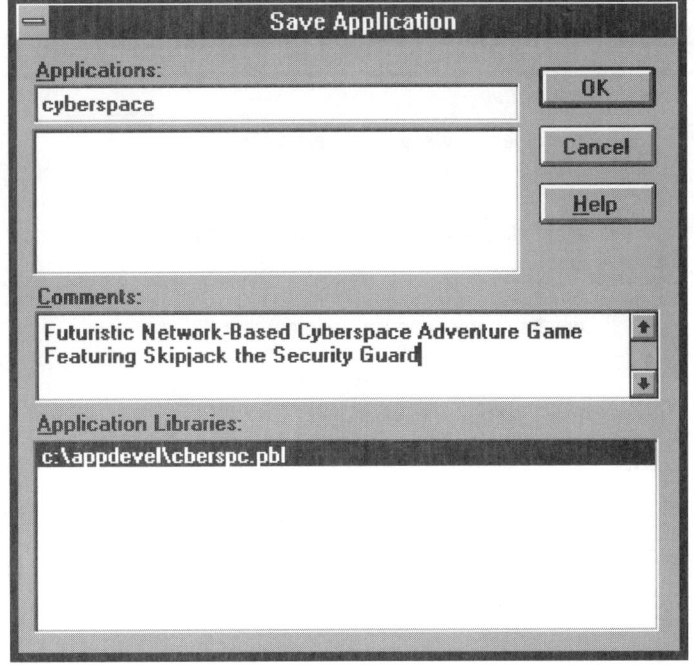

Figure 1-7: Give your new application object a name using the Save Application window.

The Library Painter PainterBar, shown in Figure 1-8 on the left side of the screen, lets you execute the most common Library Painter commands. Table 1-3 describes each icon on the Library Painter PainterBar.

Examining the contents of a library

Each PowerBuilder library file appears in the Library Painter as a small building slightly resembling a library. To open or close a library file, double-click on the small building. When a library is open, as in Figure 1-8, yellow light shines through the doorway. When a library is closed, double doors appear in the doorway.

When a library is open, each item in the library is displayed below the small building. An icon that indicates the item's type appears next to each item. To modify an item using the painter that created it, simply double-click on the item. The appropriate painter appears, containing the item. If you just want to select an item, click on it once and it will be highlighted, letting you know that it's selected.

Table 1-3: The Library Painter PainterBar icons

Icon	*Description*
	Create new PowerBuilder library file
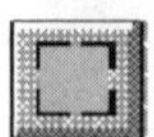	Select all items in current PowerBuilder library
	Copy items from one library to another
	Delete selected library items
	Move selected library items between libraries
	Regenerate (recompile) selected items
	Export item to a file
	Import item from a file
	Search selected items for key words
	Check in selected items
	Check out selected items
	View checkout status of items
	List PVCS registration directory

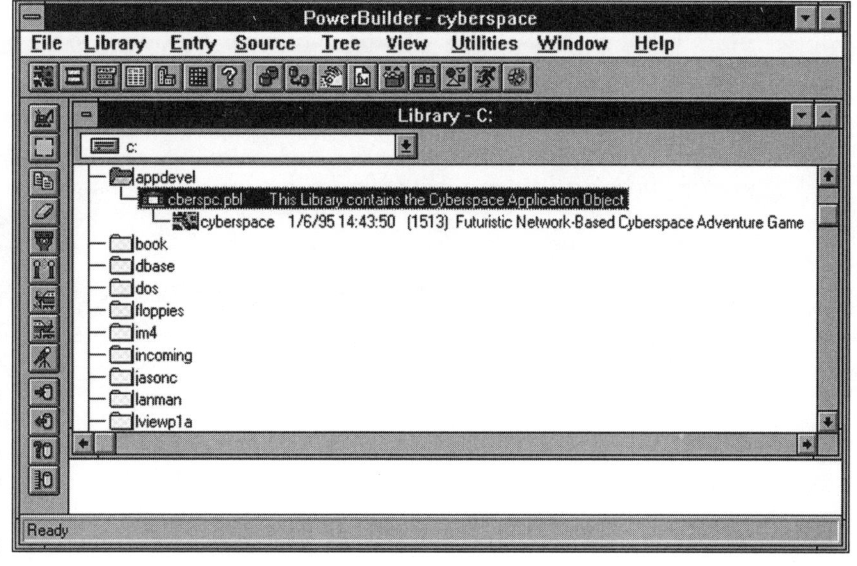

Figure 1-8: Manage the contents of your PowerBuilder libraries with the help of the Library Painter.

To select multiple items, do one of the following:

- Click on the first item you want to select and drag the mouse to highlight a range of items.
- Click on the first item you want to select and then press and hold the Control key while clicking on additional items.
- Click on the row containing the name and library icon for an open library. Then click on the 'swimming pool' icon (it's roughly the shape of a swimming pool and looks like it's filled with cool blue water) in the Library Painter PainterBar to select every item in the library. ■

To open or close a directory, double-click on the directory name. Directory names appear next to file folder icons. To change drives, select the drive letter or volume name from the drop-down list box.

When you're done using the Library Painter, you can either leave it open, so that you can switch back to it later (using the Window menu), or close it. To close the Library Painter, press Ctrl+F4 or choose Close from the Control menu on the title bar of the Library Painter.

Book burning

To delete library entries, select the entries you want to delete and click on the eraser icon in the Library Painter PainterBar. This icon will delete any selected library entries.

To delete a single library entry, either select it and click on the eraser icon, or click on the library entry with the right mouse button. The right mouse button brings up a menu with a Delete option. Choose Delete to delete the library entry.

If you want to delete an entire library, click on the library with the right mouse button and choose Delete from the menu. Or, choose Delete... from the Library menu to open the Delete Library window shown in Figure 1-9.

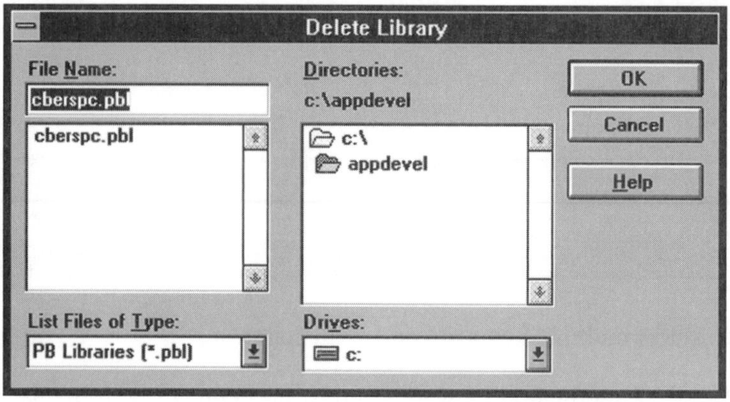

Figure 1-9: If you must delete a library, use the Delete Library dialog window.

Select the PowerBuilder library you want to delete and click on the OK button. Before you delete a library, consider the impact it will have on young children who just want a safe place to go to do their homework and learn about science, art, and literature!

Inter-library exchange

Sometimes it's fun to create lots of libraries and categorize your library entries according to size, color, purpose, or artistic value. To move library entries between libraries, click with the right mouse button on the library entry you want to move and choose the Move... menu item. A Move Library Entries window will appear listing the libraries you can move the entry into. Select a library and click on the OK button.

To move multiple library entries between libraries, select the library entries you want to move. Click on the move icon (the one that looks like a weightlifter in a red jumpsuit) in the Library Painter PainterBar or choose Move... from the Entry menu. This will open the Move Library Entries window. Choose the library into which you want to move the selected library entries and click on the OK button to move them.

Thank goodness for Xerox

Here are a few good reasons to copy a library entry:

- To create backup copies of your library entries
- You've created a particularly useful library entry and want to use it in another application
- The master versions of your library entries are stored in another directory or on a network drive and you need to make working copies

To copy a library entry, click on the entry with the right mouse button and choose Copy... from the menu. A Copy Library Entries window appears listing the libraries you can copy into. Choose a library and click on the OK button.

To copy multiple library entries, select them and click on the duplicate icon (the one that looks like two pieces of paper) in the PainterBar. Then choose a library to copy into and click the OK button.

Adding comments to describe a library entry

PowerBuilder has many features that simplify the application development process. A particularly useful one is the ability to create comments for PowerBuilder libraries and library entries. This allows you to fully document the design and technical details of your application. By using comments in this way, you can keep your documentation up to date and accessible at all times. Accurate and accessible documentation helps to reduce bugs and makes it much easier to work as a member of a development team.

The Library Painter allows you to create and maintain high-level comments. The comments you assign to libraries and library entries appear automatically in the Library Painter.

To create or modify comments, click with the right mouse button on a library or a library entry. Then choose Modify Comments... from the menu. If you modify comments for a library, the window pictured in Figure 1-10 appears. Type your comment in the Comments: section and click on the OK button. If you modify comments for a library entry, the window pictured in Figure 1-11 appears. Again, type your comments and click on the OK button.

In both comments windows, you can enter a Return character to start a new line by pressing Ctrl+Enter. You can also use the following key combinations to cut, copy, and paste text:

- Ctrl+Insert to copy selected text into the Windows clipboard
- Shift+Insert to paste the contents of the clipboard
- Shift+Delete to cut selected text into the clipboard ■

You've now sampled the simple and intuitive user interface in PowerBuilder. You'll find that the rest of PowerBuilder is just as intuitive, complete, and well thought out as the tools you've seen so far. The next chapter shows you how to use PowerBuilder's design philosophy to improve the quality and reliability of your applications. You'll also learn how to do application planning and technical design on-line using PowerBuilder.

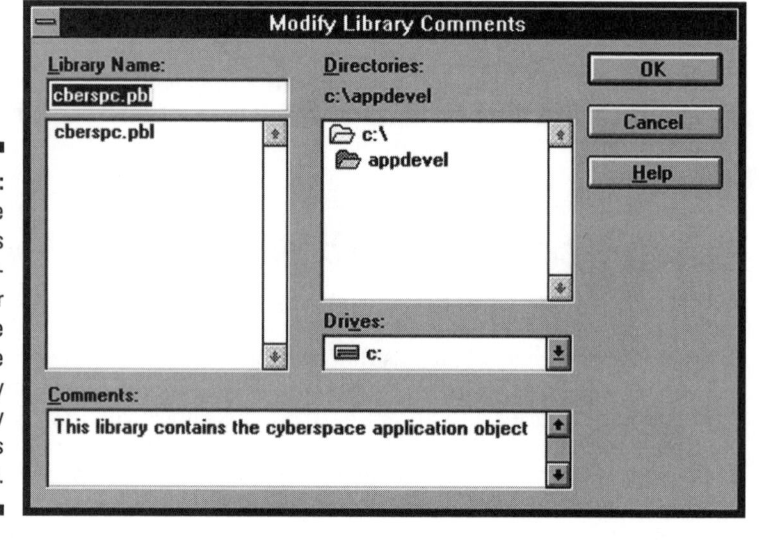

Figure 1-10: Modify the comments for a PowerBuilder library file using the Modify Library Comments window.

Figure 1-11: Modify the comments for a PowerBuilder library entry using the Modify Library Entry Comments window.

Chapter 2

A Man, a Plan, a Canal Panama

In This Chapter

- An overview of PowerBuilder programming
- Designing a superior application
- Tips to simplify your job

When things are well organized it doesn't matter which way you approach them; they work out just the same. In this chapter, you'll learn how PowerBuilder applications are organized. You'll discover the various components of a PowerBuilder application and find out what each one does. As an added feature, we've tried to write this chapter so that it reads the same forward as it does backward.

PowerBuilder in a Nutshell

It's easier to learn PowerBuilder if you start with a global perspective. (See Figure 2-1.)

PowerBuilder programming can be summarized in five general steps:

1. Create an application object.
2. Set up the database.
3. Build a user interface and reports.
4. Add detailed instructions using PowerScript.
5. Complete your program's data management features.

These five steps are described in the following sections.

Figure 2-1: A global perspective will help you understand Power-Builder.

Create an application object

You've already seen the most important component in a PowerBuilder application, the application object. An application object gives your program the ability to run by handling technical details such as event notification, error handling, and window messaging.

In addition to performing these critical tasks, the application object is responsible for other things that affect the entire application. The application object provides memory space for global variables, keeps track of global functions and global object definitions, and generally holds the whole mess together like some kind of electronic primordial soup bowl. Needless to say, an application without an application object would be a sorry state of affairs.

The application object also makes it possible to create an executable program file. For more on compiling your application, see Chapter 19.

Set up the database engine

The *database engine* is almost as important as the application object. The database engine is responsibile for all things database-related. The database engine is an expert at storing data in *database tables*, so PowerBuilder doesn't have to worry about data management. PowerBuilder simply asks the database engine to do something, and the database engine faithfully complies.

Imagine having a skilled, specialized, and reliable assistant to handle all of your filing and paperwork. With an assistant like that, you'd want to give them more responsibility, anything at all that had to do with filing or paperwork. Well, this is what is happening with database engine technology. Many database engines now track everything from the format, color, and font in which to display the data to the database commands that need to be executed when certain events occur. See Part 2 for more on information management in PowerBuilder.

There are many database engines available that work with PowerBuilder. One of them must be installed and configured in order to use PowerBuilder. Luckily, the Watcom database engine was automatically set up when you installed PowerBuilder, so you don't need to think about this right now. You'll need to know more about setting up the database engine when you're ready to deliver your finished application. Chapter 19 shows you what you'll need to know.

Most database engines come with security features such as the ability to assign users to groups and establish different access levels both by user and by group.

It's a good idea to use the security features of your database, even if your PowerBuilder application will be used by only one person. Security does more than just protect data from unauthorized tampering; it helps prevent accidental changes and makes it easy to investigate the cause of data problems. See Chapter 4 for more about database security. ■

Build a user interface and create meaningful reports

Between the application object and the database engine, it may seem like the important responsibilities are all taken care of. What is there left for you to program except a user interface? Actually, not a whole lot. Once you've added a user interface and data processing and reporting features, you're done. Most of the difficult work is done for you by PowerBuilder, freeing you up to be creative and efficient.

Part of efficient programming is being able to change what you've done easily and without introducing bugs. To help make this possible, PowerBuilder extends the same responsibility approach that it implements with the application object and database engine to each PowerBuilder component.

PowerBuilder user interfaces are based on individual *windows*. And guess what windows are responsible for? You've got it, windows are responsible for themselves, and nothing more. Your windows can have menus on them, just like most programs do. Even then the window doesn't handle the menu details; instead, a completed menu object is attached to the window and the two objects work together. For more on menus see Chapter 11.

Windows can have their own window variables and their own window functions. They can accept parameters when they're opened, and return values when they're closed. This means that windows don't need to know about global variables, global functions, other windows, or otherwise depend on external circumstances in order to function correctly. With this kind of independence built in, there are only two ways to cause a bug in a window:

- Change something incorrectly in the window
- Pass the wrong information to the window at the time the window is opened

The 5th Wave **By Rich Tennant**

" 'MORNING MR. DREXEL. I HEARD YOU SAY YOUR COMPUTERS ALL HAD BUGS, WELL, I FIGURE THEY'RE CRAWLING IN THROUGH THOSE SLOTS THEY HAVE, SO I JAMMED A COUPLE OF ROACH-DISKS IN EACH ONE. LET ME KNOW IF YOU HAVE ANY MORE PROBLEMS."

PowerBuilder lets you use all of the standard user interface controls such as list boxes, buttons, and entry fields on your windows. To make data manipulation on a window easier, there's a special data control called a *DataWindow*. For more about controls and windows see Chapters 6, 7, 9, and 10.

Using DataWindows, you can build entire data entry layouts and link them to database tables. You can also use DataWindows to create printed report layouts and display the results of queries. The same DataWindow you use to display data can be used to print that data so that the printout looks just like the screen does.

DataWindows have a graph layout feature with many graph styles. You can use DataWindows to add attractive graphs to your reports or display them on the screen. For more about DataWindows, see Part 4.

Fine-tune your application using PowerScript

PowerScript is PowerBuilder's built-in programming language. PowerScript is the language you'll use to create functions and *event scripts*. Event scripts tell PowerBuilder what to do when a particular event occurs. For example, you might write an event script to save changes to the database when a button is clicked.

Functions are PowerScript routines. You might write a function that performs special data processing or calculations and then returns a result. In technical terms, a function is like a subroutine that can accept parameters and return a value. For more on PowerScript, see Chapter 8.

PowerBuilder provides a complete interactive debugger to help you track down bugs in your PowerScript code. For more on using the debugger, see Chapter 18.

Finish up with powerful data management

PowerBuilder uses *Structured Query Language*, or SQL, to communicate with the database engine. While there are many simple and powerful ways to work with data in a PowerBuilder application — DataWindows, for example — one of the most flexible ways is to embed SQL commands within PowerScript.

If you don't know SQL yet, don't worry. There are only four important commands:

- SELECT
- UPDATE
- DELETE
- INSERT

And PowerBuilder provides an SQL painter to write the syntax for you! For information on using the SQL painter, see Chapter 4. For more on embedding SQL commands in PowerScript, see Chapter 20.

A ROSE by Any Other Name

The programming approach we alluded to previously is based on intelligently distributing the responsibilities in an application. For this reason, we like to call it *Responsibility Oriented Software Engineering*, or, as we so elegantly nicknamed it, ROSE.

Traditional programming languages are very forgiving. If you were to design a software automobile using a traditional programming language, nothing would stop you from creating headlights that have the ability to turn the wheels and lock the doors. It might even make sense to you at the time that software headlights should have these abilities. Programs like this are said to be full of *spaghetti code* because responsibilities are all jumbled together and intertwined like a plateful of spaghetti.

Spaghetti and software both begin with the letter S, but that's where their similarities should end. The headlights in a software automobile should be responsible only for illuminating the road ahead. You'll find that PowerBuilder encourages the use of a ROSE programming style.

PowerBuilder doesn't force you to program this way; it just makes it possible to do so easily. For example, you know that the application object provides memory space for global variables, so if you really want to use global variables, you can. If you still want to use global variables after reading this chapter, read it again before going on. ■

Delegating responsibility

Before you dive in and start programming, it's a good idea to identify the major responsibilities in your application and decide how to distribute them.

To make this easier, you might create design documents using the built-in file editor, or, once you're comfortable working with all of the painters, create the most important PowerBuilder components and add comments to them using the Library Painter. With your application mapped out and roughed in, you can start programming with confidence.

To access the built-in file editor, press Shift+F6 from within PowerBuilder. This will bring up the File Open window. You can either choose a file to edit and then click on the OK button or click on the Cancel button to create a new file. When you're done editing, choose Save or Save As... from the File menu.

Safety is no accident

This type of planning is simple and quick, and will help you avoid programming accidents: Don't limit your planning to the windows and other visual components in your application. Functions also need defined responsibilities.

If you find yourself expanding the duties of a function, consider creating a new function for the new duties instead. This makes it much easier to track down the cause of bugs and helps avoid spaghetti tendencies.

The promise of objects

Object orientation is an ideal. Pure object orientation is a software nirvana where objects are everywhere and everything is an object. Object-oriented databases store objects instead of just data. Objects communicate with each other using messages and requests, like "Hi there Mr. Customer object, I'm Annual Report object. Please tell me how much money you paid to Virtual Corporation this year." True object orientation is only possible if the object-oriented ideal is applied to every aspect of computing, from operating systems to databases to programming languages.

Object-oriented programming is generally misunderstood. A programming language or software development tool that uses objects or allows you to create them isn't object oriented. Yes, they're called object oriented, and no doubt they're useful and well designed software tools, but they don't implement pure *object orientation.* A better term for these tools might be *object based* rather than object oriented. In that case, PowerBuilder is an object-based development tool, and it's one of the best.

The promise of object orientation is great. Before the promise can be realized, the computer industry must answer some difficult questions such as, how can objects learn about each other dynamically; how can object-oriented databases perform as well as relational databases; and, is pure object orientation practical for everyday business applications?" The answers to these questions will answer one last question: Will pure object orientation become the standard for software development of the future?

Let PowerBuilder Be Your Guide

You can learn a lot about ROSE by looking at PowerBuilder's design. Instead of one gigantic painter that can do everything, there are several painters with well-defined responsibilities. Each painter covers a certain type of Power-Builder component.

Another good design example is the PowerScript Painter. You'll learn more about this painter later; Figure 2-2 shows what it looks like on the screen. The PowerScript Painter is used throughout PowerBuilder. Every painter that allows you to create event scripts or functions uses the PowerScript Painter. The PowerScript Painter lets you program in PowerScript, and validates your PowerScript code before saving it.

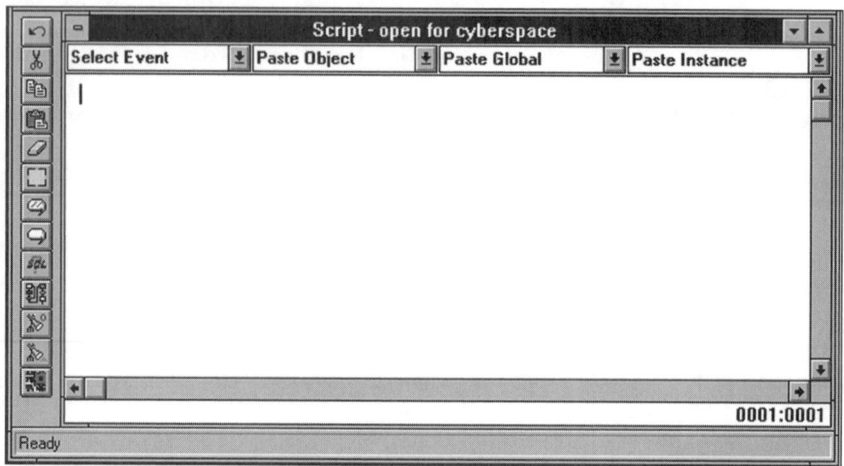

Figure 2-2: The PowerScript Painter is used by many Power-Builder painters to create and edit scripts.

Another painter that appears repeatedly is the SQL Painter. The SQL Painter lets you build queries visually and is used anywhere that a query is required — in the Query Painter, for example. Figure 2-3 shows the SQL Painter.

Both the PowerScript Painter and the SQL Painter perform the duties they've been assigned, and they perform them well. This makes it possible for other painters to call upon them to modify scripts or create SQL syntax.

Getting PowerBuilder to do your homework

Cheating is wrong, right? Here are a few ways you can cheat in PowerBuilder. If nobody finds out that you cheated, is it still wrong?

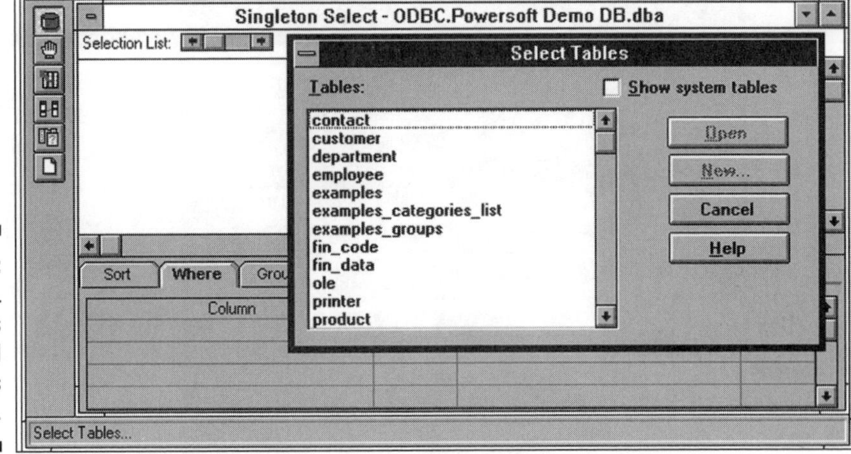

Figure 2-3: The SQL Painter lets you build queries visually.

Set default fonts in the Application Painter

In almost all of your applications, you'll want to use the same fonts consistently for things like text, headings, and labels. PowerBuilder makes this easy by allowing you to define four default fonts. Each default font applies to a different type of text:

- Normal text
- Data
- Headings
- Labels

By setting default fonts you don't need to worry about font consistency — it's handled for you automatically. To set the default fonts, do the following:

1. Start the Application Painter.
2. Click on the F icon in the PainterBar.
3. In the Select Default Fonts window (see Figure 2-4), choose the font for each of the four defaults.
4. Click on the OK button.

Once you've defined default fonts, the fonts you select are used by default in each PowerBuilder painter. You can override the default font setting simply by changing the font of text in the painter you're using.

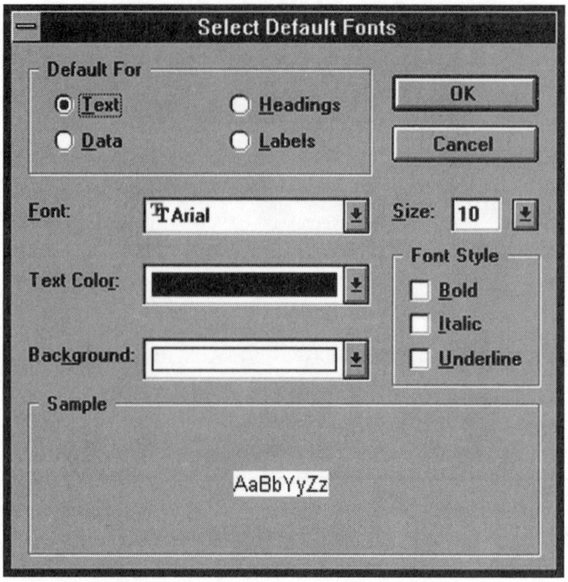

Figure 2-4: Set default fonts to provide font consistency.

Copy from the on-line help

The on-line help in PowerBuilder is a useful tool, if you know how to unlock its secrets. There are two ways to access on-line help:

- Press F1, click on a HELP button, or choose from the Help menu.
- Select a word, function name, or other text in the PowerScript Painter and press Shift+F1.

The latter will access help just for the word, function, or other text that you highlight. This is handy when you're writing in PowerScript and you'd like to access on-line help for a specific topic.

Once you're in on-line help, you can copy text to the clipboard and then paste it into your application by doing the following:

1. Click with the right mouse button and choose Copy... from the popup menu to open the Copy window (see Figure 2-5). You can also press Ctrl+Y to open the Copy window without using the mouse.
2. Select the text you want to copy by clicking and dragging across the text to highlight it.
3. Click on the Copy button.

4. Exit on-line help by choosing Exit from the File menu.
5. Position the cursor at the location you want to paste what's on the clipboard and press Shift+Insert.

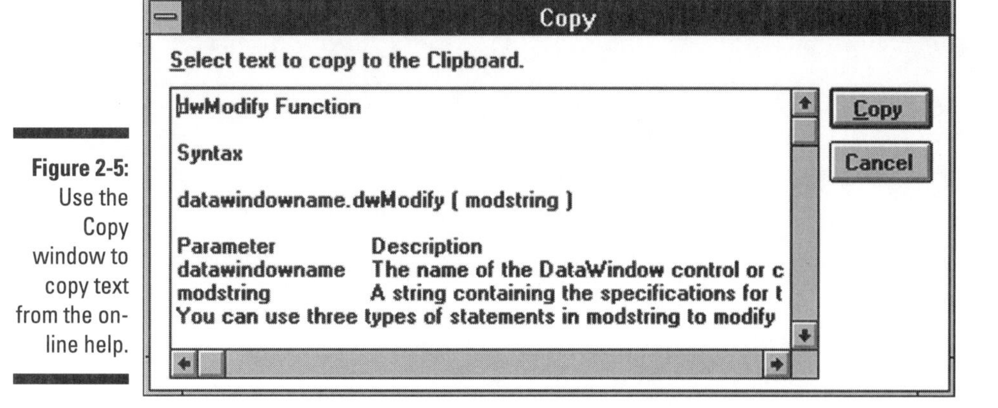

Figure 2-5: Use the Copy window to copy text from the on-line help.

Copying text from the on-line help is particularly useful when there is sample PowerScript code that you'd like to use in your application.

Learning application development tricks from PowerBuilder

PowerBuilder has a lot to teach. You've already experienced some innovative user-interface features in PowerBuilder — clicking and dragging icons to customize the PowerBar, for example. As a rule, anything that PowerBuilder does can probably be implemented in your own applications.

Part II
The Information Management Superhighway

"WHY A 4GL TOASTER? I DON'T THINK YOU'D ASK THAT QUESTION IF YOU THOUGHT A MINUTE ABOUT HOW TO BALANCE THE MAXIMIZATION OF TOAST DEVELOPMENT PRODUCTIVITY AGAINST TOASTER RESOURCE UTILIZATION IN A MULTI-DINER ENVIRONMENT."

In This Part...

Whatever you do in life, information has become important. Whether it's your bank account balance, a company's inventory, or a running total of how many people said the word "nee" in any one day, information must be saved and managed.

With the proliferation of networks has come the need for better network access to information. Here we will explain what has been done to provide that access and how PowerBuilder makes implementing that technology in your application simple.

In this part you will also learn to administer your database, add users, provide security, and use SQL for managing information. PowerBuilder provides graphic tools that allow you to build queries and views of your data. Knowing how to use these tools will form a foundation for creating database applications in PowerBuilder.

Chapter 3

Creating a Database

In This Chapter

- Understanding client-server technology
- Creating databases
- Creating tables
- Relating tables

PowerBuilder's database tool allows you to manage information using easy-to-understand graphics. In this chapter we cover what client-server technology is and why you would want to use it. Also, using the Watcom database as an example, we cover creating a database, adding tables to it, and creating relationships between the tables.

The database tool gives you complete control over the database and its tables. In a responsibility-oriented system like PowerBuilder, this tool has the responsibility of completely managing the database. It's like a built-in database administrator.

Customer-Waiter Technology

PowerBuilder uses client-server technology to make it possible to use many different database engines. Client-server is a term that means that a client application sends messages to a server program requesting that the server perform a task. In database applications, this means that a client application may request that a server application such as Watcom, Sybase, Oracle, Informix, XDB, RDB, or any of the other client-server databases available perform tasks. These may include creating databases, creating and modifying tables, querying the tables for information, or updating the information. See Figure 3-1.

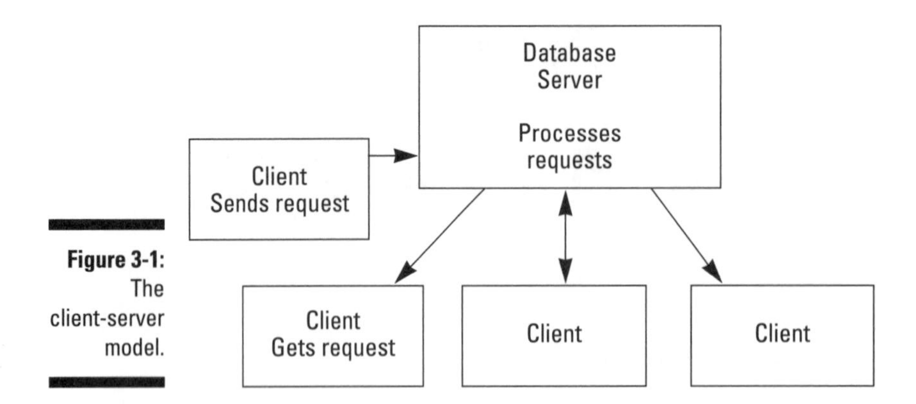

Figure 3-1: The client-server model.

In older network technologies, database programs running on a desktop computer would process information that resided somewhere else on the network. Processing a simple query required an immense amount of network traffic. This would bring most networks to their knees. Database queries over a network were painfully slow. Waiting for data was like standing in the restroom line at a rock concert.

With client-server, the client sends a query request to the server. The request is executed remotely by the server. There is no network traffic while the query is in progress. Only the results of the query are sent back to the client. Now it is possible for many users to share the data on a network at the same time without significant performance degradation. In restaurants where a client orders food from the waiter and the waiter goes to the kitchen and then orders the cook to make the food, service is faster than where the cook comes to each table and makes the food tableside. Worse, what if the waiter just brought out all the raw food and you had to cook it yourself?

Creating a database in PowerBuilder

A database is responsible for holding your information. Creating a database is nothing more than creating a shell that will hold tables. A table is the container that holds your information.

To create a database, click on the database icon in the PowerBar. This will start the Database Painter. See Figure 3-2. The existing database will be displayed in the Painter. If this is the first time you are running the Database Painter, the example database will appear.

Figure 3-2: Use the database icon to bring up the Database Painter.

The Database Painter, as shown in Figure 3-3, is used to create, manage, or delete your database. You can manage any number of databases. You can also use the Database Painter to switch between them.

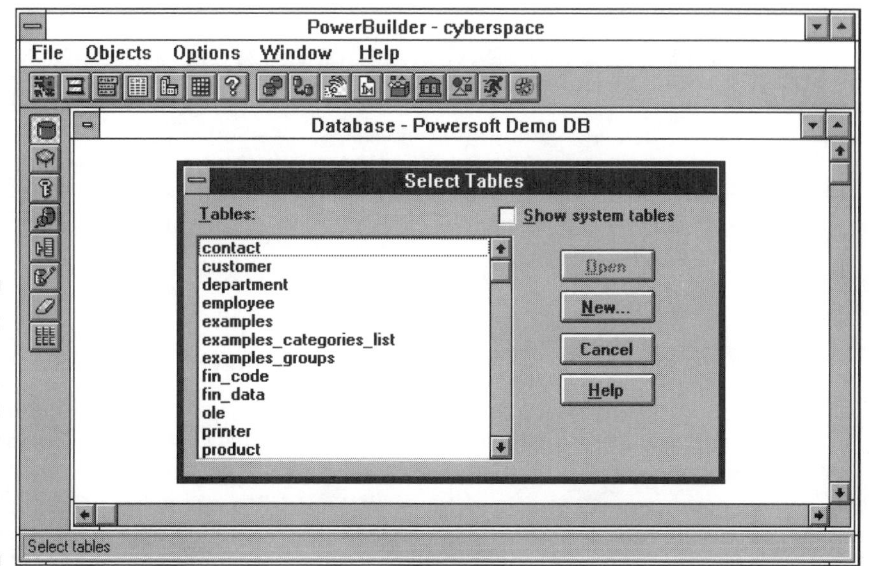

Figure 3-3: The Database Painter is where you can create or manage databases.

Follow these steps to create a new database:

1. When the Select Tables dialog appears on the screen, click the Cancel button to make the dialog go away.
2. Select File | Create Database... from the menu.
3. In the Create Local Database dialog, as shown in Figure 3-4, you must give your database a name. This name must conform to the file-naming standards of the platform you are using.
4. Click the OK button to create the database.

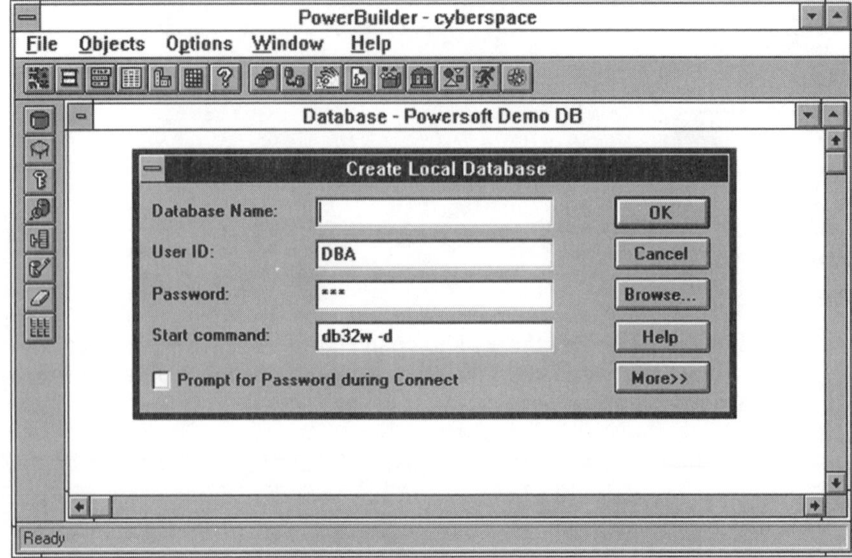

Figure 3-4: Use the Create Local Database dialog to create a new database.

You may name your database and select which directory to store it in by clicking the Browse... button. This will bring up a Create Local Database dialog box. Type in a file name, select a directory for your database, and then click the OK button.

What has four legs and can't run?

A database by itself won't do much. Its sole purpose is to contain *tables,* which are places to store your data. A database can have one or more tables.

If you have used PC databases such as dBASE or FoxPro, and you're a little confused, here is why: For many years the PC database products stored information in separate files, each called a database file. The term table was never used. Now, information is stored in a single file, a database file, and is organized into separate structures known as tables. These are called relational databases. ■

Information within a table is organized into columns. Unique information, such as last name, first name, address, and so on, each has its own column. Table 3-1 shows a sample of how information stored in a table might appear.

Table 3-1: A sample database table

LastName	*FirstName*	*Address*
McIntyre	John	2121 Angel Ct.
Adams	Grizzly	56 Clay Street
Borgia	Lucrecia	49 Ghoul Ln.
Hamilton	Al	4646 Snowball Rd.

You can see from the information in Table 3-1 that each type of information is in a separate column. Each group of information is in a distinct *row*. In Table 3-1, each row contains information about a different person.

When you create a new table, you define its columns. When you've completed creating your table and wish to add information, you add rows to the table.

Here is how you create a new table:

1. Assuming you are using the Database Painter, first bring up the Select Tables dialog box (see Figure 3-5). If it is not on the screen, select it using the Table icon. This is the top icon on the left side of the screen, as shown in Figure 3-5.
2. From the Select Tables dialog, click on the New... button. This will bring up the Create Table dialog box. See Figure 3-6.

Now that the Create Table dialog is on the screen, you can give the table a name by entering it in the Table field. Type the name MyTable.

Because PowerBuilder is a complete development tool, you can enter a comment about the table. We recommend that you use this method of on-line documentation.

To enter a table comment click the button labeled Comment in the lower-right side of the Create Table dialog. A Table Comment dialog will appear. Enter information about the use of this table in your application. For this example table you can type, "This is a sample table."

One of the things you can do is set the default fonts for your table. You can set fonts for:

- Data
- Headings (column titles that will appear in tabular displays of your data)
- Labels (column titles that will appear in freeform displays of your data)

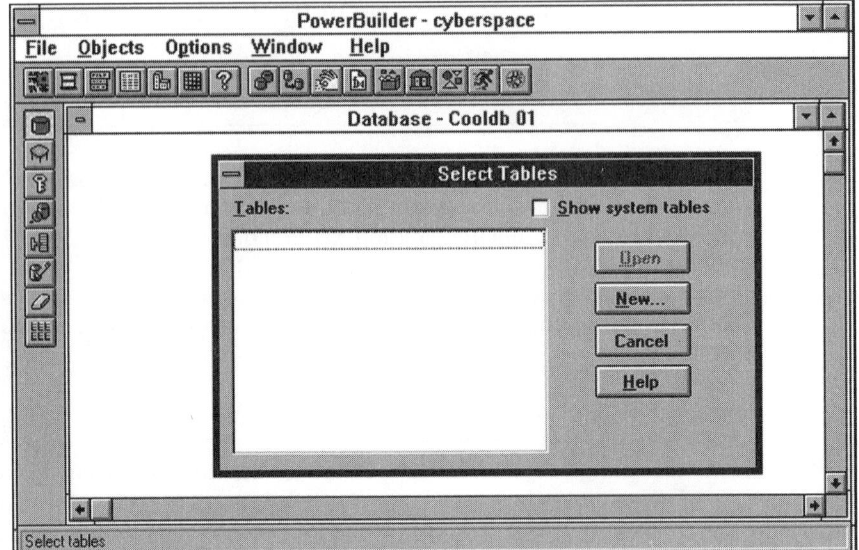

Figure 3-5: Use the Select Tables dialog to manage tables in the Database Painter.

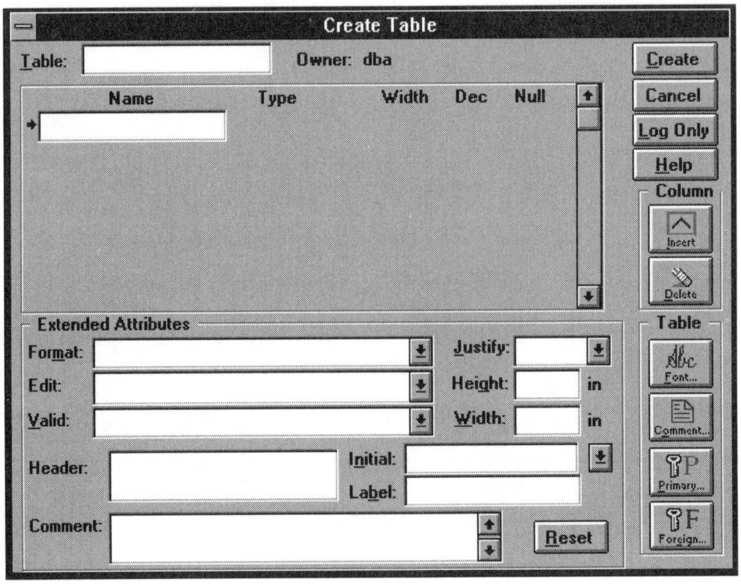

Figure 3-6: The Create Table dialog helps you create new tables.

Specifying the fonts here will save you time while developing your application. To select fonts, click the Font button in the Create Table dialog.

At this point you're ready to start defining the table's columns.

The Ancient Greeks Liked Columns — So Will You

Did you ever have one of those clear plastic coin banks? You know, the ones where quarters would go in one slot, dimes in another, nickels and pennies in theirs. What you were left with, provided you put money in it, were columns of quarters, dimes, nickels, and pennies.

Information is normally divided similarly to those coins in the bank. In the example in Table 3-1, the last name information was in a separate column from the first name information. The address information was in a third column. Tables consist of one or more columns of related information. In the bank example, all of the columns are coins. In Table 3-1, all of the columns are name and address information.

When creating a table, you define a column by giving it a name and determining the *column type*. Column types classify information based on the type of information to be stored. It can be textual information, numeric, date-related and so on. The column types vary with the database being used. Most databases support similar types. The Watcom database supports the types listed in Table 3-2.

With the Create Table dialog still on the screen we will now add columns to the table we are creating:

1. Give the column a name. The column name must be a single word, or words separated with an underscore. In the example, type lastname as the column name.
2. Select the column type from the drop-down list that appears when you click on the Type field. Select Char for the column type. Name information is character-type information.
3. Enter a width of 20 for the lastname column. For some column types, such as char or numeric, you are required to enter a column width. For other types, such as date, you cannot access this field. For the Numeric column type, you may also specify the number of decimal places accepted in this column.

4. Select No, telling the database not to accept Null values in the lastname column. (Null is the absence of a value. In numeric column types, zero is a value, and therefore not null.)

Table 3-2: Column types

Column Type	*Description*
varchar	variable-length character field
numeric	positive and negative numbers and decimals
integer	positive and negative whole numbers
smallint	a small integer
double	a really big number
binary	for storing binary information like sounds or graphics
long binary	really big binary files
date	date-related information
time	time-related information
timestamp	a date and time combination
float	a floating point number
long varchar	very long variable-length text
char	alphanumeric text

New entry fields automatically appear as you finish defining each column. To add another column, repeat the previous four steps for the new column. But before you continue on to creating another column, we'll look at how you can do more with each column by setting up its *extended attributes*. These are the customizable features of each column.

Rome wasn't built in a day

PowerBuilder, working together with the database, has made the job of creating applications easier than ever before. Each column you define in your table can have extended attributes. You can set these by filling in the bottom half of the Create Table dialog when you create or modify your table columns.

In PowerBuilder, the database is responsible for remembering how its information is normally displayed or edited, and it communicates this information to PowerBuilder.

Setting a column format

You can specify how information in a column will appear when it is displayed. For example, you can enter phone numbers without including parentheses or dashes in your table. But 9065551212 is a little hard to read. Creating a format that will show this information as a phone number, (906) 555-1212, will save users from having to enter the extra symbols. It will also save disk space in large databases. Defining a format when creating a column will save you from having to format the data in the column each time it is used in the program.

To create a format for a column, enter one or more of the formatting characters listed in Table 3-3 in the configuration you want your data to appear. Some examples follow.

Create formats for each data type using these formatting characters. Here are some examples:

String:

```
(@@@) @@@-@@@@
```

This is a typical phone number format: (906) 555-1212

Numbers:

```
#,##0
```

This is a format that places a comma in the number if it exceeds three digits: 1,234

Dates:

```
mmmm d, yyyy
```

This formats the date with the full month name, the day without a preceding zero, and the year with the century: January 25, 1995

Color me

Color can add accent and power to your information. A few of the ways color can be used are:

- To display negative numbers in red, setting them apart from other numbers
- To color customer names by region
- To flag delinquent accounts

Table 3-3: Formatting characters

Characters	*Data Type*	*Usage*
@	String	Any alpha-numeric character
single quote	all	Surrounds literal characters you want to appear within your data
backslash	all	Precedes a character that normally has a special meaning, such as @, if you want the character to appear in your data.
#	Numeric	Represents a single number
$	Numeric	Displays a dollar sign in the data
%	Numeric	Displays a percent sign in the data
0 zero	Numeric	Represents a numeric value
- or /	Date	Separators
d	Date	Day with no preceding zero
dd	Date	Day with a preceding zero
ddd	Date	Three-letter day name abbreviation
dddd	Date	The full day name
m	Date	Month with no preceding zero
mm	Date	Month with a preceding zero
mmm	Date	Three-letter month abbreviation
mmmm	Date	Full month name
yy	Date	Year without century
yyyy	Date	Year with century
: or /	Time	Separators
h	Time	Hour with no preceding zero
hh	Time	Hour with a preceding zero
m	Time	Minute with no preceding zero
mm	Time	Minute with a preceding zero
s	Time	Seconds with no preceding zero
ss	Time	Seconds with a preceding zero
AM/PM or am/pm	Time	Displays appropriate Ante or Post Meridian in either upper- or lowercase

With a little creativity and the ability to color your data, your programs will become easier and more fun to use. The great part is that it requires no programming. Just add a little color to your data formats.

Adding color is easy. Simply precede the format with a color name in brackets. Here is an example:

```
[Blue] @@@-@@-@@@@
```

This is a format for a blue social security number.

The colors you can use are:

- Black
- Blue
- Cyan
- Green
- Magenta
- Red
- White
- Yellow

More powerful than a speeding locomotive

Your data can change formats based on its value. Each format has different sections separated by a semicolon.

- String formats have two sections. The first section is for normal text. The second is for Null values.
- Numeric formats have four sections. The first section is for positive numbers, the second is for negative numbers, the third is for a zero value, and the fourth is for a Null value.
- Date formats, like string formats, have two sections. The first formats a date value; the second format is for a Null value.
- Time formats have two sections. The first is for formatting time values; the second is for Null values.

Here is an example that formats a number based on all four possible data values:

```
[Black] #,##0;[Red] (#,##0);[Blue] 'Zero';[Green] 'No value'
```

In this example, positive numbers display as black, and with a comma if greater than three digits. Negative numbers are red and are surrounded with parentheses. The word zero is printed in blue if the value is zero; the words No Value are printed in green if there is a Null value.

Editing with style

You have just learned how the database keeps track of how its data is displayed. It can also keep track of how its data is edited. This is done using an *edit style*.

You can select a style from the drop-down list that appears when you click in the Edit field. You may choose one of the styles listed or create your own.

To create your own edit style select Objects | Edit Style Maintenance... from the PowerBuilder menu. This will bring up the Edit Styles dialog (see Figure 3-7).

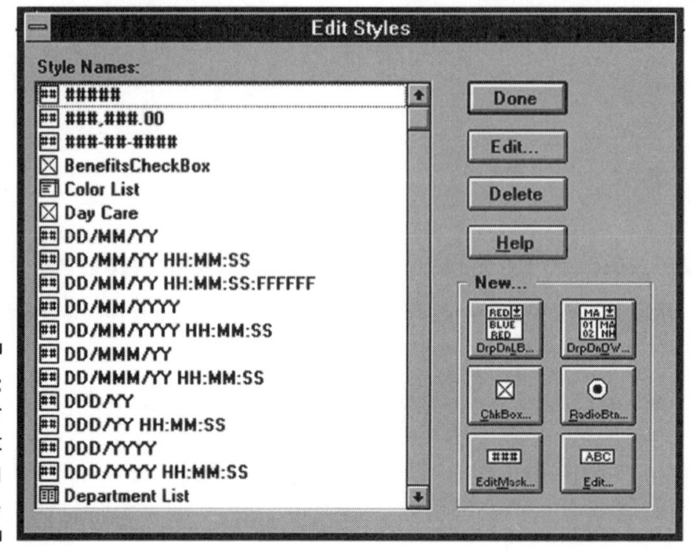

Figure 3-7: Create or modify edit styles using this dialog.

You can choose to edit your data in one of the following formats:

- Drop-Down List Box
- Drop-Down Data Window
- Check Box
- Radio Button
- Edit Mask
- Single-Line Edit

Each of these edit styles will be explained in greater detail throughout this book.

Validity is next to godliness

The extended attributes, stored in the database repository, not only store how the data is edited or displayed, it can store *validation rules*. These are PowerBuilder expressions used to validate user-entered data. To select a validation rule, you must have created one first.

To create or modify validation rules:

1. Select Objects | Validation Maintenance... from the PowerBuilder menu. This brings up the Validation Rules dialog box, as shown in Figure 3-8.
2. Select a validation rule to modify or click the New... button. This brings up the Input Validation dialog box.
3. Construct your validation expression in the Input Validation dialog box, as shown in Figure 3-9.

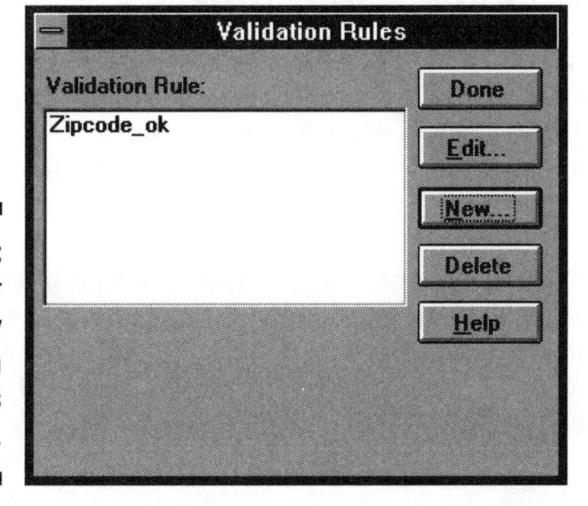

Figure 3-8: Create or modify validation rules in this dialog box.

When creating an input validation, you must include a reference to the column. You can add this into the expression by clicking the @col button provided, or type it manually. You may also select from the function list, which is provided in the list box to help you construct your expression.

Once a validation rule has been saved, you may select this rule for your column. You may also use this validation rule in other parts of your program.

Figure 3-9: Construct an input validation expression in this dialog box.

Specifying custom headers and labels

Column names can often become cryptic. You may specify a header or label that will replace the column name whenever it would normally appear in your program. For example, you may have a column named GROSS_AN_SALARY. You can specify a header or label that might be more meaningful, such as Gross Annual Salary.

Headers and labels are similar. Wherever a column title would normally appear, in reports, for example, the header or label will appear as the title instead. Headers appear above columns of data; labels appear to the side.

Enter the new header and label information in the fields provided in the Create Table dialog.

You can set the font for headers and labels by clicking the Font button in the Create Table dialog. This will set the default font for all column headers and labels. You can always override these default settings later if necessary.

Who, what, why, when, and where

So far, you have learned many of the important attributes used to customize how PowerBuilder handles the data in each column. Here are a few more attributes you should know about:

- Set the initial value. When adding new data to a table you can set the initial value the user is presented with.
- You can set the height and width of the control used to edit the data with the Height and Width attributes.
- Add a comment to each column. This is an important step in documenting your program. PowerBuilder allows you to comment on each part of an application. We recommend you take every opportunity to do so.

Remember that it is much easier to have the database remember all of these things than to try and remember them yourself. Let the database and PowerBuilder do your work for you.

Finish creating the example table following the steps outlined above. Add the columns listed in Table 3-4.

Table 3-4: Structure of the sample table MyTable

Name	*Type*	*Width*	*Dec*	*Null*
lastname	Char	20		No
firstname	Char	15		No
id_number	Char	5		No
age	Numeric	3	0	No

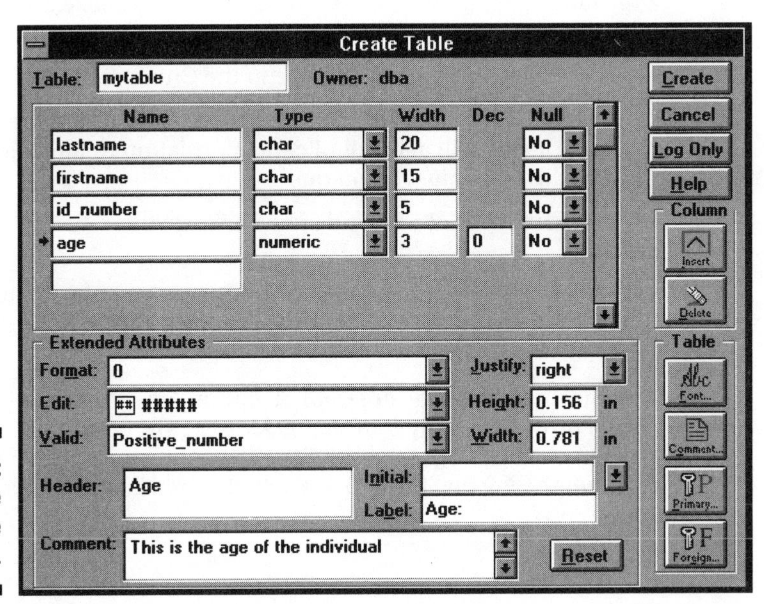

Figure 3-10: A complete table definition.

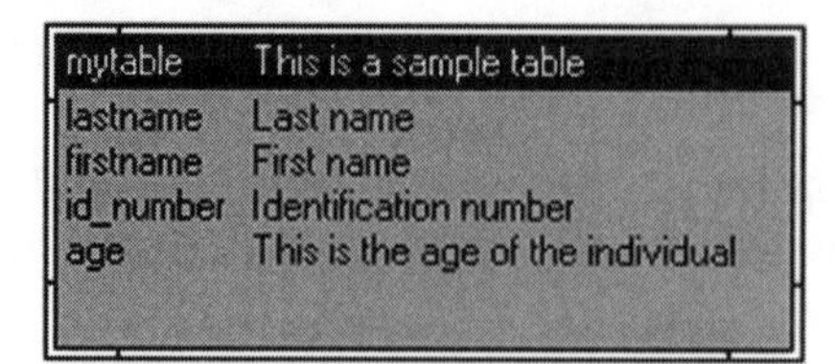
mytable	This is a sample table
lastname	Last name
firstname	First name
id_number	Identification number
age	This is the age of the individual

Figure 3-11: The newly created table appears in the Database Painter.

The Create Table dialog should look like Figure 3-10.

When you have finished defining all of the columns in the table and adding extended attributes, click on the Create button to have PowerBuilder create this table in your database. When asked if you want to define a Primary key, answer No for now. The completed table will appear in the Database Painter, as shown in Figure 3-11. Notice how the table and each column is commented.

Creating indexes

Indexes are special lookup files used by the database to find information in a table rapidly. You can create indexes by following these steps:

1. Open at least one table in the Database Painter.
2. Click the index icon in the toolbar on the left. It looks like a key. This will bring up the Create Index dialog.
3. Give the index a name by entering one in the Create Index field.
4. Click the radio button next to either Unique or Duplicate to choose whether your index will allow duplicate information to be added or if all entries into the table must be unique.
5. Choose the sort order of your index by clicking either Ascending or Descending.
6. Select the column or columns you want indexed from the list box at the bottom of the dialog box. They will appear in the Index on box as they are selected.
7. You can then complete the creation of your index by either clicking the OK button or the Log Only button. Clicking the OK button will create your index. Clicking Log Only will place the command to create the index within the log file, but will not actually create the index.

You may choose to add more than one index. It is important to note that before you can add data to a table you must have added at least one index or a primary key. Primary keys are explained at the end of this chapter. If you are creating an example by following this book, you should create an index at this time. ■

Manipulating data in a table

You have seen how to create the structure of a table by defining its columns. Now you'll learn how to add rows of data to a table.

The Database Painter (which was shown in Figure 3-3) has built-in tools for editing data in the development environment. Click on the Preview icon, shown in Figure 3-12, to start the Data Manipulation tool.

Figure 3-12: Clicking the Preview icon starts the Data Manipulation tool.

When the Manipulation tool is started, the database is queried for its data. The results are displayed in the Manipulation tool. Data is displayed in rows beneath the column headers. In our example, there is no data in the table yet. Therefore, the column headers appear with no data beneath them.

To add rows of data, click the Insert Row icon in the toolbar on the left (see Figure 3-13). This icon looks very similar to the Preview Icon. An empty row will appear.

If you are not able to add rows by clicking on the Insert Row icon, make sure that you have previously created an index or defined a Primary key. You will not be able to add rows without at least one of these. ■

Sorting Out Your Relationships

Most databases have more than one table. One of the features of relational databases is that you can set relationships between tables. To see how these relationships work in PowerBuilder you should create another table. Follow the steps described previously for creating tables. Your new sample table should be named INFO, and have the structure listed in Table 3-5.

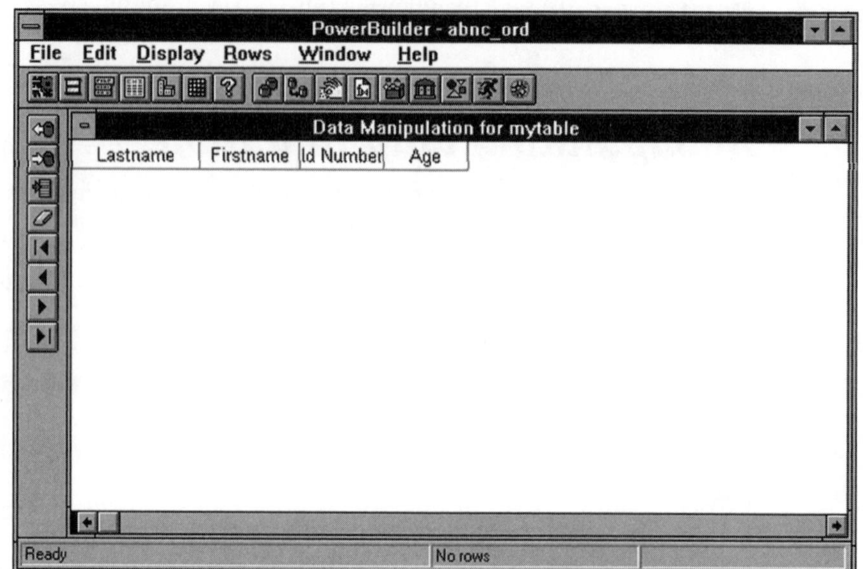

Figure 3-13: Add new rows by clicking the Insert icon.

Table 3-5: The structure for the sample table named INFO

Name	*Type*	*Width*	*Dec*	*Null*
id_number	Char	5		No
Date	Date			No
Hours	Numeric	2	0	No

Notice that this new table has a column with the same name, type, and width as a column in the first table we created. As you may have guessed, the id_number column will be used to create a relationship between the two tables.

Setting relationships

You will want to form relationships between tables so that you can connect tables with related information. When tracking employee information, for example, it is not necessary to store the employee's name in each table. Several tables containing employee information need only have some unique bit of information, such as the employee ID number in common. Therefore, a timecard table, having many rows of information for each employee, can form a relationship with an employee-information table containing the employee's name, social security number, employee ID number, and so on.

A table containing information such as the employee's name is considered the *parent table*. A second table containing one or more rows of information about the employee is considered a *child table*. In PowerBuilder, relationships between parent and child tables are created by defining *key columns*. A key column is one, such as the employee ID number, that both the parent and child have in common. The parent table defines a key known as the *primary key*. Defining a primary key tells the database that this table can act as a parent table. To form a relationship with a parent, child tables define their keys as *foreign keys*.

Each table can have only one column defined as a primary key. A table may have one or more columns defined as foreign keys. Also, a table may be both a parent and a child table, containing both a primary and foreign keys. ■

To define a primary key in a table:

1. In the Database Painter, double-click the open table where you want to define a primary key. The Alter Table dialog will appear, containing the table information.
2. Click the Primary button in the lower-right corner of the Alter Table dialog. This button has a key and the letter P on it. This will bring up the Primary Key Definition dialog.
3. Select from the list the column you want to define as the primary key. It will appear in the Key Columns box. Your primary key can be made up of more than one column. Continue selecting columns until your primary key is correctly defined.
4. Click the OK button to define your primary key.
5. Click the Alter button in the Alter Table dialog to complete the definition of the primary key. Your table will now appear in the Database Painter with the primary key identified by an icon (see Figure 3-14).

All right, you've let the database know that your table can be a parent. It's time for a child. Making children in PowerBuilder isn't nearly as much fun as making human children. But, it's faster and they don't cry in the middle of the night. To create a child table you must define a foreign key in the table you wish to be the child. It's rather like an adoption.

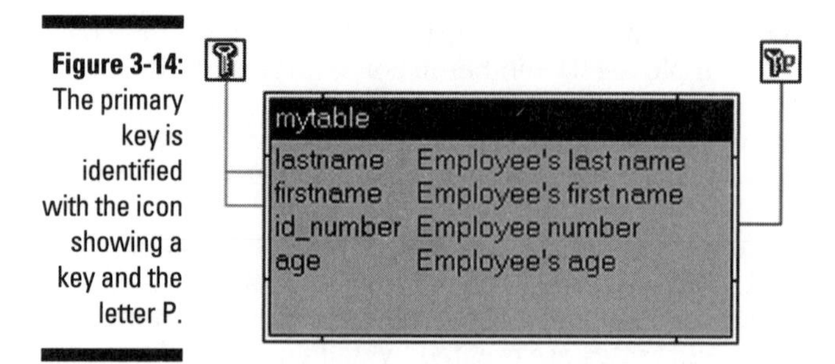

Figure 3-14: The primary key is identified with the icon showing a key and the letter P.

To create a foreign key:

1. Double-click the open table to bring up the Alter Table dialog.
2. Click the Foreign button in the lower-right corner of the Alter Table dialog. It has a yellow key and the letter F. This will bring up the Foreign Key Selection dialog. If no foreign keys exist, your only option is to click the New... button. If foreign keys exist, you may select them to be modified.
3. You must give your foreign key a name. Since a table can have many foreign keys, each must have a unique name. Enter a name in the Foreign Key Name field.
4. Select a column or columns that you want defined as the foreign key from the Select Columns list. Remember, they must match a previously defined primary key. The selected columns will appear in the Foreign Key Columns box.
5. Select the table from the drop-down list that contains the primary key. In other words, select the parent table from the list. The matching primary key column will be automatically inserted in the Primary Key Columns box.
6. Select the behavior you wish to happen to rows in the child table when a row is deleted in the parent table by clicking the radio button next to the specific behavior.
7. Click the OK button. This will return you to the Foreign Key selection dialog. You will notice that your newly defined foreign key is now displayed in the list box.
8. Click the Done key. This will return you to the Alter Table dialog.
9. Click the Alter button. This will return you to the Database Painter. Figure 3-15 shows that there is now a line connecting the parent and child tables. This line points from the primary key to the foreign key icon that now marks the foreign key in the child table.

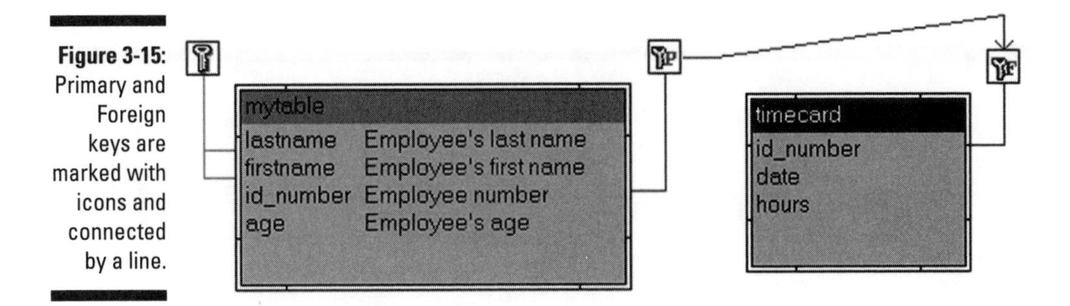

Figure 3-15: Primary and Foreign keys are marked with icons and connected by a line.

PowerBuilder makes working with databases simple. No matter what database you are using, the Database Painter gives you a common interface to each one. Each of the databases you may be using may have different capabilities. PowerBuilder is set up to take advantage of each of these abilities. You should refer to the technical manuals of your database to learn more about it.

Summary

In this chapter you have learned how to create a database and add tables to it. You have also learned how to add indexes and set relationships between tables by defining primary and foreign keys. You can use the Database Painter to administer your database while developing applications in PowerBuilder. You can also use this painter to edit the data contained in the tables.

In the next chapter you will learn more about administering databases and how to use SQL (Structured Query Language) to issue commands to your database.

Chapter 4

Database Handling

In This Chapter

- Adding users
- Adding groups
- Setting up security
- Using the SQL Painter to communicate with the database

In the last chapter you learned how to create a database, put tables in it, and fill it with data. This is a little like going out to buy a puppy. Puppies are fun and they lick your face. But very soon after getting your puppy you find that some very important dog handling must occur. Learning to handle your new puppy and training it to respond to your needs and desires will lead to many years of happiness for both of you. Learning to handle your database will bring the same kind of happiness. That is, if databases can be said to be happy.

Learning proper database administration and learning to communicate effectively with your database will make your job much easier. PowerBuilder's Database Painter allows you to administer and communicate with your database in the same simple manner you used to create it.

This chapter will show you how to administer your database — setting up table security, maintaining users, and setting up and maintaining groups of users — using tools included in the Database Painter. You will also learn how to use SQL, a structured query language, to communicate with your database.

Adding Users

The databases that work with PowerBuilder employ user IDs and groups to control access to information stored in tables. You may choose to have everyone use a single user ID, or give each user a unique ID. By giving a unique ID to each user, you can control security at the individual user level.

Using the Database Administration Painter you can maintain the list of users allowed access to the database. To add a user:

1. Start the Database Painter by clicking on the Database Painter icon in the PowerBar.
2. Click the Cancel button in the Select Tables window.
3. From the PowerBuilder menu, select Objects | Database Administration... This starts the Database Administration Painter.
4. From the PowerBuilder menu, select Objects | Maintain Users... This brings up the Maintain Users dialog. All current users will be listed in this dialog.
5. To add a user click the New... button. This brings up the Create User dialog.
6. Enter the User ID in the field provided. For example, type the following name in the User ID field:

   ```
   zaphod
   ```

7. Enter a password for the user, and then re-enter it in the next field. Entering the password twice verifies that you have entered the password you intended. For example, type the following password:

   ```
   samplepw
   ```

8. Click the OK button to create this user. You will be returned to the Maintain Users dialog, where you should now see the new user's name in the list box.
9. When you are finished adding users, click the Done button to return to the Database Administration Painter.

Figure 4-1 shows the users listed in the Maintain Users dialog. You can continue adding users, change the passwords of existing users, or delete users using the buttons in this dialog box.

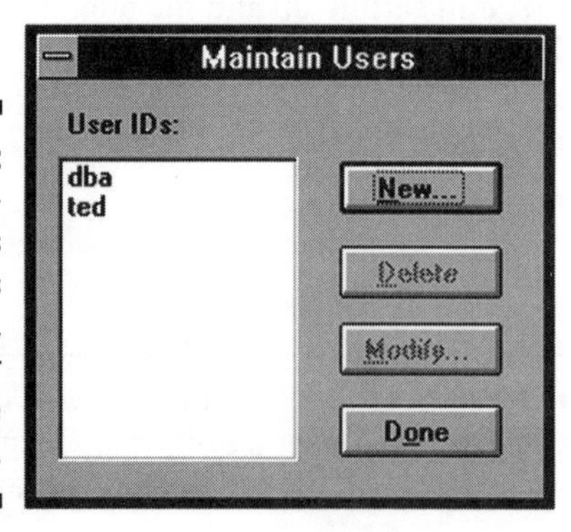

Figure 4-1: The Maintain Users dialog lets you add, change, or delete users.

Forming a user group

Humans, being social animals, are always forming groups. Ants form colonies, geese form gaggles, and humans form user groups. This isn't the kind of user group that meets at the local all-night restaurant to discuss when the new release of their favorite software is due out and how many bugs it is expected to have. The type of group you as the database administrator define is one in which you define different levels of security for different groups of users.

Creating a group is a two-step process. First, you must create a new user whose name is actually the name of the group. This new group will be a user of the database. Then you add users to the the new group (or define the group) by choosing which of the already existing users will belong to the group.

You must have added users following the steps given previously before they can be added to a group. Remember, you must also add the group as a user before you can define the members of the group.

To create a group:

1. Start the Database Painter by clicking on the Database Painter icon in the PowerBar. When the Select Tables dialog appears, click the Cancel button.
2. From the PowerBuilder menu, select Objects | Database Administration... This starts the Database Administration Painter.
3. From the PowerBuilder menu, select Objects | Maintain Users...
4. Add the new group as a user by clicking the New... button.
5. Enter the group name in the User ID field.
6. Enter a password for the new group.
7. Click the OK button to create this user.
8. Click the Done button to return to the Database Administration Painter.
9. From the PowerBuilder menu, select Objects | Maintain Groups... This will bring up the Maintain Groups dialog.
10. To form a new group, click the New Group... button. This will bring up the Create Group dialog.
11. Enter the name of the group you previously added as a user in step 5. You will automatically return to the Maintain Groups dialog. You will see the new group name in the Group Names box.

12. Now you must add users to your group. In the User Names box, highlight the users you want included. Add them to the Group members box by clicking on the << arrow. To remove them as members click on the >> arrow.
13. When you are finished adding members to your group, click the Done button.

You have now added users and created groups. The reason you added users and created groups is so you can control security. This next section shows you how.

Calling security

Allowing users or groups different access to the database tables can be very important for:

- Protecting confidential information
- Maintaining data integrity
- Departmentalizing information

These are only a few of the many reasons to set up security at the user and group levels.

Security is set up for each individual table. To save you a lot of work, PowerBuilder allows you to set up security for many tables at the same time using the Table Security dialog. See Figure 4-2.

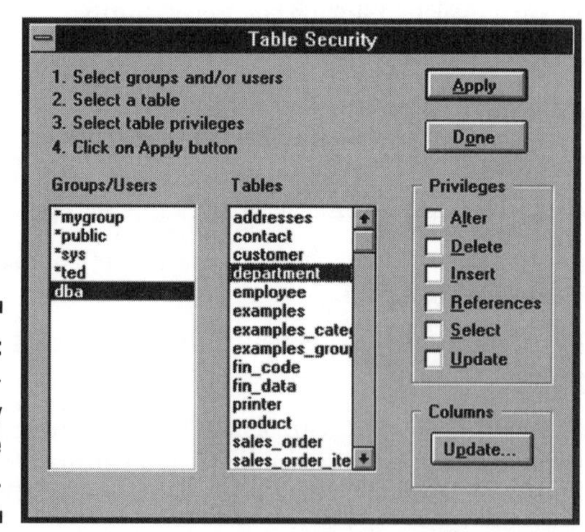

Figure 4-2: Set up security for many tables at the same time.

1. Start the Database Painter by clicking on the Database Painter icon in the PowerBar.
2. From the PowerBuilder menu, select Objects | Database Administration... This starts the Database Administration Painter.
3. From the PowerBuilder menu, select Objects | Table Security... This brings up the Table Security dialog, as shown in Figure 4-2.
4. Select the groups or users you want to set security for.
5. Select the table on which you want to place security for the groups and users selected in step 4.
6. Select the privileges you want to confer to your groups and users by clicking the checkboxes next to the privileges.
7. You can give update privileges for one, several, or all of the columns in a table. Click the Update button and select the columns you want to be updateable. Click the OK button in the Column Security dialog.
8. When you have finished defining security you must click on the Apply button. This will apply all of your security changes to the database. Because you can only select one table at a time, repeat steps 5 through 8 for each table.
9. Click the Done button to return to the Database Administration Painter.

Remember, defining good security will save you a great deal of work later. You can protect your work, and the work of the people entering the data, by restricting access to those users who need add, change, and delete access. ■

"Garçon!," "La Cuenta!," and Other Server Commands

PowerBuilder uses a language called SQL (pronounced "sequel" by many), or Structured Query Language, to communicate with your database. Many people become apprehensive when they hear the word language. While you don't need to be a SQL wizard to use PowerBuilder, it does help to know the basic elements of SQL.

SQL is an industry-defined standard language for communicating with databases. Its commands allow you to:

- Administer the database
- Add, change, and delete data
- Create views of your data through queries

Even though each database uses standard SQL, they all have added their own enhancements to the language to control special features unique to their products. Refer to the database user manual for a complete SQL syntax guide.

Talking to the database through an interpreter

PowerBuilder provides a complete SQL Painter to help you build SQL commands. To start the SQL Painter, click the SQL icon. This icon is available in the toolbar of several painters.

To use the SQL Painter in the Database Administration Painter:

1. Start the Database Painter by clicking the Database Painter icon in the PowerBar.
2. Select the tables you want opened.
3. Click the Database Administration icon in the Database Painter toolbar. It shows a pencil and a green drum that somehow represents the database. I've heard of Janitor in a Drum, but database in a drum?
4. Click the SQL icon in the Database Administration Painter. The SQL Painter will load. See Figure 4-3.

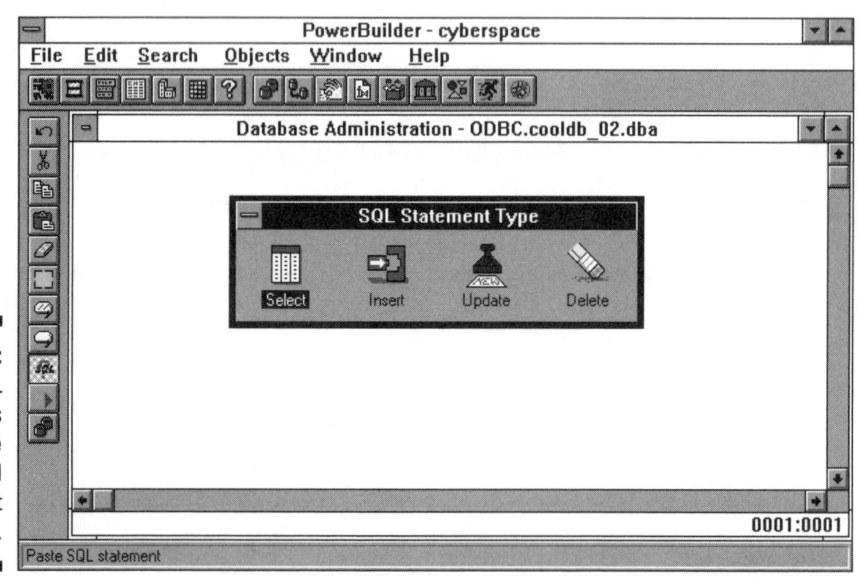

Figure 4-3: The SQL painter is available from several different painters.

You can see from Figure 4-3 that there are four commands available to you in the SQL Painter. No, you didn't get shortchanged. These four commands are the heart of the SQL language. With these four commands you can do anything you want with the data in your tables. Table 4-1 gives you a brief description of each command.

Table 4-1: The SQL commands available in the SQL Painter

SQL Command	*Description*
Select	Retrieves rows of data from your table in response to query criteria
Insert	Inserts rows of data into your table
Update	Allows you to change data in your tables
Delete	Removes rows from your table

It is important to know some basic facts about each of these commands:

- They all talk to tables; therefore, they need to know which table they are acting on.
- The Select, Insert, and Update commands involve columns; they need to know the columns' names.
- Select, Update, and Delete have a scope; therefore they need to know which rows you are referring to.

The SQL Painter will help you construct these commands so that each of the important elements is included.

Applying SQL

With many other programs, now would be the time to do your yoga, meditation, or whatever you do to lower your blood pressure. However, PowerBuilder has made working with SQL so easy that there is no need for heart palpitations.

To begin, we will cover the most commonly used SQL command, the Select statement. Use the Select statement to query information from your table. After you issue a Select statement, the database returns a *result set*. The result set consists of the rows in the database table or tables that match the criteria specified in the Select statement. To use the SQL Painter to construct a select statement:

1. Double-click the Select icon with your mouse. This will bring up the Select Tables dialog. (See Figure 4-4.)
2. Select the tables from the list by clicking on them. Then click on the Open button. You will notice that each table's structure appears in the SQL Painter with a line connecting the key fields. (Figure 4-5)
3. Click on the column names to select which columns you want in your query. Notice that they appear across the top of the SQL Painter. The order in which you select them is the order in which they will appear. (See Figure 4-4.)

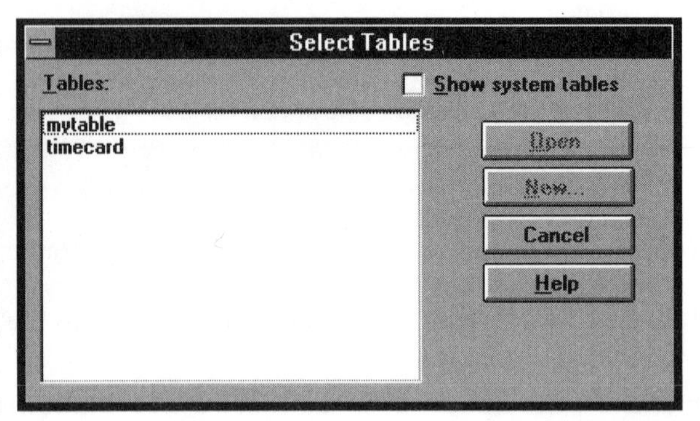

Figure 4-4: Open the tables by selecting them from the list in the Select Tables dialog.

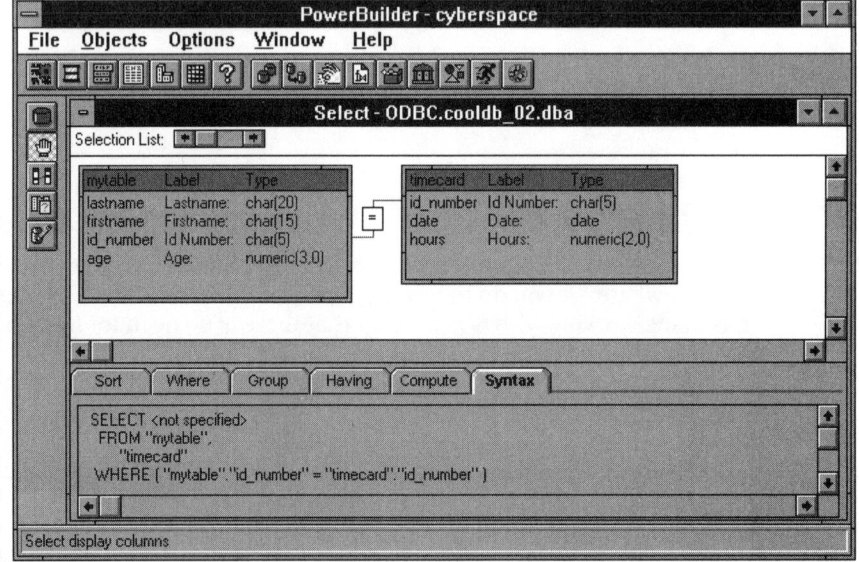

Figure 4-5: The SQL syntax is displayed at the bottom of the SQL Painter when you click the Syntax tab.

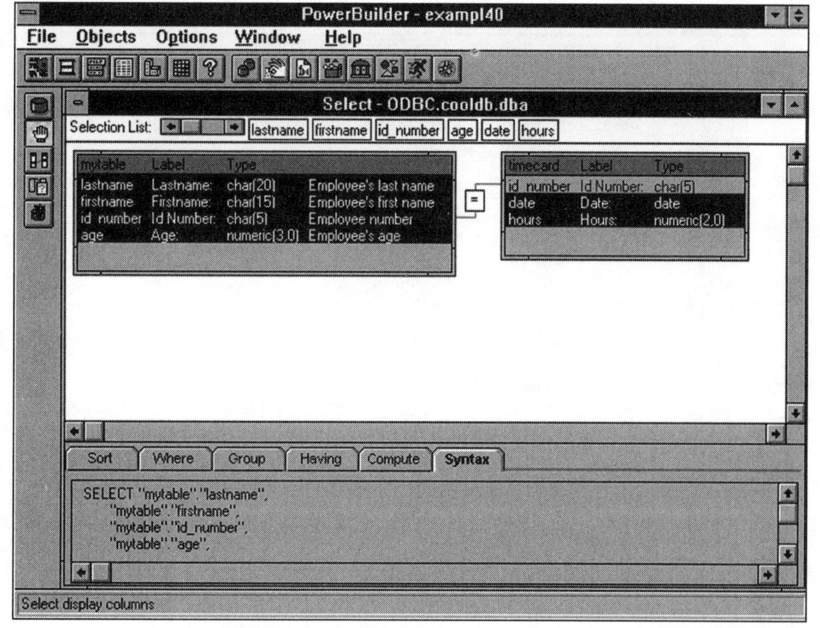

Figure 4-6: This is a graphical representation of a simple Select statement.

You have now constructed a SQL Select statement. You can view the syntax of your Select statement at the bottom of the SQL Painter. Now you need to send the Select statement to the database.

Executing SQL

When you exit the SQL Painter, the syntax of your SQL statement will be pasted into whatever tool the SQL Painter was called from. In our example, we called the SQL Painter from the Database Administration Painter. When we return to this painter, our Select statement will be pasted there.

Click on the Database Administrator icon in the tool bar. This will close the SQL Painter and return you to the Database Administration Painter with the SQL query you have created (Figure 4-7).

The last step is to execute the Select statement. Executing the statement means sending it to the database for proper handling. When the database receives a select statement it knows to perform a query and return a result set.

To execute this Select statement, click on the Execute icon. The icon looks like the play button on your VCR. Once you have clicked the icon the results will appear in a Select window, as in Figure 4-8.

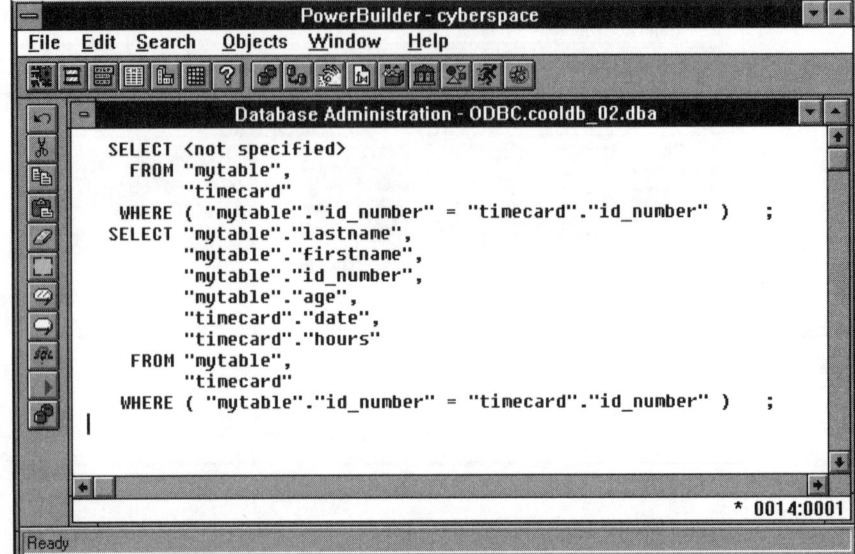

Figure 4-7: This is the syntax for the graphics in Figure 4-6.

Select 1

Lastname	Firstname	Id Number	Age	Date	Hours
Bowditch	Nate	10010	95	9/9/94	8
Swift	Tom	10011	15	9/9/94	9
Franklin	Ben	10012	73	9/9/94	6
Cohen	Ishmael	10013	35	9/9/94	10
Hati	Vivek	10014	30	9/9/94	8
Tupelo	Honey	10015	20	9/9/94	8

Figure 4-8: The results of your queries appear in a Select window.

Santa is not a valid SQL clause

The Select statement in the previous section was a simple query. The Select statement can be simple or very complex. You can construct complex queries by adding *clauses*. A clause is a component of a SQL statement that constructs, limits, or formats the result set. Table 4-2 lists some common Select statement clauses. You should refer to your database manual for complete Select statement syntax.

Table 4-2: Components of a Select statement

Clause	*Description*
Join	Joins two tables together with a Where clause
Union	Combines the results of two Select statements
Sort	Sorts the Select statement's results
Where	Used to limit which rows appear in the result set; also used when a value in one table has some relationship to a value in another table; used with Join to join the tables
Group	Defines groups into which results are separated
Having	Restricts the selection of groups

We will now use the SQL Painter to create another Select statement that includes some of the clauses listed in Table 4-2.

1. From the Database Administration Painter, click the SQL icon. This will start the SQL painter.
2. Choose Select as the SQL Statement Type by double-clicking the Select icon.
3 Open both tables by highlighting them (by clicking on them with your mouse). When you have selected the tables you want, click the Open button.
4. Select the columns you wish to appear in the result set by clicking on them in the order you want them to appear.
5. Click the Sort tab at the bottom of the SQL Painter. Click and drag the id_number column from the list of columns to the box on the right. The column name will now appear with a checkbox labeled Ascending (see Figure 4-9) next to it. Unchecking this box will cause the sort to be done in descending order.
6. Click the Where tab. The Where clause can be used either to limit which rows will be in the result set or to join tables. We'll use it to join our two tables.
7. Click the first empty row beneath Column and choose a column name. For this example, choose mytable.id_number. Notice that the table name precedes the column name and the two are separated by a dot.

8. The default operator is an equal sign. You may select other operators but, for our example, we will use the equal sign.

9. In the Value column type

```
timecard.id_number
```

This will join the two tables with the primary and foreign keys (see Figure 4-10). For more on keys, refer back to Chapter 3.

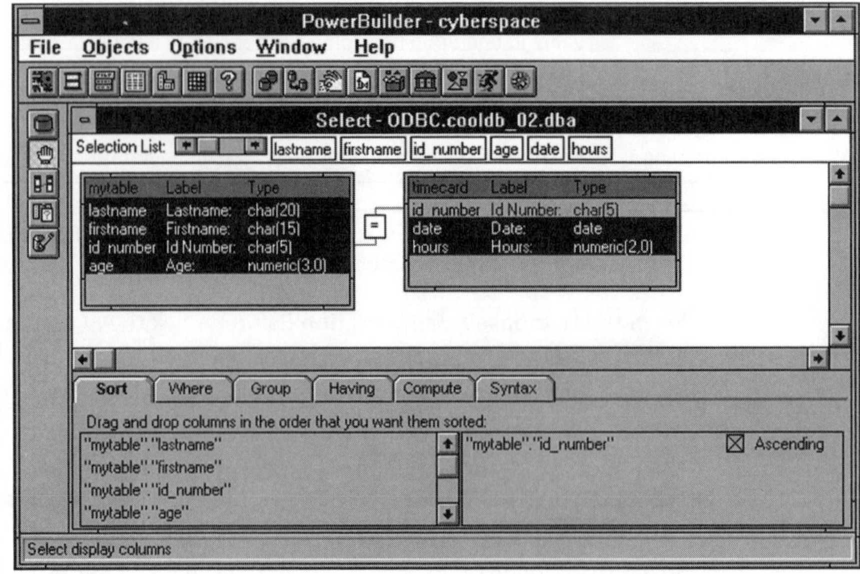

Figure 4-9: The sort columns are dragged to the box on the right.

Another, simpler way is to click the Join icon. There are many ways of doing the same thing in PowerBuilder. As you become comfortable, you will begin to decide which way works best for you.

Even though there are more tabs to choose from, the Sort and Where clauses are the only ones that make sense for this example. Now return to the Database Administration Painter with this SQL statement and execute it.

In other, more complete data tables, you may choose to have the results appear grouped. For these cases, click the Group tab to define the groups.

When information in a result set is grouped, you may further limit the information in your result set by specifying a Having clause. To do this in your Select statement, define the group first and then click the Having tab to define the Having clause.

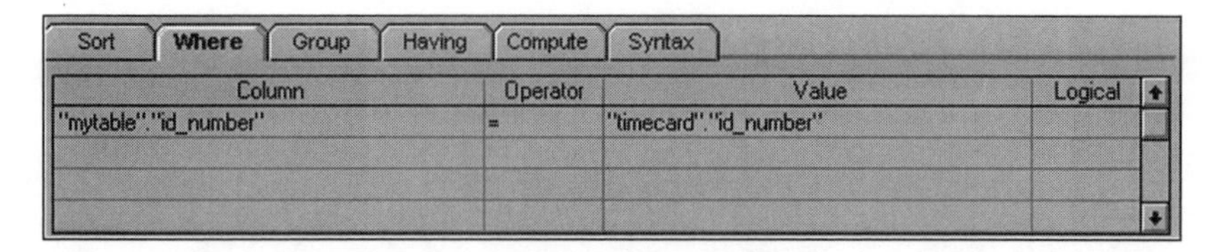

Figure 4-10: The Where clause can limit rows or join tables.

Something from nothing

You may notice in Figure 4-10 that there is a Compute Tab. Clicking this tab allows you to create a computed column. As you become more familiar with using SQL, you may want to try creating computed columns. Here is how to do it:

1. Click the Compute tab.
2. Click with your right mouse button in the Computed Columns box to add column names and functions.

Using the sample table, mytable, try creating a computed column using the firstname and lastname columns.

1. Click with the right mouse button in the Computed Columns box and select Columns...
2. Select mytable.firstname. It will appear in the Computed Columns box.
3. For this example we are going to concatenate (put together) the first and last names, so insert a plus sign after the firstname column.
4. Click with the right mouse button in the Computed Columns box and select Columns...
5. Select mytable.lastname. The computed column will now read: mytable.firstname + mytable.lastname.

The computed column is now defined. The database will treat this computed column as any other column while selecting information from a table. You can't add or delete information in computed columns.

The example we used where two names are concatenated can be improved by removing the trailing spaces in the name columns using the TRIM( ) function. More PowerScript functions will be covered throughout this book. It will look like this: TRIM(first_name). When you remove the extra spaces, you will have to concatenate in a single space before you add the last name: TRIM(first_name) + " " + last_name. ■

Safe inserting

The ability to add new data to a table is an important feature in any database. You have already seen how you can use the Database Painter to add and edit information. You may choose to use the Preview tool for quick administrative access to your data. However, in order to develop applications, you will want to become familiar with how SQL inserts data into your table.

To insert data using the SQL Painter:

1. From the Database Administration Painter, click the SQL icon.
2. Double-click the Insert icon in the SQL Statement Type dialog box.
3. Select the table or tables into which you want to insert rows of data and click the Open button.
4. Enter the new values next to the appropriate column names in the Insert Column Values dialog. (See Figure 4-11.)
5. When you are finished adding values, click the OK button.

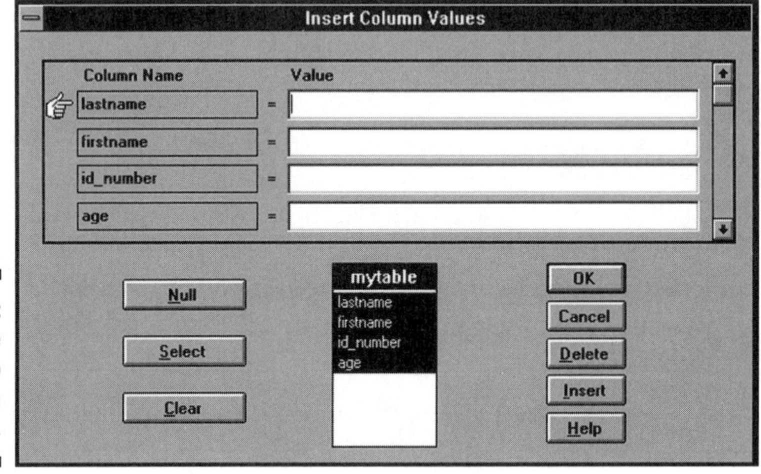

Figure 4-11: Fill in the values to insert data into a table.

Make sure you know which columns will accept Null values. If you leave blank a column that requires values, you will get an error message. In columns where Null values are not allowed, you can't fill in just some of the data. ■

You can use the Null button to insert the word Null into your column. This is useful if:

- You forget how to spell Null
- You don't want to let go of your mouse
- Number of keystrokes is a productivity issue
- You're lazy

On a more useful note, you can insert the result of a Select statement. Clicking the Select button will take you into the familiar Select SQL Painter, except that now the window is titled Insert From Select.

The trick to inserting from a Select statement is that the columns in the result set must match the columns in the Insert statement.

Before you hit that OK button to return to the Database Administration Painter with your Insert statement, there are a couple more buttons to address. The Delete button will remove the selected column. The Insert button will insert a blank column before the selected column. This is useful only if all your column names are not displayed. You can use delete and insert to change the order of column names.

Updating does not mean dating in Beverly Hills

You can use the SQL Painter to change values already stored in a table. The terms used in SQL aren't always the most obvious. No one consulted us before they created this standard language. As you've learned, insert means add new rows of data; update means replace column values with new ones. To use the SQL Painter to change values:

1. From the Database Administration Painter, click the SQL icon.
2. Double-click the Update icon in the SQL Statement Type dialog box.
3. Select the table or tables in which you want to update rows of data, and click the Open button.
4. Select a column name from the list. It will then appear in the blank box near the top of the Update Column Values dialog (Figure 4-12). Enter the new value next to the column name. It's not necessary to supply new values for all the columns.

Make sure that the type of data you're entering matches the column type. Also, make sure that character data is enclosed in quotes. ■

You can use the operator buttons supplied to help you construct complex values. There is the amazing Null button to amuse you. Also, if you get tired of the Null button, there is a two-step process involving the Clear button for removing what you've typed in the values fields.

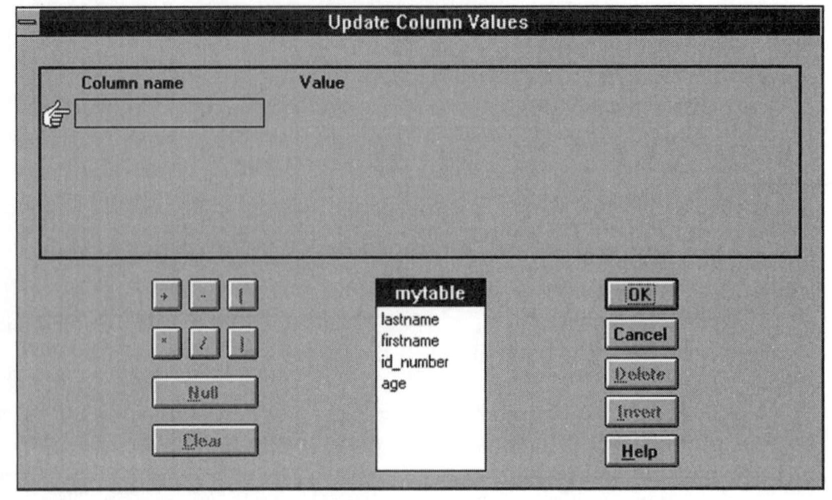

Figure 4-12: Column names appear as you select them.

You may also use the Insert and Delete buttons in your Update statement to remove columns or to change their order.

Dial "M" for delete

Deleting data from your table doesn't have to be murder. In fact, the SQL Painter makes removing those nasty rows quite easy. We could say as easy as 1-2-3 but that's another product.

Important: Back up your data often. Deleting rows of data permanently removes that information from your table. Restoring this data can be a cumbersome task. If records are accidentally removed, it's possible to restore your database table from a backup copy. You may also use your transaction log to reconstruct data entered through PowerBuilder. You should refer to your database manual for more information on restoring information using transaction logs. ■

To remove rows of data from your table using the SQL Painter:

1. From the Database Administration Painter, click the SQL icon.
2. Double-click the Delete icon in the SQL Statement Type dialog box.
3. Select the table or tables from which you want to delete rows.
4. Select the Where tab in the Delete window.
5. Click on a box beneath the Column header and select a column name from the list. In this example we will choose the column mytable.lastname.
6. Choose an operator. The default is the equal sign.

7. Enter a value that will create a valid expression. For example, Smith. This creates the expression:

```
mytable.lastname = "Smith"
```

All rows where the last name equals Smith will be deleted. See Figure 4-13.

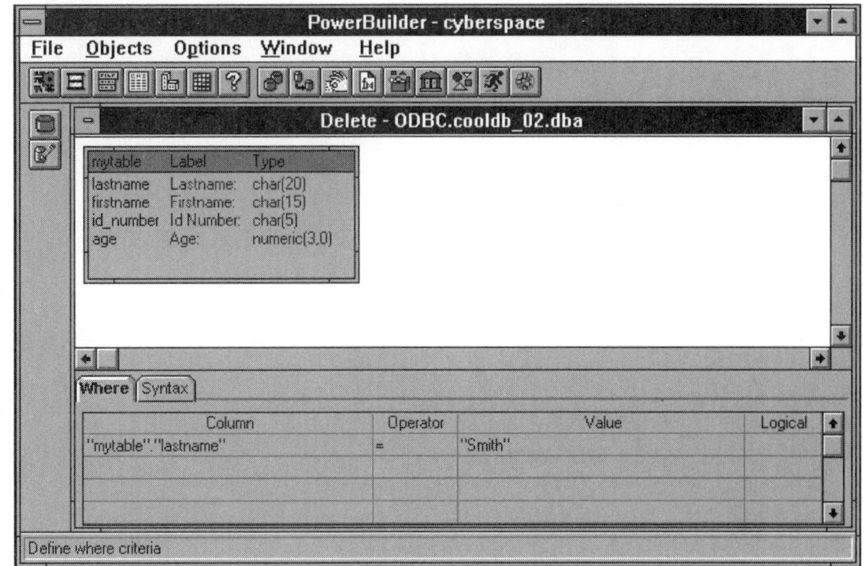

Figure 4-13: The Where clause is the only thing you specify for a Delete statement.

The Delete statement is the easiest to use of the four SQL statements available in the SQL Painter. There are no columns to select, no order to specify. You simply limit the number of rows you want deleted by specifying a Where clause.

Be warned that not specifying a Where clause will permanently delete every row in your table. It's a good idea to have a cup of coffee before specifying deletes that could wipe out all of your data!

Summary

Database administration is now simple with the graphic tools provided in PowerBuilder. The Database Administration Painter allows you to create security for your tables, while the SQL Painter gives you the ability to add, change, and delete data. The SQL Painter also helps construct complex queries using the Select statement. The next chapter will take you further into viewing and querying your data.

Chapter 5

Views and Queries

In This Chapter

- Creating views
- Using views like tables
- Creating and using queries

Powerful database applications include not only the ability to add, change, and delete data, but the ability to easily retrieve data from the database. Views and queries make your programming easier. There is no need to produce SQL syntax over and over when you build an application. You can create views that look like tables or create queries, which are saved SQL Select statements, that you can use over and over when developing applications.

Using these tools simplifies application development, which reduces the number of bugs, and makes it easier for teams to work together. It also makes changing an application simpler — you can make changes in one place instead of throughout the entire application.

Vista Point 500 Metres

A view is a way of looking at the information in your tables. It's a little tricky, so here's a strange analogy:

> KPDR TV decides to take the world's first remote group picture. They set up mini-cams all over the country to take group pictures in each location. A bunch of happy, smiling faces stare expectantly into the camera at each site. However, the tricky camera operators zoom in on only one person from each group. They send the feed live via satellite to New York, where creative technicians put all of the images into a super graphic workstation and compose one group picture from all of the individual shots. So while these

participants are grinning and twiddling their thumbs, thinking they are part of their local group, only one of them is actually being featured in a composite picture created artificially by a TV station with nothing better to do.

A view is like the preceding example. You have all these columns that are part of this little group of columns called a table. Now some creative application developer like yourself puts together something that looks like a table, but is really a picture of columns from other tables.

To create a view, take columns from several tables and give this set of columns a name, just as you would a table. The things to remember about a view are:

- It looks like a table.
- It acts like a table.
- You can query it like a table.
- It isn't a table; it's another way of accessing the data in your tables.

A Kodak picture place

You may be asking yourself why you would want to create a view. One word: SIMPLICITY! If you have a query you are always performing, or an SQL statement you continually execute, to see one particular set of data, you can now see the data as though it were a special table. You never have to run your query or execute that SQL syntax again. PowerBuilder performs this magic behind the scenes. This is especially useful if you have many people working on the same PowerBuilder application. You reduce your application development time, and minimize the possibility of introducing bugs with incorrect syntax.

To create a view:

1. Open the Database Painter by clicking on the Database Painter icon.
2. Click the Cancel button in the Select Tables dialog to close this dialog.
3. Click the View Painter icon.
4. Open the tables that have the columns you need for your view. To do this, highlight the tables by clicking on them, and then click the Open button.
5. Select the columns you want to appear in your view by clicking on the column names. The column names will appear across the top of the window as you select them. See Figure 5-1.

6. Set the Sort, Group, Where, and Having criteria. See the next section for details on setting these criteria.
7. Click the Database Painter icon; when the Save View Definition dialog pops up, enter a name for your view. This is similar to naming a table.

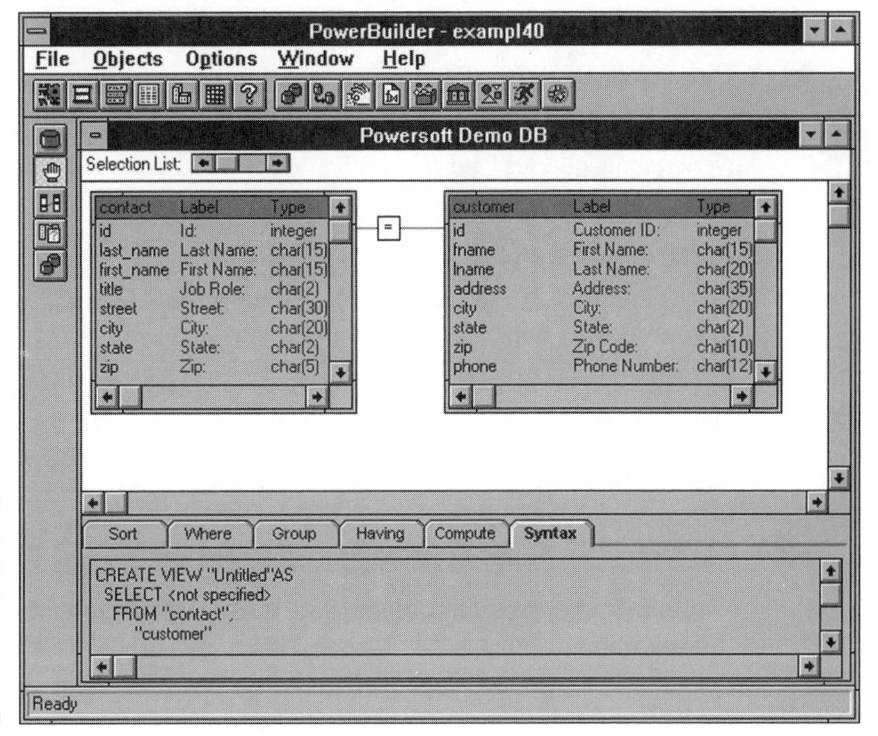

Figure 5-1: Select columns by clicking on the column names.

You can include computed columns in your view. Select the Compute tab and enter the criteria to create the computed field.

When creating computed columns, you can click in the Computed Columns box with your right mouse button to be able to select Columns, Functions, or Arguments. We cover creating a computed column in greater detail in Chapter 4. ■

Setting the criteria for a view

A view is a subset of information that you wish to look at as though it were a table. Before, we said that you could take one or more columns from several different tables and create a view out of them. This is true; but the exciting part is that you don't have to include all the data from those columns.

For example, if you have a goose farm and are tracking goose products, you may want to limit your view to products made from down. You can specify criteria that will show only those products in your view. However, if you specify the criteria incorrectly, you may end up with a big goose egg.

It isn't absolutely critical that you specify criteria when creating a view. You can simply select the columns and view all of the information contained in them. You can then limit what you see in the view by creating a query. We cover creating queries later in this chapter. ■

Sorting your view

The first criteria you can set up for your view is the sort order. You can sort your view by one or more columns. The column you select first denotes the primary sort order, and then each column you subsequently select is sorted in the same order in which it was selected. For example, if I choose the lastname column as the primary column and the firstname column as the secondary, names are sorted by lastname and then by firstname. See Table 5-1.

Table 5-1: The result of columns sorted by lastname and then by firstname

lastname	*firstname*
Anderson	Alice
Anderson	Sven
Baker	Judy
Carlson	Peter
Carlson	Robert
Carlson	Zaean

To specify the sort order:

1. Click the Sort tab.
2. With your left mouse button, click on a column name in the list of columns. Holding the left mouse button down, drag the column name into the empty box to the right.

3. Continue selecting and dragging columns to the box on the right until you have selected all of the columns on which you want the view to be sorted.

Limiting the data in your view

As we said earlier, it isn't necessary to view all of the data from the columns in your view. You can limit what data appears in your view. Just as when you take a photograph, you can choose what appears in the picture (or view), except for those sneaky kids sticking their tongues out at the last second.

Use a Where clause to limit what your view shows. A Where clause limits the data shown to rows of the column *where* it matches your criteria. Where last-name equals "Carlson" would have limited the rows in Table 5-1 to the last three, as shown in Table 5-2.

Table 5-2: The result of using a Where clause to limit the rows viewed in a table

lastname	*firstname*
Carlson	Peter
Carlson	Robert
Carlson	Zaean

Now let's create a Where clause. Remember that the Where clause consists of three basic components — a column name, a relational operator, and a value to compare the column name against. You can create compound Where clauses by joining many small clauses together with logical operators such as AND and OR. For example:

```
SKY = "BLUE" AND TEMPERATURE < 70
```

When creating compound Where clauses, put each small clause on a different line with the logical operator at the end to join it to the clause on the next line. The last clause has no logical operator at the end. ■

To create a Where clause:

1. Select the Where tab.
2. When you click in the Column box, a drop-down listbox appears. Select a column name from the list.

3. Select the operator necessary to build your criteria. Clicking in the operator box gives you a list of choices. The default operator is an equal sign.
4. Enter a value. Clicking with the right mouse button allows you to choose columns, functions, and arguments. You may also enter a value. Remember to enclose character-type information in quotes.
5. (Optional) If you are building a compound Where clause, select a logical operator from the list that appears when you click in the Logical box. Then enter a new Where clause, starting with step 1. You may continue steps 1 through 5 until your Where clause is complete.

It's important to remember why you are creating a view — to make developing your application easier. If there is a regular set of data you need to look at in your application, create a view rather than repeating the same query throughout your application to extract this set of data. ■

Encounter groups

Grouping your data is another way of organizing it. It is similar to sorting the data, except that you can limit which groups you see in a view by issuing a *Having clause*. See the next section for more information on the Having clause.

To create a group:

1. Click on the Group tab.
2. Select the column by which you want the data grouped, by State, for example. Click and drag the column name to the box on the right.

You can create subgroups by selecting additional column names and dragging them to the box on the right. The groups are created in the same order they are selected.

The haves and the have nots

The Having clause is meant to be used with Groups. You can include or exclude groups from your view by specifying criteria in a Having clause. If the group meets the criteria you specify, it is included in the view.

To create a Having clause, click on the Having tab and follow the same directions for creating a Where clause. The Having clause is a Where clause for groups.

Including computed columns in a view

A view is a special way of looking at data. You can make it even more meaningful by adding computed columns. Whenever you find yourself performing the same calculations on your data over and over again, consider creating a computed column. A computed column in your view also allows the user to query against that column as though it were a column in a table.

To create a computed column in your view:

1. Click the Computed tab.
2. Create the calculation whose result will appear as the data in your computed column. Normally, this calculation includes one or more columns. Remember, you can click the right mouse button to select column names, functions, or arguments.
3. Create a name for your new column and enter it in the box labeled Alias.

Remember that you are creating a view or a computed column in order to make your application easier to develop. It's easy to forget to use these labor-saving devices. Looking for ways to use them must become part of your development strategy. ■

Saving the view

Before you save your view, you may want to preview the results of your handiwork. Selecting Preview from the Options menu will give you a sneak preview of what your view will look like. It's also a good way to check your work — you'll receive an error message if there are any errors.

You can also enhance your view by changing the names of the columns before saving your definition. The column name is known as its alias. Select Modify from the Options menu and then Column Aliases and do what?

When you have completed the process of creating your View, you can either click on the Database Painter icon or select Return to Database Painter from the File menu. Then the Save View Definition dialog appears, asking you to enter a name for your view. Once you have entered the name, you must choose either the Create or Log Only button.

The Create button will send your definition to the database and your view will be created. Pushing the Log Only button will create the definition in the log file without sending a request to the database to create this view.

Your view will appear in the Database Painter as a table. There is no way visually to tell the difference between a table and a view in the Database Painter.

Using views

Views can be used like tables. Anything you can do with a table you can do with a view. Think of it as a virtual table. You can insert, update, and delete information.

Using the view in the DBA notepad

You can use your view in the DBA Notepad in the same manner you use tables. You can create SQL statements that join tables and views, or choose to administer the data in a view just as you would a table.

Important: Remember that a view is *not* a table. It is another way to view the data stored in other tables. Making changes to the data in a view changes the data in the tables themselves. ■

Commenting your view

It is very important that you add comments to your newly created view, since it will appear in PowerBuilder like a table. Commenting makes working together in an environment with many programmers easier. Because views don't behave exactly like tables, commenting will prevent confusion.

It's always a good idea to comment everything in PowerBuilder that can be commented. Let PowerBuilder keep track of your system documentation. When the documentation is on-line and attached to each component of the program, it's easier to refer to and easier to change. It's a wonderful feature. Make sure you take advantage of it. ■

To comment your view:

1. In the Database Painter, click on the title bar of the table with your right mouse button.
2. Select Comment… from the popup menu.
3. Enter a comment in the Comments for (Table Name) dialog. Hit OK when you are finished. The comment now appears in the title bar of the table. (See Figure 5-2.)

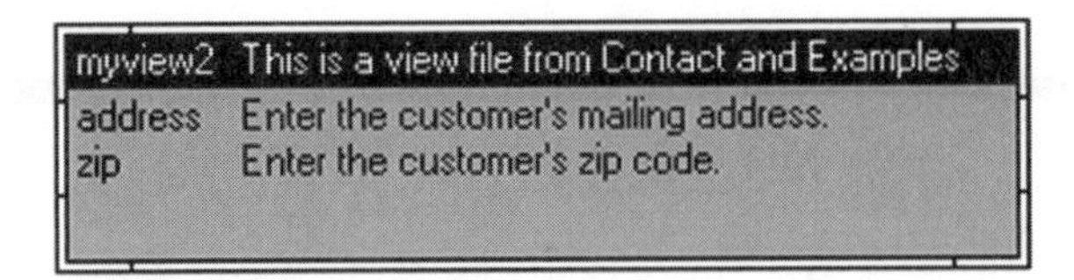

Figure 5-2: You can't tell the views from the tables without a comment.

Popping the Question

You've learned how you can make application development easier by creating a view of your data. Another tool is similar to a view, yet different. You create a view with a SQL statement and it hangs around looking like a table. A query is a SQL statement that hangs around looking like a SQL statement. Once again, you don't have to be a wizard with the SQL syntax. The graphic interface makes creating these statements simple.

As we cover other PowerBuilder tools later in this book, we will revisit queries to see how to use them to make application development even easier. So for starters, you need to know that you create queries with the Query Painter.

Building queries with the Query Painter

Unlike views, queries are not part of the database. Therefore, the icon for the Query Painter is part of the PowerBar, not the Database Painter. It's the yellow hand picking information out of a document. It also looks like it's making the OK sign. So OK, let's get started making queries. Here's how:

1. Click the Query icon in the PowerBar.
2. From the Select Query dialog, either select a query or click on the New button. The Select Tables dialog will appear.
3. When creating new queries, select the tables from which you want to retrieve information. To do this, click on the table names in the Select Tables dialog and then click the Open button to open them.
4. Select the columns you want included in your query from the open tables by clicking on the column names.
5. Set the selection criteria exactly as previously described in setting criteria for a view.

When you have finished building the query, you can preview the results by clicking on the Preview icon in the PainterBar. You may have to go back and forth, adjusting your query until you have just the results you want. It is much easier to test your query while still in the Query Painter than it is to test it live in your application.

When you have several tables open, it can be difficult to view them all. You can move them around the screen by clicking on them with your mouse and dragging them to a new location on the screen. If space is an issue, you can hide the toolbox (the one at the bottom of the screen that has the criteria tabs). To do this, simply click the Hide Toolbox icon in the PainterBar. Click it again to unhide the toolbox. Dragging your mouse across each different icon will display each function in the status bar at the bottom of the PowerBuilder window. ■

Don't get into a retrieval argument

Queries can be dynamic. You can create queries that change based on information you feed them at runtime. The information you supply to your query is called a *retrieval argument.* If you're writing an application for anthropologists, you may want to provide the ability to query by names of tribes. If the user enters "Yanomano," this value becomes a retrieval argument. It returns all rows in the tables where a tribe column equals "Yanomano."

Cool! You want to know how to do this, don't you? Here goes:

1. Select Retrieval Arguments... from the Objects menu. The Specify Retrieval Arguments dialog appears.
2. Enter a name for your retrieval argument. In the previous example, the retrieval argument might be named TRIBE_NAME.
3. Enter the type of the retrieval argument. This should match the column type with which you intend to use this argument. In our example, TRIBE_NAME is the String type.
4. You may choose to add additional retrieval arguments. If so, click the Add button. A new row will appear where you can enter the next argument.
5. Click the OK button when you have finished adding arguments.

You can insert and delete arguments from your list by clicking on the row you want deleted or on the row before which you want to insert a row, and then clicking either the Delete or Insert button.

To exit and save your query, press Ctrl+F4 or choose Close from the File menu. You will be prompted to name your query if it is the first time you have saved it. Make sure you specify in which PowerBuilder library you want the query saved.

Take this opportunity to add a comment to your query. As you are becoming aware, a PowerBuilder application can have many components. To keep track of them, their uses, and how they fit into the whole plan, it's a good idea to comment everything. Another good reason is that your application will be self-documenting.

Using queries

You can use a Query as a data source for *DataWindows* (remember, DataWindows are special data-handling controls). When you create a DataWindow you have several choices for filling it with data. Most of the choices involve using a SQL query to retrieve data. If you have already defined this SQL statement and have saved it as a query, you can tell PowerBuilder to use this saved query as the source for your data.

Just as there are many roads up a mountain, there are many queries that can lead to the same query results. The way you create SQL queries can greatly affect the efficiency of your database query. Optimizing a fairly complex query can be a challenging task. Once a query is optimized though, you will want to use that version of the query every time this data retrieval is required.

In a responsibility-oriented system, this makes the query responsible for getting the data from the database, and the DataWindow responsible for displaying that data in DataWindow format. Here are some sensible reasons for using queries:

- A team of programmers can share complex queries, thus standardizing a query.
- The ability to reuse queries simplifies application development..
- Use Responsibility Oriented System Engineering principles to create your application.

You can assign a query to a custom toolbar icon. This makes repetitive database querying simple. Of course, one of your big goals is to make your application easy for the end-user. Why not treat yourself well, too. Make your own life easier by customizing your work environment.

If you are a project leader, you'll want to create as many productivity devices as possible. Assigning a query to a custom toolbar icon ensures that your entire team sees the same data by standardizing the query used to retrieve data from the database.

To assign a query to a Custom Toolbar icon:

1. Open the customize window for the toolbar in which you want your custom icon to appear by clicking with your right mouse button anywhere on the toolbar. Select Customize… from the popup menu.
2. Click the Custom radio button at the top of the Customize dialog. This changes the Selected Palette of icons to the custom icons.
3. You must choose an unassigned icon for your query. Some custom icons already have tasks assigned to them. An available icon shows the description "Unassigned custom icon" in the Description area when you click on it. Choose one of these.
4. Click and drag an icon from the Selected Palette to the Current toolbar area. To drag an icon, you must hold the left mouse button down while moving the icon.
5. When the Toolbar Item Command dialog appears, you will have three fields to fill in. The first field, Command Line:, is filled in automatically when you click the Query… button and select the query you want to assign to your icon.
6. Whatever you type in the Item Text: field will appear whenever your mouse cursor moves over the icon. The small yellow popup text description will display the contents of this field.
7. Microhelp will appear in the status bar at the bottom of the PowerBuilder window whenever you place the mouse cursor over the icon. This should include any help you want to provide for this icon.
8. Select OK in the Toolbar Item Command dialog, and then again in the Customize dialog.

Your new Custom Query icon now appears in the toolbar you have just customized.

Summary

We have just covered Views and Queries. The moral of this chapter is this: You are a programmer; you can make computers work for you. This is your chance to do just that. Don't let computers control you. Dominate and control them. They are your slaves. Creating views and saving them as part of the database and creating queries that simplify your application development are both good examples of how to use PowerBuilder with the elegance of a truly outstanding programmer. It may seem as though all you have done so far is play with the database. Take heart, creating as many labor-saving tools, such as Views and Queries, will take the work out of the programming. This makes developing applications faster and more fun.

Part III

GUI Programming in PowerBuilder

"A CONSULTANT TOLD US THAT POLYESTER CAN CAUSE SHORTS IN THE SYSTEM, SO WE'RE TRYING AN ALL LEATHER AND LATEX DATA ENTRY DEPARTMENT."

In This Part...

One of the most compelling reasons to use PowerBuilder is that it makes building a graphical user interface, or GUI, for your database application fast and simple. Although our seemingly endless quest for faster and simpler compels us to eat horrible food, travel altogether too much, and purchase every new electronic gizmo that comes along, when it comes to building database interfaces, faster and simpler really *is* better.

Part 3 introduces the painters and tools that make building a user interface fast and simple.

Chapter 6

Window Painting

In This Chapter

- Creating windows using the Window Painter
- Adding buttons, text, and other controls

Several science-fiction writers have imagined a future so filled with crime and despair and so overpopulated and overbuilt that people replace the windows in their homes with peaceful, computer-generated images. You can help civilization avoid such a fate by creating user-friendly PowerBuilder applications.

The powerful people of the future will grow up using computer software. If that software is easy to use and well designed, then each day will be filled with joy and happiness for these young computer users. This will translate directly to an optimistic and well-adjusted population that comprehends an essential truth:

> User Interfaces are for users, not for programmers.

It Starts with a Window, You See

User interfaces are created using *windows*. Think of a window as an information presentation tool and as a navigation control panel. A window is at once a traffic sign, a dashboard, and a steering wheel. To create or modify a window, use the *Window Painter.*

Click on the Window icon in the PowerBar to start the Window Painter. The Select Window dialog appears, as shown in Figure 6-1. To modify an existing window, select the window name from the list box and click on the OK button. To create a new window, click on the New button.

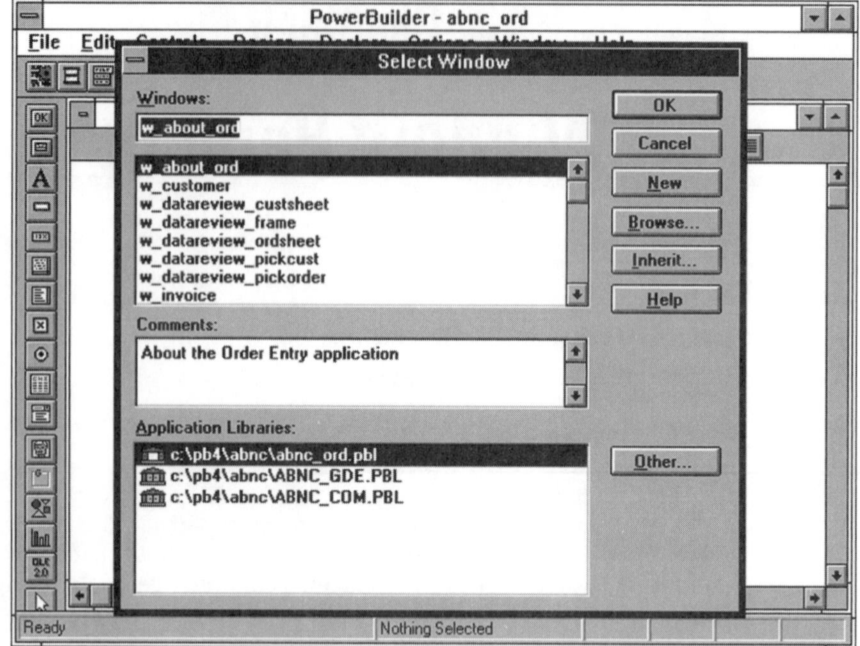

Figure 6-1: Select a window to modify in the Window Painter.

Once you've selected the window you want to modify, the Window Painter appears on the screen. If you click on the New button in the Select Window, a blank window will appear in the Window Painter (see Figure 6-2). The rectangular mass that looks like it has a bad case of chicken pox is the blank window.

The Window Painter PainterBar also appears. In Figure 6-2 the PainterBar is on the left side of the screen. As with other PainterBars, you can customize and reposition the Window Painter PainterBar. Click on the PainterBar with the right mouse button to customize or reposition it.

Setting the attributes of a window

There's more to that blank window than meets the eye. Even before you start adding text and user interface elements, there's a virtual treasure chest full of attributes that can be changed, such as:

- The type of window
- The window's size and position
- The window's color

- Whether the window has a Control menu
- Whether the window has minimize/maximize arrows
- Whether the window has a title bar

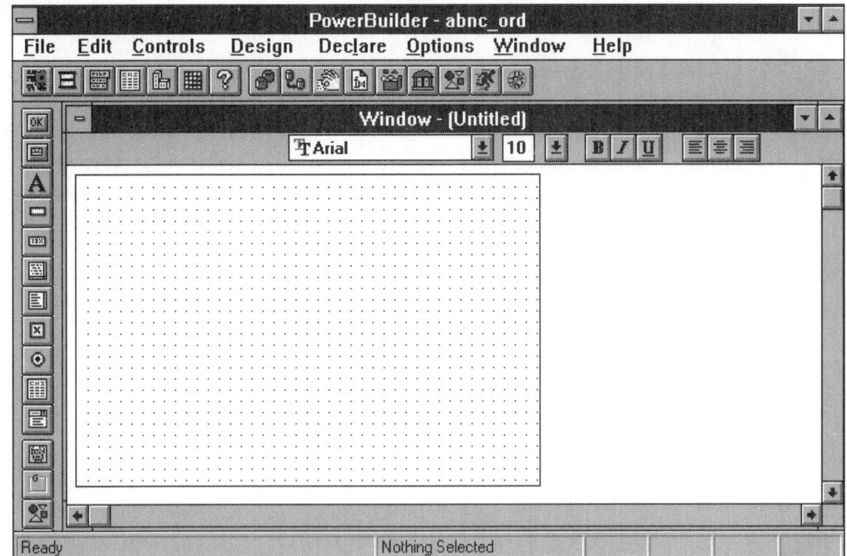

Figure 6-2: Create and modify windows with the Window Painter.

To change the attributes of your window, double-click on the window with the left mouse button. This opens the Window Style window shown in Figure 6-3. Another way to open this window is to choose Window Style... from the Design menu.

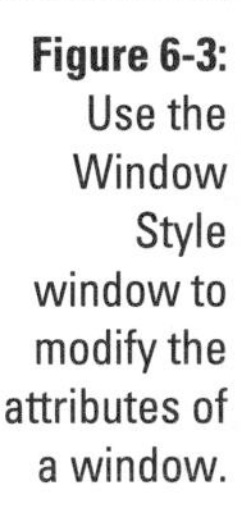

Figure 6-3: Use the Window Style window to modify the attributes of a window.

The miniature window graphic that appears just to the left of the buttons on the Window Style window gives you a general idea of what your window will look like. Changes to attributes such as Controls menu, HScroll Bar, and VScroll Bar cause corresponding changes to this graphic.

Figure 6-4: For a faster and simpler way to change a window's attributes, try clicking on the window with the right mouse button. The window attribute popup menu appears, allowing you to change attributes without opening another window. Selecting a menu item with an arrow next to it brings up another menu full of colors, style options, or window types.

The following sections briefly describe the most important window attributes. Although the attributes of a window can have an effect on your program, you normally won't spend much time thinking about them, so neither will we.

Getting it in position

Windows have several position attributes that determine how large the window is and where it will appear on the screen. To change the position of a window, do one of the following:

- Choose Position... from the Window Attribute popup menu.
- Choose Window Position... from the Design menu.

The Window Position window, shown in Figure 6-5, appears on the screen. This window allows you to change all of the window's position attributes; the rectangles at the bottom of the screen show you where the window will appear on the screen.

When it absolutely, positively has to be there

Two attributes control whether or not a window can be used when it's opened. They are:

- Enabled
- Visible

When the Enabled checkbox has a check in it, the window can be used. Without the check, the window is disabled. The user can't do anything with a disabled window. Click on the Enabled checkbox to switch between enabled and disabled.

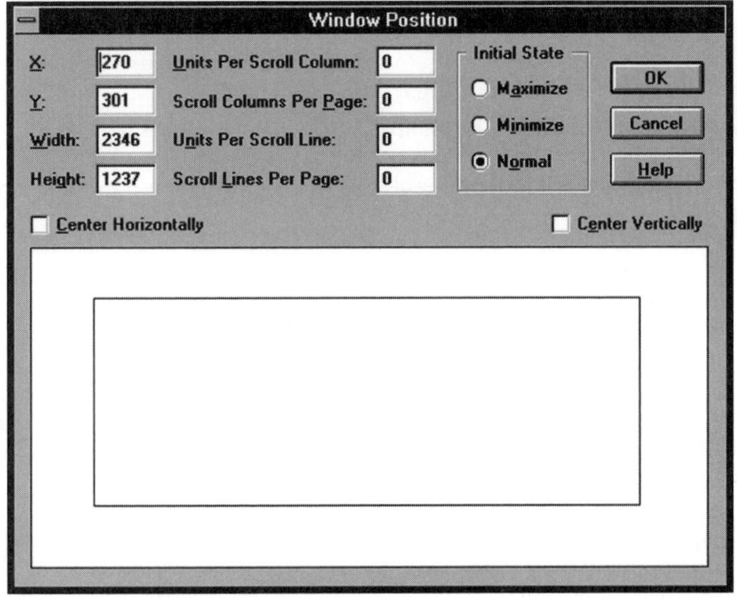

Figure 6-5: Tell your window where it can go using the Window Position window.

To make the window invisible, uncheck the Visible checkbox. The Visible attribute determines whether or not the window displays on the screen when it's opened. If the window is invisible, the user won't even know that it's there, much less do anything with it.

Invisible windows can come in very handy. The neat thing about an invisible window is that you can make it visible again while your program is running. Chapter 8 shows you how to do this. Try to think of creative ways to use invisible windows in your programs.

You can affect changes on a window that is invisible. It can be used as a work area, or prepared to make a grand appearance. You may want windows to be active and ready to appear rather than going through lengthy open procedures. Then, when windows appear, they will "pop" onto the screen. ■

What's your type?

Each window is one of six window types. A window's type controls how the window interacts with other windows and with the user. The six window types are:

- Main
- Child
- Popup
- Response
- MDI Frame
- MDI Frame with Microhelp

Main windows are independent, like the castaways in the book *Swiss Family Robinson*.

Child windows are dependent on a Main window and, like a soldier who will not break the chain of command, a Child window will not display outside of a Main window.

Popup windows are opened by other windows. They're like servants called upon to perform a task and then dismissed when the task is complete. Unlike a Child window, a Popup window can display outside of the window that opened it.

Response windows are selfish, demanding brutes that won't leave you alone until you hand over your lunch money. Response windows force the user to respond, usually with the click of a button, before the user can do anything else in the application.

To set a window's type, click on one of the Window Type radio buttons in the Window Style window (see Figure 6-3).

A MDI window is a particular style of window that allows you to open several windows, called sheets, within it. We cover MDI windows in greater detail in Chapter 23.

Saving the window

When you're done making changes to the current window, choose Save from the File menu to save your work. If this is the first time you've saved the window, the Save Window appears (see Figure 6-6).

Give your window a name by typing in the Entry field. Add any comments that you want in the Comments: section. Select the PowerBuilder library file to save the window in, and then click on the OK button.

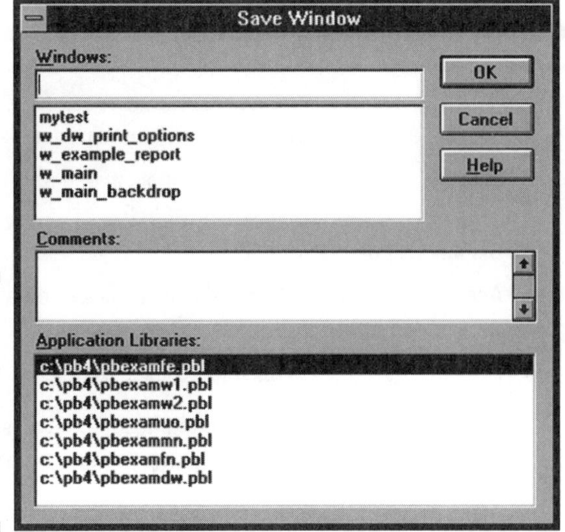

Figure 6-6: Save the window using the Save Window dialog.

User Interface Controls

Blank windows don't make for an attractive and functional user interface. The user needs things to click on, point at, scroll through, type in, and make fun of if a window is going to provide a meaningful user interface. *Controls* provide these things in the form of buttons, list boxes, entry fields, and other clickable, scrollable, readable, and usable visual objects.

More controls than you can count on one hand

There are many types of controls; each one serves a particular purpose. Table 6-1 describes the purpose of each control type.

The Window Painter PainterBar contains an icon for each type of control listed in Table 6-1.

To find out which control type a PainterBar icon represents, click on the icon with the left mouse button. A message describing the icon you clicked on appears in the bottom-left corner of the screen. ■

Table 6-1: Control types and their purposes

Control Type	*Purpose*
CommandButton	Provide a button the user can click on to perform an action
PictureButton	Provide a fancy button with a graphic image on it that the user can click on to perform an action
StaticText	Display text on the window
SingleLineEdit	Allow the user to enter or edit a single line of data
EditMask	Allow the user to enter data in a specified format
MultiLineEdit	Let the user enter or edit multiple lines of data
ListBox	Display a list or allow the user to choose from a list
CheckBox	Allow the user to choose one of two possible settings
RadioButton	Allow the user to choose one out of several selections
DataWindow	Display data from database tables or allow the user to modify data
DropDownListBox	Allow the user to select from a drop-down list
Picture	Display a picture
GroupBox	Group several controls together
UserObject	Do whatever the custom object is designed to do
Graph	Display a graph
OLE 2.0	Give the user a simple interface to OLE 2.0 objects

Each of the control types on the PainterBar can also be found under the Controls menu. There are several geometric shapes that are loosely referred to as controls. These shapes aren't really controls in the classic control sense. It may be more correct to refer to them as *shape objects* or *visually appealing additions to an otherwise dull screen*. They do, however, appear in the Controls menu, so let's call them controls. These shape controls are:

- Line
- Oval
- Rectangle
- RoundRectangle

Finally, there are two controls in the Controls menu that don't appear in the default PainterBar:

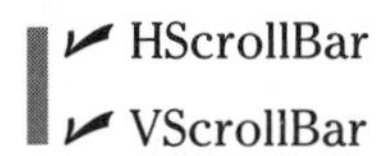

- HScrollBar
- VScrollBar

These two controls, the horizontal and vertical scroll bars, can be used to let the user scroll through a range of values.

Adding controls to a window

To add a control to a window, first select the control type by doing one of the following:

- Click on the control type's icon in the PainterBar.
- Select the control type from the Controls menu.

Then, click on the window in the location you want the control to appear. Once you've added a control to the window, there are two things you can do to set the attributes of the new control:

- Click on the control with the right mouse button to access a Control Attribute popup menu similar to the Window Attribute popup menu.
- Double-click on the control or choose Name... from the Control Attribute popup menu to open a Control Attribute window.

The popup menu or control window that appears depends on the type of control you click on. Some of the most common attributes are:

- Control's color — black and white is boring; add some color.
- Border around the control — set a border around the control if you want.
- Control's name — give a name to the control so you can reference it by name.
- Enabled — check this attribute if you want the user to be able to click on the control.
- Visible — check this attribute if the control should be visible.

For a complete list of attributes for a control type and a description of each one, do the following:

1. Open the On-line Help Index by choosing Help Index from the Help menu or by pressing F1.
2. Click on the Search button to open the Search window, as shown in Figure 6-7.
3. Type the name of the control type you want help on and, when you see the control type highlight in the list box, press Enter. In Figure 6-7, we typed CommandButton.
4. Highlight the "Attributes of..." topic and click on the Go To button.

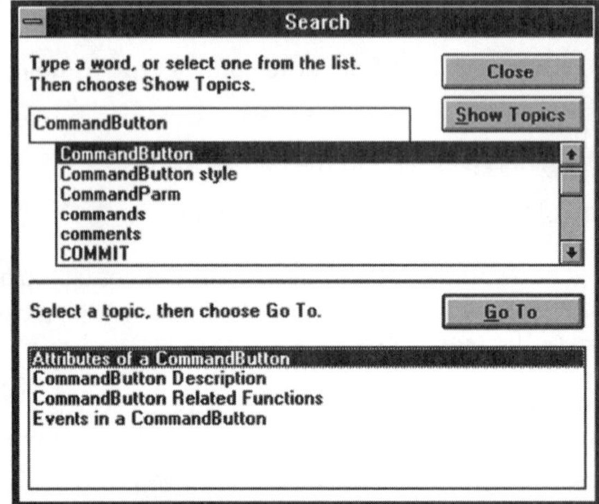

Figure 6-7: Use On-Line help to find out about the attributes of a control.

Later chapters of this book go into more detail about many of the control types. Anything that we don't cover you can find quickly in the On-line Help. The following sections explain several things you need to know when working with controls in the Window Painter.

Setting the tab order

Each control on a window has a position in the *tab order*. The tab order determines which control receives focus next when the user presses the Tab key. To see the tab order for the controls on your window, choose Tab Order from the Design menu.

When you enter Tab Order mode, numbers display on the top-right corner of each control. The control with the lowest number is first in the tab order, while the control with the highest number is last. Controls with a zero tab order aren't included in the tab order, which means they'll be skipped when the user presses the Tab key.

To change the tab order of a control, click on the control's tab order number and type a new number. Tab order numbers are saved as factors of 10, but you can change them to any number; PowerBuilder will convert them back to factors of 10 when you're finished making changes.

To exit Tab Order mode, choose Tab Order from the Design menu again.

Selecting controls

You can select one control at a time by clicking on a control with the left mouse button. However, sometimes you want to select several controls at once. There are several ways to select more than one control.

The fastest way is called *lassoing.* Click on an empty spot on the window and drag the mouse pointer across the window. This produces a rectangle that outlines the selected area. Any control inside that rectangle when you release the mouse button is then selected.

If lassoing selects too many controls, you can select them one by one instead. Click on the first control with the left mouse button and then click on additional controls while holding down the Control key. You can also click and drag while holding down the Control key.

A selected control displays four black boxes, one in each corner. To deselect a selected control, press and hold the Control key and click on the control with the left mouse button. The black boxes disappear; the control is no longer selected. ■

Another way to select controls one by one is to open the Control List window. Choose Control List... from the Edit menu. The window shown in Figure 6-8 appears, listing each control on the window. Highlight the controls you want to select by clicking on them with the left mouse button. Click on the Select button to select them.

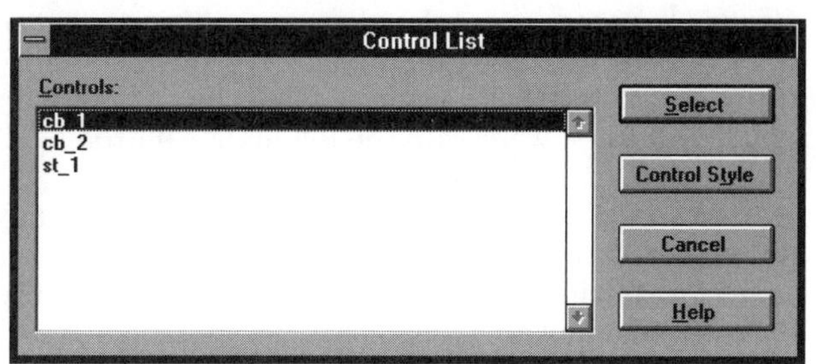

Figure 6-8: Use the Control List window to select from a list of controls.

Press Ctrl+A or choose Select All from the Edit menu to select every control on the window in one fell swoop.

Aligning controls

You'll spend a considerable amount of time adjusting the layout of controls on a window. So much time, in fact, that you'll start wishing for a way to align controls vertically and horizontally with a simple menu selection. When you start wishing something like this, consult your astrologer to make sure the planets are aligned, then read the following paragraphs.

To align controls, first click on the control you want to align other controls with. Then press and hold the Control key while you select the controls you want to align. Choose Align Controls from the Edit menu and then select from the popup menu that appears (see Figure 6-9). Each diagram illustrates a different alignment method. Click on the one you want with the left mouse button.

Be careful, lasooing the controls can give you unpredictable results when trying to align controls. Alignment is based on the first selected control. When lasooing, you can never be sure which control is selected first. ■

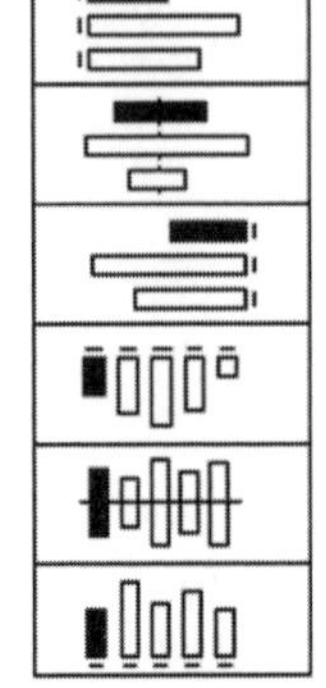

Figure 6-9: Align controls using the Align Controls popup menu.

To change the size of controls so that they are the same size vertically or horizontally, first click on a control that has the size you want. Then press and hold the Control key while you select the controls you want to resize. Now choose Size Controls from the Edit menu and select from the popup menu, as shown in Figure 6-10. Each diagram illustrates a different sizing method. Click on the one you want with the left mouse button.

To space controls evenly, first click on one control with the left mouse button. Then press and hold the Control key while you click on a control that is the right distance from the first control. Keep holding down the Control key while you select the remaining controls that you want to space evenly. Then choose Space Controls from the Edit menu and select from the popup menu, as shown in Figure 6-11. You know the routine by now.

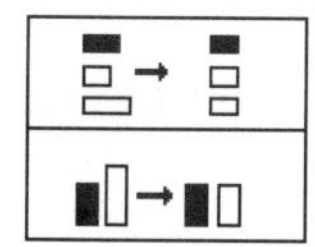

Figure 6-10: Size controls using the Size Controls popup menu.

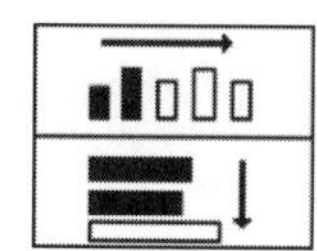

Figure 6-11: Use the Space Controls popup menu to space controls evenly.

Grid your teeth and bear it

The window grid gives you a visual reference point for placing controls. In addition to displaying guidelines on the window, you can tell PowerBuilder to align controls automatically by *snapping* them to the grid. You don't actually hear a snapping sound when a control snaps to the grid, but the analogy is a good one. When a control is close to a grid line it sort of jumps (or snaps) to align with that line. To fool around with the window grid, choose Grid... from the Design menu and use the Alignment Grid window shown in Figure 6-12.

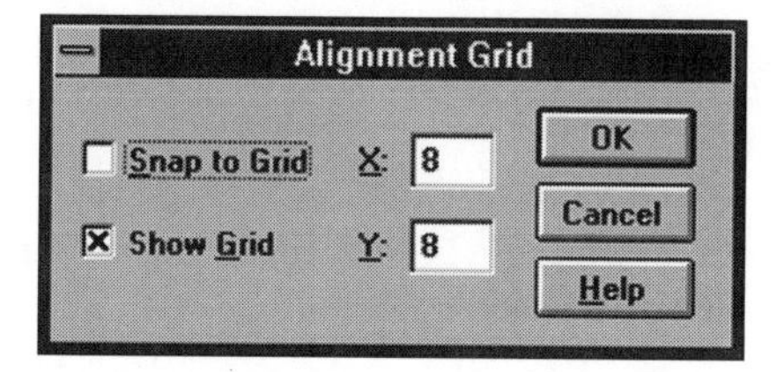

Figure 6-12: Change window grid settings using the Alignment Grid window.

Adding wisdom to each control

A *tag value* is a special tidbit of text that you assign to a control. The tag value of a control can be accessed later for whatever purpose your scheming mind can think of. For example, you could store short instructions for each control and display them later when the user of your program needs help.

To edit the tag values for the controls on your window, choose Tag List... from the Edit menu. The Edit Tag Values window, shown in Figure 6-13, appears on the screen.

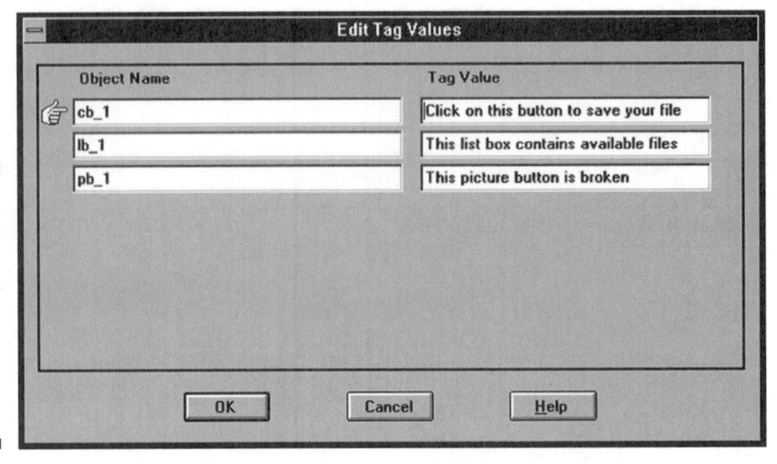

Figure 6-13: Add tag values so that your controls will seem like fortune cookies.

The Object Name column displays the name of each control, while the Tag Value column displays the current tag value. Click on the tag value you want to edit and type any changes. Then click the OK button.

Deleting a control

To delete a control, select it and press the Delete key; or select it and click on the Eraser icon in the PainterBar.

If you didn't really want to delete a control, you can undo the deletion by choosing Undo from the Edit menu.

Summary

This chapter introduced the first step in building a graphical user interface for your application, creating windows. You've also learned how to use controls on a window. The next chapter introduces PowerScript coding, which you will use to build more complex user interfaces.

Chapter 7

Windows Is a Happening Place

In This Chapter

- Telling controls what to do with PowerScript
- Giving your windows a head start on life

The Windows environment is full of *events*. An event is something that happens, such as the click of the mouse, the press of a key, or the collapse of Communism. Events normally cause something to happen. For example, a mouse click may cause a button to depress, the press of a key may cause a letter to appear on the screen, or the collapse of Communism may cause the former USSR to embrace democracy and a free market economy.

Getting Started with PowerScript

PowerScript is the built-in programming language in PowerBuilder. You can use PowerScript to write programs that will execute when a particular event occurs. These PowerScript programs are called *event scripts*.

Event scripts are created using the *PowerScript Painter*. To open the PowerScript Painter from the Window Painter, click with the right mouse button on the window or on a control. Then choose Script... from the popup menu. The PowerScript Painter appears, as shown in Figure 7-1.

Select the event you want to create an event script for by choosing from the Select Event drop-down list box. In Figure 7-1, the PowerScript Painter is displaying a blank event script for the open event of a window named Untitled.

To return to the Window Painter, click on the Window icon in the PowerScript Painter PainterBar. The Window icon is the icon on the bottom of the PainterBar.

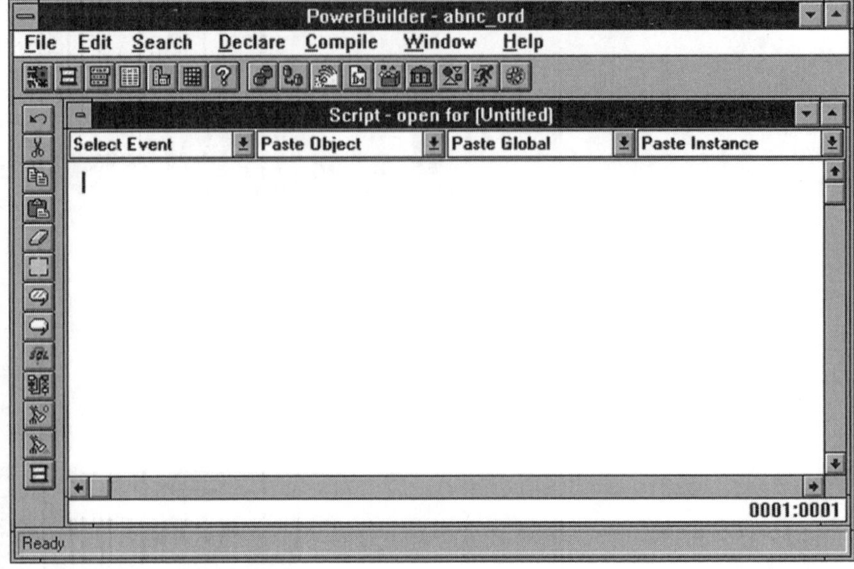

Figure 7-1: Create event scripts using the PowerScript Painter.

Events occur all over the place in a PowerBuilder application, including in windows and controls. Each window and each control on a window can have many event scripts. To access the event scripts in a control, click on the control with the right mouse button and choose Script... from the popup menu. Click on the window to access its event scripts.

Working with controls in an event script

PowerScript gives you the ability to work with controls in an event script. You can do many things with controls in PowerScript, including:

- Read the contents of control attributes
- Invoke control functions
- Modify control attributes

You need to know the control's name in order to do any of these things. You also need to know the name of the attribute or function. Once you know these two things, combine them using *dot notation* to write a PowerScript instruction, like this:

```
ControlName.AttributeNameORFunctionName
```

For example, the text attribute of a CommandButton named cb_1 can be modified to read "Push Yourself" by combining dot notation with the equal sign, like this:

```
cb_1.text = "Push Yourself"
```

Or, the tag value that you learned about in the preceding section can be set to "Tag, you're it!" like this:

```
cb_1.tag = "Tag, you're it!"
```

One of the most common types of event scripts is one written for the *clicked* event of a CommandButton. A clicked event occurs when the user clicks with the left mouse button. The following section shows you how to create a simple clicked event script for a CommandButton.

Writing programs in the event they're needed

This example builds a complete sample application that opens one window containing two controls. The first step is to create a new application object. Even if you've already created an application object, create a new one anyway. There's no limit to the number of applications you can build at one time in PowerBuilder. But, you can have only one application current at any one time.

To create an application object, close any painters that are currently open and click on the Application Painter icon in the PowerBar. Then choose New... from the File menu. ■

When the Select New Application Library window appears, type the following and click on the OK button:

```
sample.pbl
```

When the Save Application window appears, type the following and click on the OK button:

```
experiment
```

Click on the No button when asked about generating an Application Template. Now do the following to create a new window:

1. Click on the Window Painter icon in the PowerBar.
2. Click on the New button in the Select Window window to create a new window.
3. Click on the StaticText icon in the PainterBar (the large *A*). Then click on the blank window to add a StaticText control.
4. Double-click on the new StaticText control to open the StaticText window. Change the Name: field to st_foo and change the Text: field to Foo Bar (see Figure 7-2).
5. Click on the OK button to accept the changes.

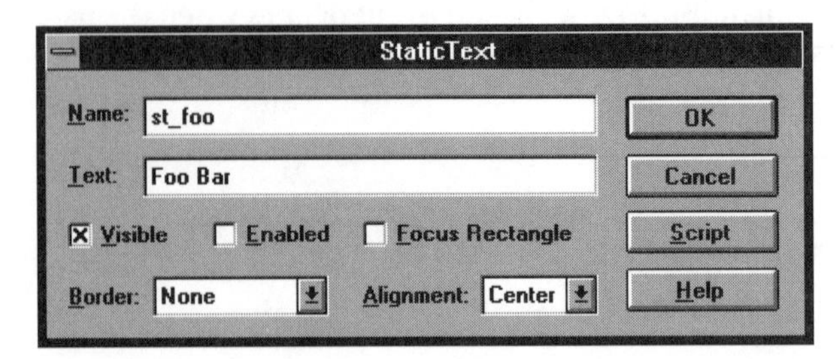

Figure 7-2: Set the attributes of a StaticText control using the StaticText window.

Now add a CommandButton by doing the following:

1. Click on the CommandButton icon in the PainterBar.
2. Click on the window to add a new CommandButton control.
3. Double-click on the new CommandButton control to open the CommandButton window. Change the Name: field to cb_button and change the Text: field to Just Do It (see Figure 7-3).
4. Click on the Script button to open the PowerScript Painter.
5. Click on the Select Event drop-down list box and choose clicked from the list to make sure that you're modifying the clicked event script. The title bar on the script window should read:

   ```
   Script - clicked for cb_button
   ```

6. Type the following in the clicked event script:

   ```
   st_foo.text = "Done!"
   ```

7. Click on the Window icon in the PainterBar to return to the Window Painter. The event script you just created is saved automatically in the CommandButton when you leave the PowerScript Painter.
8. Save the new window by choosing Save from the File menu, and typing the following window name then clicking on the OK button:

```
foowin
```

9. Close the Window Painter by choosing Close from the File menu.

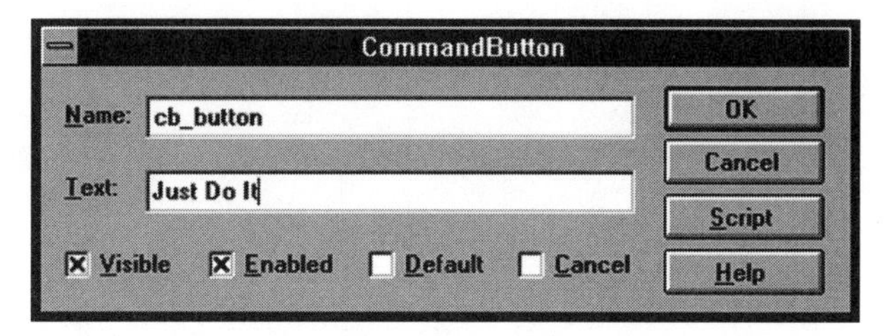

Figure 7-3: Set the attributes of a CommandButton control through the CommandButton window.

The event scripts in a window are only stored in memory until the window is saved. After making changes to event scripts be sure to save the window. ■

Now that you've created a new window, you need to tell the application object that it should open the window. Do the following:

1. Click on the Application Painter icon to open the Application Painter.
2. Click on the Script icon in the PainterBar. The Script icon is the one that looks like a blank piece of paper.
3. When the PowerScript Painter appears, choose open from the Select Event drop-down list box. This selects the event script that is executed when the application opens. The title bar on the script window should now read, "Script — open for experiment."
4. Type the following line and then click on the Application icon in the PainterBar to return to the Application Painter:

```
Open(foowin)
```

5. Choose Save from the File menu to save the changes you just made to the application object.

The application is ready to run. Click on the Run icon (the blue picture of a humanoid running) in the PowerBar to run the application. When the application opens, the open event script is executed, and foowin is displayed on the screen. Click on the Just Do It button to see what happens (see Figure 7-4).

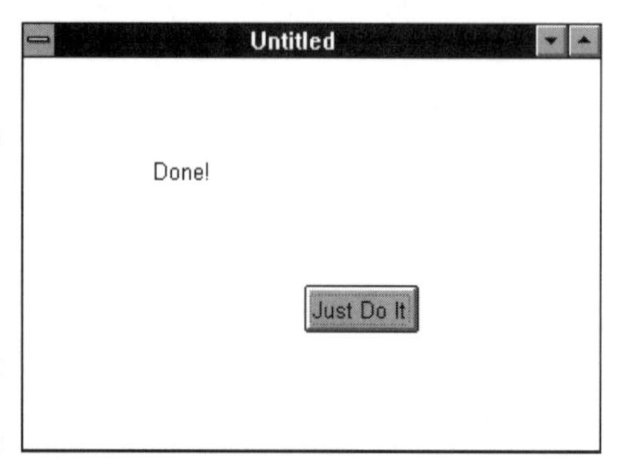

Figure 7-4: A change occurs when you click on the Just Do It button.

When you're done, choose Close from the window's Controls menu or press Alt+F4 to close the window. With the window closed, the application has nothing more to do, so it quits automatically. You're taken back to the Application Painter.

Ancestor Worship

Inheritance allows you to continue building where your relatives left off. You accept the product of your ancestors' lives and, one hopes, use it to produce more with your life. PowerBuilder lets you do the same thing with windows.

When you create a new window, you can begin by inheriting from an existing window. Window inheritance is different from human inheritance. When a window inherits from another window, the descendant window becomes an exact duplicate of the ancestor. Then you can modify the descendant window without affecting the ancestor window.

Inherit the window

To use window inheritance when creating a new window, you must choose a window to inherit from. Click on the Window Painter icon in the PowerBar. When the window titled Select Window appears, click on the Inherit... button. A window titled Inherit From Window appears, as shown in Figure 7-5. Use this window to select the window from which you want to inherit.

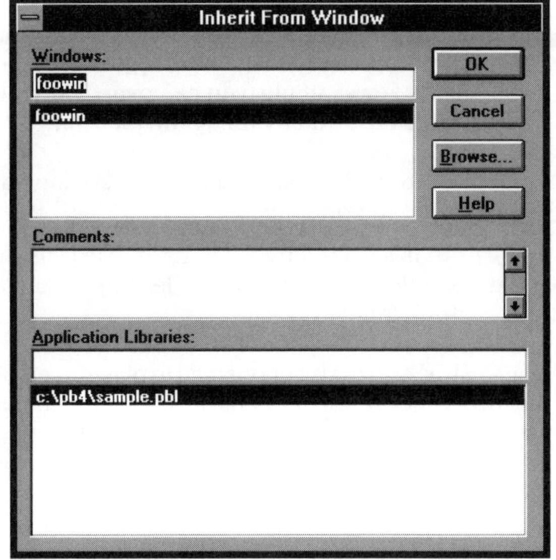

Figure 7-5: Choose a window from which to inherit using Inherit From Window.

Select foowin and click on the OK button. PowerBuilder creates a new window and takes you to the Window Painter. The new window looks exactly like the window called foowin — the new window has inherited the settings, controls, and scripts from foowin.

You can now add controls and scripts to the new window without affecting foowin. When you're done adding to the new window, save it and give it a name.

In the window called foowin, the clicked event script in the CommandButton changes the text displayed in a StaticText control. By default, the CommandButton in the new, descendant window does the same thing. However, in the new window, it doesn't have to stop there. You can *extend* the CommandButton's clicked event script in the descendant window. Or, if you want to keep the CommandButton but you don't want to keep its clicked event script, you can *override* the script. The following section tells how to do both.

The pane of childbirth

Every event script in an ancestor window can be either extended or overridden. When a script is extended, the ancestor window's script is executed first, then the descendant's script is executed. When a script is overridden, the ancestor's script isn't executed at all; only the descendant's script runs.

By default, the event scripts in the ancestor window are all extended. To override the ancestor window's event script, open the PowerScript Painter for the event script you want to change. Then choose Override Ancestor Script from the Compile menu. For example, you can override the clicked event for the Just Do It CommandButton by doing the following:

1. With the right mouse button, click on the Just Do It CommandButton and choose Script... from the popup menu.
2. The clicked event script is selected by default. Choose Override Ancestor Script from the Compile menu. This overrides the clicked event script from the ancestor window, foowin.

You can display the ancestor's script by choosing Display Ancestor Script... from the Compile menu. A window appears on the screen containing the script in the ancestor window's clicked event (see Figure 7-6).

3. Type in a new script, such as:

```
st_foo.text = "SPAM"
```

4. Click on the Window icon in the PainterBar to accept your changes to the clicked event script and return to the Window Painter.
5. Save the window by choosing Save from the File menu. If you haven't given your window a name yet, do so when prompted for one.

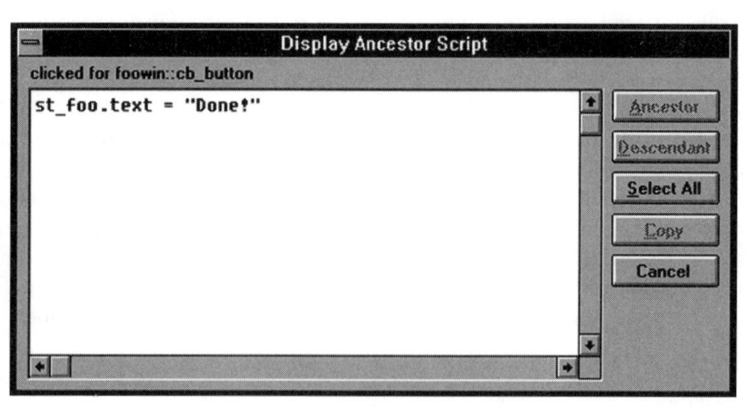

Figure 7-6: View an ancestor window's event script using the Display Ancestor Script window.

You've now replaced the previous CommandButton clicked event script with a new one. To try out the changes you've made, open the Application Painter and click on the Script icon in the PainterBar. Notice that the Script icon no longer looks like a blank piece of paper; it looks like it has writing on it! This is because it now has the open event script that you added in the previous section — and it shows you how smart it is by changing the icon's appearance.

The open event script appears on the screen, containing the following:

```
Open(foowin)
```

Replace foowin with the name of your descendant window and click on the Application icon in the PainterBar to accept your changes and return to the Application Painter. Choose Save from the File menu to save your changes to the application object. Now click on the icon that looks like a running humanoid in the PowerBar to run your application.

Click on the Just Do It button to see what happens. By the way, SPAM is a good meat to bring along on sailing trips or other outdoor excursions. It may not be the best food in the world, but it won't spoil and it's the closest thing to a hamburger that you'll find in the middle of the ocean.

Summary

In this chapter you began to write PowerScript code in events. The next chapter goes into detail about the PowerScript language. With a better understanding of PowerScript, you'll be able to build complex user interfaces in no time.

Chapter 8

PowerScripting

In This Chapter

- Exploring PowerBuilder events
- Using PowerScript functions
- Learning PowerScript language essentials
- Using scope
- Creating user-defined functions

In the first seven chapters of this book, you have learned how to use Painters to create portions of your application. PowerScripting is the next step. This is the step that makes your application really do something. PowerScript is a complete application development language. You can use PowerScript to:

- Perform mathematical calculations
- Control program flow using branching statements and loops
- Manipulate data, such as string manipulation and type conversion
- Move data between windows
- Manage the user interface

PowerScript gives programmers access to a number of functions and program control statements.

Where and When to PowerScript

You add PowerScript to *event scripts* and *user-defined functions*. An event script is a series of commands that are executed when a particular event occurs. An event is a signal that something, such as a mouse click or a key press, has occurred.

You can write applications that require new or custom functions. PowerBuilder allows you to write user-defined functions. A user defined function is one that you write using PowerScript. It can accept arguments, process information, and return values. PowerScript comes complete with many functions already built in.

Windows and controls all have events to which PowerScript can be added to give them new abilities. CommandButtons, for example, do nothing when pushed unless a script is added to the clicked event. As an example, Table 8-1 lists the events available for a CommandButton control.

Table 8-1: Events for a CommandButton control

Event	*Description*
Clicked	The mouse was clicked on the CommandButton.
Constructor	The CommandButton is being constructed.
Destructor	The CommandButton is being removed from memory.
Dragdrop	The CommandButton has been dropped on a target object.
Dragenter	A CommandButton enters a target object.
Dragleave	A CommandButton leaves a target object.
Dragwithin	A CommandButton is within a target object.
Getfocus	This event occurs before a selected CommandButton becomes active or gains focus.
Losefocus	This event occurs when a CommandButton is no longer active or selected, or loses focus.
Other	Any Windows event that is not a PowerBuilder event occurs.
Rbuttondown	The right mouse button is clicked on the CommandButton.

Using PowerScript in events

Programming in PowerScript is like designing parts of a car. When you push on the padded section in the middle of your steering wheel, you expect the horn to honk; when you push the button with the picture of a light on it, you hope the headlights come on. This same idea applies when adding scripts to events.

When you click on a button you expect the clicked event script to run. When you give focus to a control or open a window, the event script associated with these events should run. Of course, if there are no scripts connected with these events, nothing happens.

You can think of events as hard-wired switches. If your house had switches that turned on and off whenever it became dark or light, when doors opened and closed, or when activated by a clock, you could imagine all sorts of things to do with these switches. In fact, with enough different types of switches, you could get pretty imaginative. As we have shown in Table 8-1, each window and control comes with quite a number of different events. And if these aren't enough, you can create your own custom events.

To add PowerScript to an event:

1. Double-click on the object to which you would like to add script. If you are adding script to a CommandButton, a dialog box similar to the one in Figure 8-1 will appear.
2. Click on the Script button. An empty editor screen will appear.
3. In the upper-left corner of the editor is a drop-down list box titled Select Event. Click on this list box to select the event to which you want to add script. The title bar of the Editor window always lets you know what event you are adding script to.

Figure 8-1: Click on the Script button to add event scripts.

After you have added scripts to an event, you may notice that a small Script icon appears next to the event name in the Select Event list box. This lets you know which events have scripts associated with them.

Begin adding PowerScript in the editor provided. When you have finished, PowerBuilder will check your script for any obvious compilation errors and then help you correct them.

It is possible to write PowerScript in a different editor and use the Windows clipboard to cut and paste the text. Even though that's a bit more work, to some people it's worth it. Editors are always a matter of comfort and personal taste. ■

Using the PowerScript functions

PowerScript functions are the workhorses of the language. There are ten different types of PowerScript functions. They are listed in Table 8-2.

Table 8-2: The ten types of PowerScript functions

Function type	*Description*
Date	Returns date information or compares two dates.
DDE	Provides Dynamic Data Exchange capability.
Numeric	Manipulates numbers.
Object	Provides information about or makes changes to objects.
Print	Makes print capabilities available.
Special	Controls the PowerBuilder environment and provides special language support.
String	Manipulates and provides information about character strings.
Text File	Allows you to read and write text files.
Time	Returns time information or compares two times.
Type Conversion	Changes data from one type to another.

There are functions to do just about anything you might want to do. PowerBuilder objects, such as windows and controls, have functions called *methods*. A method is a function that works only on its object. For example, a window has an Open function. Running this function opens a window on the screen.

When using methods, you must precede the method with the name of the object and a dot. For instance, if you have created a window called BigPain, and while the program is running you want to hide it, the function call would look like this:

```
BigPain.Hide()
```

Each object type — windows and controls — has a full set of methods. They are used to accomplish the following:

- Control the object's appearance
- Change the object's values
- Provide information on the object's values
- Change the object's location on the screen

The PowerScript functions are the heart of the language. You should become familiar with the functions of each object as you use them in your application.

If you are upgrading from PowerBuilder version 2 or 3, you will find that some of the function names have changed. For example, DataWindow functions no longer begin with the letters dw. Also, object names precede the function. This was not required in version 2 and earlier.

Learning PowerScript Essentials

As in any programming language, the functions do all of the work; but there are other elements of the language, known as *statements*. There are several types of statements in the PowerScript language, they are:

- Assignment statements, which assign values to variables and objects
- Expressions, which evaluate one or more PowerBuilder values using operators for their result value
- Branching statements, which direct the flow of a PowerScript program
- Special statements, which can stop either a PowerScript program or PowerBuilder application from running

Operators

What's life without a few characters? Operators are special characters that are used to do the following things:

- Compare numbers, text, and boolean values
- Combine boolean values and expressions
- Manipulate character strings
- Perform mathematical calculations

When you compare values — is one greater than six, for example — you get a boolean value, that is, true or false, back from evaluating the statement. To compare values, you use *relational operators*. Relational operators are also known as comparison operators. Table 8-3 gives you a list of the relational operators and how they are used.

You use logical operators when you combine boolean values. Three logical operators are described in Table 8-4.

Table 8-3: The relational operators

Operator	*Use*	*Example*
=	Evaluates whether one value is equal to another. In the example, the return value is FALSE.	"Blue" = "Green"
>	Evaluates whether one value is greater than another value. In the example, the return value is TRUE.	5 > 3
>=	Evaluates whether one value is greater than or equal to another value. The example returns FALSE.	12 >= 16
<	Evaluates whether one value is less than another value. The example returns TRUE.	7 < 10
<=	Evaluates whether one value is less than or equal to another value. The example returns TRUE.	15 <= 15
<>	Evaluates whether one value is not equal to another value. The example returns TRUE.	12 <> 67

Table 8-4: The logical operators

Operator	*Description*
AND	Returns TRUE only if both values being combined are TRUE.
OR	Returns TRUE if either or both values are TRUE.
NOT	TRUE values are changed to FALSE and FALSE values to TRUE when the value is preceded by a NOT.

You can add character strings together. This process is known as *concatenation*. It's called this so you won't confuse adding numbers with adding character strings. The plus sign is used to concatenate strings. Here is an example:

```
"Blue" + " " + "Grass"
```

"Blue Grass" results from this concatenation.

You can see that it uses the plus sign to concatenate the strings. This is the only operator used with strings. If you want to subtract portions of a string, there are special string-handling functions for that. Sorry, no string subtraction operators. You will also notice that single quotes are used when you want to include double quotes as part of the string.

Speaking of subtraction, we would be remiss if we didn't cover the math operators. They are pretty much as you would expect, (+) plus sign, (-) minus sign, (*) multiplication, (/) division, and (^) exponential.

There is always the question of whether operators need spaces before and after them. The only operator that requires this is the minus sign. Programs read easier with spaces before and after the operators, but sometimes an expression can get very long with all the spaces included. You have to use your judgement. Just remember that the minus sign needs them. ■

Assignment statements

Some of the operators have more than one job. You have already seen how the plus sign is both an arithmetic operator and a string concatenation goody. The equal sign has more than one job too.

The equal sign is used in *assignment statements*. An assignment statement is one in which you let something, such as a variable or a control, have a value. It's like giving them a pet. "Here is your little value, now take good care of it."

Here is an example in which you will assign a value to a StaticText control. These controls have attributes known as *text attributes* that store the values displayed on the screen. To change this value, simply assign a new one with the assignment operator:

```
st_1.text = "Worf has a receding hair line."
```

Attributes are values belonging to an object, such as a control or a window, that store information such as its shape, color, value, or any other important features. You can change any of these attributes by using the assignment statement. Start with the name of the object, a dot, and then the attribute. Slap in an equal sign followed by the new value and you're set. It doesn't get any easier than this! You can refer to Help to list attributes for any object. ■

Expressions

"I want to learn PowerBuilder in the worst way possible."

Now here is an expression often heard throughout the United States. It confounds people in other countries who wonder why anyone would want to do things in the "worst way." Why not the "best way"? Well, you're reading this book, so you have obviously chosen the best way possible.

An expression is a statement, not unlike the preceding quote. We are talking about computers now. An expression is a statement that is understood by the computer. Expressions are used to:

- Perform math
- Concatenate strings
- Logically evaluate values

When math is performed, it forms an expression with a result. For example:

```
2 + 2
```

This is an expression whose result is 4. You can create a much more complex mathematical equation. It will still be an expression with some result.

String concatenations also return a result. You have seen how "Blue" + " " + "Grass" results in "Blue Grass." Concatenations can also be quite complex. Once again, there is still only one return value or result.

When expressions are used to logically evaluate values, they return either TRUE or FALSE, boolean values. Here is an example:

```
2 = 2
```

This isn't an assignment statement since you can't store a value to the number 2. It's sort of stuck with the value of 2. Instead, this expression is evaluating equality. Is 2 equal to 2? Without a lot of calculus or deep conceptualizing it can be said the 2 does equal 2. This expression now results in TRUE. Here is an example of an expression that returns FALSE:

```
"Blue" = "Pig"
```

This has nothing to do with either the color or the farm animal. This expression simply evaluates whether the characters B, l, u, and e are equal to the letters P, i, and g. Since each letter is equal to some ASCII value, the answer is no.

For more information on ASCII values, you can refer to the many charts that exist. Essentially, all printable characters — and a few that aren't printable — have been assigned a numeric value. It is with this numeric value that letters are evaluated. Since "B" and "b" have different ASCII values, "B" is not equal to "b". I guess this finally answers the question, "To B or not to b?"

They went that-a-way

What would life be without decisions? We make decisions all the time. We make a decision based on events, like the alarm going off in the morning. We make decisions about what to have for breakfast. And on and on. It's possible to make decisions in your program using PowerScript.

If you want it your way

One of the most common ways to make a decision in a program is with the *IF statement*. An IF statement decides, based on the expression you provide it, whether or not the PowerScript code within the statement should be executed. Expressions used in an IF statement evaluate to TRUE or FALSE. If the statement evaluates to TRUE, the PowerScript code gets executed.

There are three parts to an IF statement:

- The expression
- The body, containing the PowerScript code
- The end statement

Here is a sample IF statement:

```
IF SLE_1.TEXT = "Boogie" THEN
   SLE_2.TEXT = "Woogie"
END IF
```

In the preceding example, there are three parts to the first line of the IF statement. Of course, the word IF; then the expression that must evaluate to TRUE or FALSE followed by the word THEN. This can be read, "If it is true that the text attribute of SingleLineEdit (SLE) number 2 is equal to the character string, Boogie, then..."

If you aren't an experienced programmer, you might be confused about the expression in the first line of the IF statement and the assignment statement in the second line. They look very similar. The fact is, if the expression in the first line were to appear all by itself, it would be considered an assignment statement. Because it appeared where only an expression can appear, PowerBuilder knows that this is an expression and not an assignment statement. ■

So if it's TRUE that SLE_1's text attribute is "Boogie" then we will set SLE_2's text attribute to "Woogie." See Figure 8-2 to see what this might look like.

The IF statement ends with the words END IF. When the expression in an IF statement evaluates to FALSE, the PowerScript code is skipped and the program continues with whatever comes after the END IF.

In our example, there is only one line of PowerScript code within the IF statement. You can include any number of lines. You can even include more IF statements.

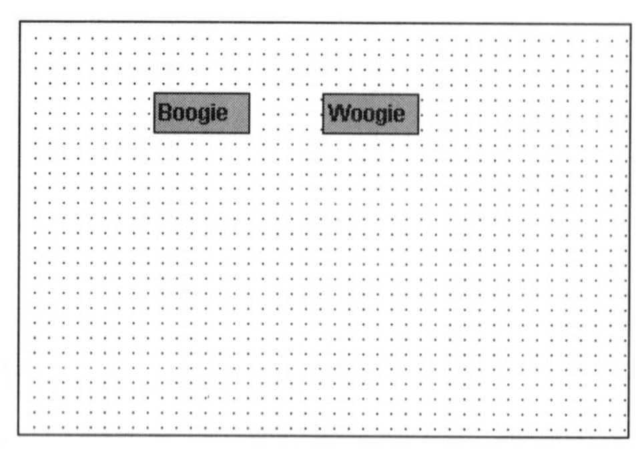

Figure 8-2: Boogie Woogie with SingleLineEdits.

Some of the decisions you make during the day are either/or types of decisions. "If we have milk and it hasn't curdled, I will eat cereal for breakfast; otherwise I will eat eggs and bacon, against my doctor's wishes." You can make the same kind of decision, though not about your breakfast, in PowerScript. All you have to do is include an ELSE statement in your IF.

Here is an example that shows you how to make the SingleLineEdit number 2 say "Rock and Roll" if SingleLineEdit number 1 doesn't say "Boogie":

```
IF SLE_1.TEXT = "Boogie" THEN
   SLE_2.TEXT = "Woogie"
ELSE
   SLE_2.TEXT = "Rock and Roll"
END IF
```

Figure 8-3 shows how this might look.

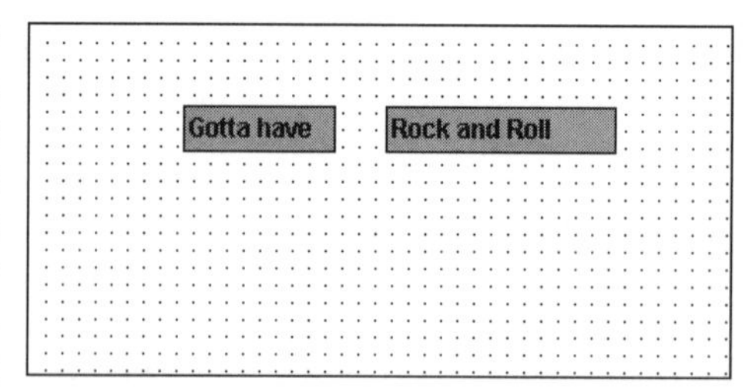

Figure 8-3: If it isn't Boogie Woogie it's gotta be Rock and Roll.

If you want it easier...

When IF statements are simple one line, do this or do that, like our first example, you can put them on one line. The END IF is then understood, and not written. Here is that same example:

```
IF SLE_1.TEXT = "Boogie" THEN SLE_2.TEXT = "Woogie"
```

You can include an ELSE statement like this:

```
IF SLE_1.TEXT = "A" THEN SLE_2.TEXT = "B" ELSE SLE_2.TEXT = "C"
```

You still don't include the END IF.

Another way to write an IF statement on a single line is using the IF( ) function. Use this function in cases where you need a single value and writing a line of code isn't possible, such as in a DataWindow or in the next example.

There are three parameters to an IF( ) function:

```
IF(expression, TRUE value, FALSE value)
```

When the *expression* evaluates to TRUE, the *TRUE value* is returned. When the *expression* evaluates to FALSE, the *FALSE value* is returned. Here is an example that embeds an IF( ) function in a string concatenation.

```
"The weather is " + IF(SPIN1.Value < 60, "cold", "warm") + "."
```

If the value of the Spin control is less than 60, the sentence will read, "The weather is cold." Otherwise, "The weather is warm."

Choosy mothers choose GIF

If you don't like to limit yourself to only two choices, you're going to love this next feature. You can have your program choose from many possibilities.

You may be writing an application that needs to know what graphic type you are using. Here's an example that will add the appropriate file extension to your file name depending on the graphic type you choose.

```
CHOOSE CASE
   CASE SLE_1.TEXT = "TIFF"
      SLE_2.TEXT = TRIM(SLE_2.TEXT) + ".TIF"
   CASE SLE_1.TEXT = "GIF"
      SLE_2.TEXT = TRIM(SLE_2.TEXT) + ".GIF"
   CASE SLE_1.TEXT = "WINDOWS BITMAP"
      SLE_2.TEXT = TRIM(SLE_2.TEXT) + ".BMP"
   CASE ELSE
      MESSAGEBOX("ALERT", "INVALID GRAPHIC FORMAT", StopSign!, OK!)
END CHOOSE
```

This example makes a choice based on the text entered in SingleLineEdit number 1 (SLE_1). Based on its decision, it takes the text from SingleLineEdit number 2 (SLE_2), uses the TRIM( ) function to trim off any trailing spaces, and then concatenates the correct extension.

In the event that none of the expressions after each of the CASE statements evaluates to TRUE, the code following the CASE ELSE statement is run. In this case, it displays an error message with a stop sign and an OK button.

There are three requirements for a CHOOSE CASE statement:

- It must begin with the words CHOOSE CASE.
- It must contain one or more CASE expressions. This is the word CASE followed by a valid expression.
- It must end with the words END CHOOSE.

The CASE ELSE statement is optional. It is used very much like the ELSE in part of an IF statement. When all ELSE has failed, do this...

Throw 'em for a loop

"Round and round she goes. Where she stops nobody knows!"

— *Las Vegas Croupier named Bert*

Whenever you need to perform the same code over and over, there is a PowerScript loop for you. There are two basic types of loops, *DO loops* and *FOR loops*. No matter what style of loop you use, they have the same basic idea. An expression is evaluated and if it evaluates to TRUE, the program continues looping.

The DO loop has several different configurations. Table 8-5 lists them for you.

Table 8-5: The DO loops

Loop	*Description*
DO While ... Loop	Expression evaluated at the beginning of the loop; loops while expression is TRUE.
Do Until ... Loop	Expression evaluated at the beginning of the loop; loops until the expression becomes FALSE.
Do ... Loop Until	Expression evaluated at the end of each loop. The code in this loop will always be executed at least once. Loops until the expression is FALSE.
Do ... Loop While	Expression evaluated at the end of each loop. The code in this loop will always be executed at least once. Loops while the expression is TRUE.

In the DO loops, the expressions are evaluated either at the beginning or at the end of each loop. When expressions are evaluated at the end of the loop, the PowerScript code within the loop is always executed at least one time. Here is how they look:

```
DO WHILE expression
   PowerScript code
LOOP

DO UNTIL expression
   PowerScript code
LOOP

DO
   PowerScript code
LOOP WHILE expression

DO
   PowerScript code
LOOP UNTIL expression
```

When using the Script Painter you can paste the syntax for loops with the Paste Statement icon. This is the icon that looks like several geometric symbols connected with lines. Using Paste Statement you can save time and eliminate possible syntax bugs. ■

A FOR loop is designed to loop a certain number of times. You tell a FOR loop just how many times you want it to loop and its automatic counter keeps track of how many times it has looped. The FOR loop is quite versatile. It has seven basic parts to it:

1. It begins with the word FOR (so does "For He's a Jolly Good Fellow," and you sing that over and over, too).
2. Next there is a counter that keeps track of the loop's progress. It is called the *iteration counter.*
3. The number with which to begin counting.
4. The number at which to stop.
5. There is an optional step value. It begins with the word STEP and is followed by the value you wish to count by. The FOR Loop can count by twos, fives, or any value you want.
6. Next comes the PowerScript code you want executed.
7. Lastly, the keyword NEXT appears after the PowerScript code in the loop. When the loop has finished, the line of code following the NEXT statement will begin executing.

Here is how the FOR loop looks in action:

```
FOR i = 1 TO 20 STEP 2
   PowerScript code
NEXT
```

In this example, the letter i is the iteration counter. The number one is where the iteration counter begins. The number twenty is where it stops, and the loop will count by twos. So, this FOR loop will loop ten times.

There are two key words that you can use with either DO loops or FOR loops. The key word CONTINUE placed in a loop will pass control to either the LOOP or NEXT statement. Figure 8-4 shows how it works.

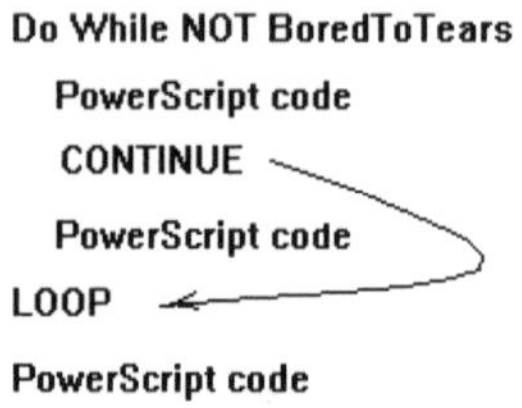

```
Do While NOT BoredToTears
   PowerScript code
   CONTINUE
   PowerScript code
LOOP
PowerScript code
```

Figure 8-4: CONTINUE passes control to the LOOP statement.

The second key word is EXIT. This key word will cause the program to stop looping and start executing PowerScript code on the line following the end of the loop. See Figure 8-5.

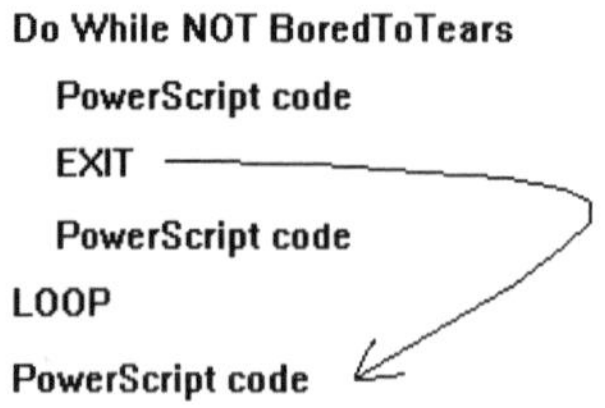

```
Do While NOT BoredToTears
   PowerScript code
   EXIT
   PowerScript code
LOOP
PowerScript code
```

Figure 8-5: EXIT is like a "Get out of the loop FREE card."

If loops have you going in circles, you're doing something right. There are many different possibilities from which to choose. A good rule of thumb in choosing between a DO loop and a FOR loop is: If you know how many times you need to loop, use a FOR loop. Even this isn't written in stone. You can always exit out of the loop prematurely by using the EXIT command if necessary.

Variables: Variations on a Theme

Do you own a suitcase? If not, you probably own a gunny sack or some other contrivance for putting stuff in and carrying it around. Variables are a little like suitcases for data. They have little name tags so they won't get lost, and they change type depending on what you put in them. For example, if you put in a razor and some aftershave, you call it a shave kit. If you put in mascara and eye liner, you call it a cosmetics case. If you put explosives in it and try to board a plane, you'll be arrested.

The real definition of a variable is boring. Here it is: A named memory location. Be that as it may, they are incredibly useful tools. You can temporarily store information in memory, and give that value or information a temporary name.

Creating variables

Creating a variable is a two-step process:

- Create the variable by declaring it.
- Put something in the variable by using an assignment statement.

The first step, declaring the variable, creates a place in memory and sets the type. So if you say you're going to use the bag for cosmetics, it's a cosmetics bag before the lipstick goes in. Declaring a variable is easy. Begin with the variable type and follow it with a variable name, like this:

```
Numeric     MyNumber
String      MyString
Character   MyChar
```

There are seventeen different data types in PowerBuilder. You can find a data type to meet almost any need. In this example, we have created three variables — one a numeric type called MyNumber, another a string type called MyString, and lastly, a character type called MyChar.

Assigning values to variables

For the second step, we store a value in the variable. To do this, we use the assignment operator (=). You must store the correct type of information into the container you have created. You wouldn't want to store SPAM in your shave kit. In other words, numbers go in a numeric variable, characters in a character variable. Here is what it looks like:

```
MyNumber = 6
Mchar = "A"
MyString = "Give me a lever and I'll pry the keys off my keyboard."
```

Assigning values to declared variables is all it takes to create variables for your application.

Array of Hope

An *array* is a special type of variable. The way to imagine the difference between a variable and an array is that a variable is like a guitar case and an array is like an egg carton. You can store one guitar in a guitar case; you can store several eggs in an egg carton.

Declaring arrays

You identify each *element* of an array with an *index number*. An element is one of the values stored in an array, and the index number identifies its place in the array. You create an array by declaring it as you would any variable. When you declare the variable, you can either fix how many elements will be in the array, or you can leave it at a variable length. To declare a fixed-length array, do the following:

1. Start with the data type.
2. Enter the name of the array.
3. Enclose the number of elements in brackets after the array name, like this:

   ```
   Int MyEggs[4]
   ```

This example creates a fixed array of integers four elements long. To create a variable length array, leave out the number of elements, like this:

```
Int MyEggs[]
```

The array will increase in size as you assign values to the elements. It's quite simple to assign values to elements. It's very much like assigning values to any variable. The only difference is that you must include the element number when you assign a value. Here is how we can assign values to each of the four elements of our sample array:

```
MyEggs[1] = 5
MyEggs[2] = 3
MyEggs[3] = 17
MyEggs[4] = 12
```

To reference a value stored in an array element, just include its index number. In this example, we store the value of an array element into another variable:

```
Int MyValue

MyValue = MyEggs[3]
```

Multi-dimensional arrays

So far we have been talking about arrays that have only one dimension. In other words, the values string out in a line, one after another. You can also have arrays that have more than one dimension, like the cups in an egg carton. Figure 8-6 shows a multi-dimensional array of five elements by five elements.

	1	2	3	4	5
1	1,1	1,2	1,3	1,4	1,5
2	2,1	2,2	2,3	2,4	2,5
3	3,1	3,2	3,3	3,4	3,5
4	4,1	4,2	4,3	4,4	4,5
5	5,1	5,2	5,3	5,4	5,5

Figure 8-6: Element 2,4 is highlighted in this 5-by-5 array.

This is how you would declare the array in Figure 8-6 and how you would reference the highlighted element:

```
String        MyArray[5,5]
String        MyVariable

MyVariable = MyArray[2,4]
```

This procedure for declaring arrays is the same for each variable type, with one exception. The decimal type is declared in a special way. You should refer to the On-line Help for exact instructions on declaring a decimal array.

Earthquake-Proof Structures

A *stucture* is a versatile type of PowerScript variable. A structure allows you to group related variables under one name. It's like having an office building with the name Law Offices; then, inside, you have about forty different law firms.

Creating and using structures is a three-step process. First, you create the structure, which is actually a new data type. Then you declare a variable of the new structure type; lastly, you assign values to the variables.

Creating a structure

The variables in a structure do not all have to be the same type, as they do in an array. You can group variables of any type together into a structure.

PowerBuilder provides an easy way to create structures. To create a structure:

1. Click on the Structure icon in the PowerBar. It is the one that looks like a building. This brings up the Structure Painter.
2. In the Select Structure dialog, click the New button. This will bring up the New Structure dialog.
3. This step is similar to creating a database table. Enter a variable name in the field provided.
4. Select a variable type (see Figure 8-7).
5. Continue adding variables by repeating steps 3 and 4 until you have finished. Then click the OK button.
6. When prompted to name your structure, enter a name that is meaningful for this group of variables.
7. When you have finished typing the name you should add a comment in the Comments: box. It is important to document every part of your PowerBuilder application. Now click the OK button.

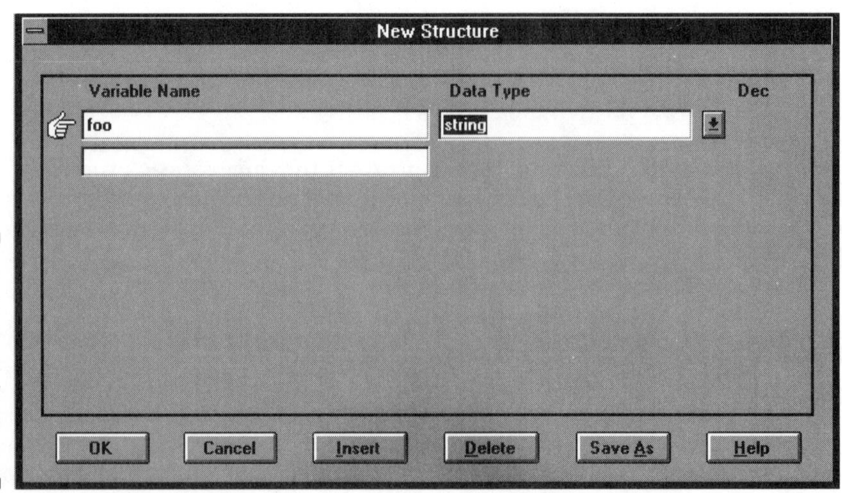

Figure 8-7: Create a structure using the New Structure window.

Your structure is now ready to use. Structures are especially handy for moving information around between PowerBuilder objects. We will cover this in more detail in Chapter 10.

Structures can also be declared at the window and user object level. This way, you can store information in structures for use within a window or user object. ■

Declaring new structures

Once you have created a structure, you have created a new data type. Just as you would declare a variable of type integer or string, you can now declare an integer of type MyStruct or whatever you named your structure in the preceding section.

Here is an example in which we have created a structure called MyStuff. This structure has three variables, ANIMAL, VEGETABLE, and MINERAL. They are all string type variables.

```
MyStuff Goodies
```

There is now a structure called Goodies. It has three variables, just as we designed when we created MyStuff.

Using structures

Using a structure is easy. Use the variables in a structure as you would any other variable. Just remember to always precede the variable name with the name of the structure and a dot. Here is an example of assigning a value:

```
MyStuff Goodies
Goodies.ANIMAL = "Bear"
Goodies.VEGETABLE = "Carrot"
Goodies.MINERAL = "Lead"
```

A common mistake is forgetting that the structure you create is only a template. You must declare a variable using your new structure, as in the previous example. ■

I Think You Need Scope

Scope is defined in the Webster's dictionary as "space for movement or activity; opportunity for operation." Variables in PowerBuilder have scope.

Determining a variable's scope determines its area of operation. This is an area in an application where the variable can be seen and used by other portions of the program.

It's like having a little kid. Everyone in the family knows your kid. When they come to your house they pinch the kid's cheek and say how cute it is. School-aged kids have a wider scope. They are known by others outside the family. They now have two areas they can operate in, school and home. Then there is the adolescent, young-adult-type kid. They think they rule the world. They are known to everyone — the cop that brought them home after a particularly fun night, all the unattached kids of the opposite sex, teachers, neighbors who have moved because of the loud music, and of course, the family who loves them. Their scope is global, unless they're grounded.

A variable can have different levels of scope, depending on where it is created; they are:

- Global
- Local
- Shared
- Instance

Getting the big picture on global variables

Any script in the entire application can see global variables. The application object, all of its windows, all the objects on the windows, and functions can see a global variable.

Global variables are a temptation! It is certainly convenient to have a variable that can be seen from everywhere in the application. But this makes the application object responsible for keeping track of variables that it shouldn't care about.

Besides violating the idea of responsibility-oriented software engineering, using global variables is dangerous. It is easy for different parts of the program to accidentally change the values in variables. Global variables can be a debugging nightmare. Use global variables if you must, but use them sparingly.

Keeping local variables to yourself

Local variables are seen and used only by the objects that create them. For example, a button script variable is created by a button script, used in that script, and then removed from memory when the script is finished running. You can use the same names for variables used locally in different scripts. This will save you from having to think of different names for variables that do the same thing in each script. An example of this is the integer variable i. This is commonly used as a counter variables in FOR loops.

```
FOR i = 1 TO SomeAmount
```

As long as the variable, i, is a local variable, it can be used safely in different scripts.

Be careful when using variable names over again in the same script. You must reset or clear the value in the variable before you reuse it another time, unless the previous value is needed.

Instant gratification with instance variables

Declare an instance variable when you need to add an attribute to an object. Any type of variable can be used as an instance variable. The instance variables of an object are accessed just like built-in attributes, such as:

```
ObjectName.InstanceVariable
```

When more than one instance of an object is created in your application, each instance will contain its own version of the object's instance variables.

Stick around for shared variables

Shared variables, also known as static variables, are much like instance variables. The main difference is that when opening more than one instance of an object, only one copy of the shared variable exists. Each instance of the object is able to change this single value. When using instance variables, each object has its own set where it stores values used only in that instance of the object. Applications, windows, and menus can have shared variables.

Writing the User Defined Function

PowerScript is rich with functions. There is a function to do just about anything you might need to have done. You can think of PowerScript functions as motors, gears, strings, and pulleys, all tools to get the job done. You can take all these tools and construct new, more complex tools. These are called *user-defined functions,* or simply UDFs. Think of UDFs as robots made from motors and gears. Create these tools whenever you need to perform the same task in many different places in your application.

You can create your own functions at two levels. You can have application-level functions available to all objects in your application, or you can have object functions, such as windows, menus, and user objects.

Window functions are available to other parts of your application by using dot notation. This is a good way to communicate with the window from other parts of the program.

Therefore, use window functions when the task to be performed is unique to the operations of that window. If your task can be used by more than one window, consider making this an application-level object.

The process for creating application-level and window-level functions is slightly different.

To create an application-level user-defined function:

1. Select the Function Painter icon from the toolbar.
2. Click the New button in the Select Function dialog.
3. Enter a name for your function in the New Function dialog.
4. Enter a return value type from the list box on the right side of the New Function dialog (see Figure 8-8). You can choose to return no value by choosing [None] from the list.
5. Optionally, you can add arguments that are passed to the function. Type a name for the variable, choose a type, and select whether to pass the variable by value or by reference.
6. Click the OK button to bring up the Function Editor. Write your function by entering as many valid PowerScript statements as you wish. Paste arguments by selecting them from the list provided.
7. Click the Return icon when you're finished creating your function. PowerBuilder then checks your function for syntax errors. If it gets a clean bill of health, your function is now ready to use.

Creating a window-level function is very similar. While in the Window Painter follow these steps:

1. Select Window Functions... from the Declare menu.
2. Click the New button from the Select Function in Window dialog.
3. Follow the steps for application-level functions, starting at step 3, to complete creating your window-level function.

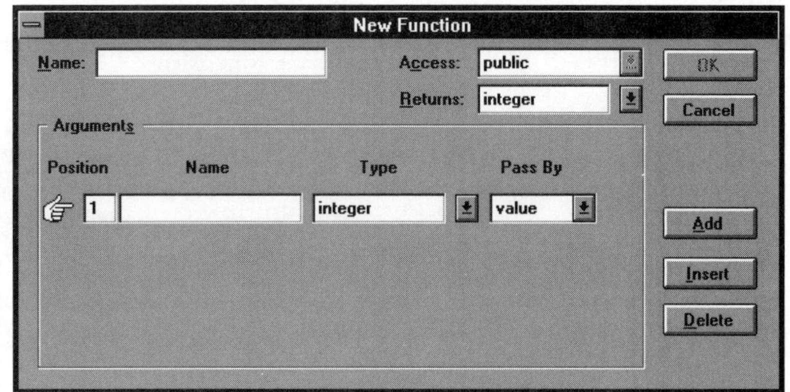

Figure 8-8: Use the New Function window to define new functions.

The window and any of its controls can now use your function.

Arguments to functions can be passed by value or by reference. When passing a value by value, you actually send the value along to the function. When you pass by reference, you are passing a pointer to the place in memory where the value is stored.

When a value is passed by reference, if it is changed in the function, it is also changed in memory. This way, when the function completes its processing, the value remains changed. A variable passed by value is changed only while the function is executing. If you want a variable passed by value to change when the function quits, you must pass the new value back as a return value. ■

Summary

Becoming fluent in PowerScript, as in any language, takes practice. PowerBuilder has a rich language that allows you to create powerful applications quickly with a minimum amount of programming. In the next chapter you will learn how to put PowerScript to good use in creating data-entry screens.

Chapter 9

Building Data-Entry Screens

In This Chapter

- Getting a new picture of data-entry screens
- Crafting data-entry screens with controls
- Reading the contents of data-entry controls

You have now learned how to paint windows and write scripts for events using PowerScript. In this chapter we will use these skills to create powerful data-entry screens.

Simplifying data entry is one of the more important parts of developing an application. Good data-entry screens are:

- Easy to use
- Able to check for errors
- Pleasant to look at for long periods of time

By building good data-entry screens, you can increase the productivity of your tool, decrease the likelihood of errors in the data, and create long-lasting friends in the user community. Creating this type of screen is more of an art than a science. You could say that data-entry screens are crafted rather than programmed into existence.

Crafting data-entry screens requires that you use the visual programming methods described in Chapter 6 and the non-visual scripting methods described in Chapter 8. Feel free to refer back to those chapters as we explore data-entry screens.

Enter Data, Stage Right

The idea of a data-entry screen brings to mind a user mindlessly keying data in to the appropriate fields. That might have been the way it was in the past, but not anymore. Data entry is now an interactive manipulation of information. Drop-down selection lists, important lookup information, and graphic data representations are all part of entering information. Instead of typing information, a user might drag it from one window into another. He might select information from a list of choices or create an entry by clicking on graphic representations of information.

When you design a data-entry screen, it is easy to get into the trap of trying to figure out how you are going to collect all that text onto one or two screens. This is an old text-based habit. Instead, ask yourself:

- What is the easiest way to accept data from a user?
- What will make this program fun to use?
- How can I keep the user from entering wrong information?

The list can go on and on. Force yourself to expand the way you think about data-entry screens; your programs will become works of art.

Choosing the Right Data-Entry Controls

Controls are the tools we use to craft our data-entry screens. Even though you can use any control you wish, certain controls are better for this than others. It's like painting a landscape — you can use any color, but if you are striving for reality, you probably won't use hot pink and lime green (unless, of course, they match your couch).

We will cover some of the more obvious data-entry controls, and then some of the not so obvious.

For the textually timid...

The most commonly thought of control for data entry is the single line edit. This control allows you to capture one line of text information. These controls are great, but, before you get carried away thinking that this is the only control you will ever need, think back to all those tests in school. Whether it was Sister Marie Formaldehyde or Mr. Macacque on your back, you hated those essay questions. You loved multiple-choice questions on tests because you knew that there was at least some chance of getting the right answer. The same is true in data entry. You can have the user either type the information, or, when possible, select it.

When typing is the option of choice, and there is only one line of information to type, use a SingleLineEdit control (see Figure 9-1).

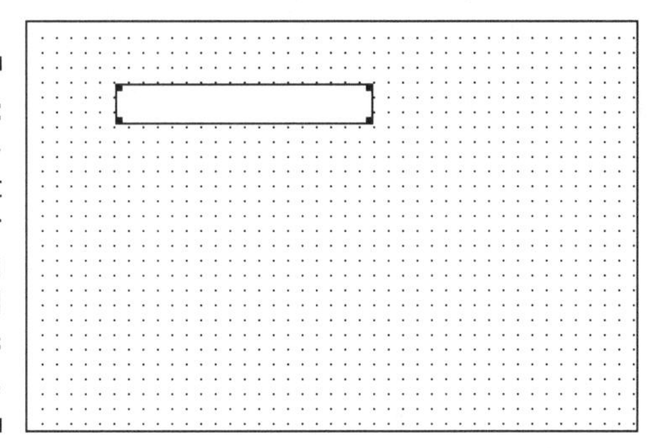

Figure 9-1: Use SingleLineEdit controls for entering small amounts of text.

To add and configure SingleLineEdit controls:

1. Click the SingleLineEdit Control icon on the Painter Bar.
2. Click on the window where you would like the SingleLineEdit control to appear. You can adjust the placement with the mouse any time you want.
3. At this point, you can choose either to double-click the SingleLineEdit control or to click on it with the right mouse button. These steps assume double-clicking. This brings up the SingleLineEdit dialog (see Figure 9-2).
4. As you can see in Figure 9-2, the SingleLineEdit's default name is sle_1. You may choose to give it a more meaningful name.
5. If you want a default value to appear in the SingleLineEdit, fill in the Text: field.
6. Finish setting each of the other parameters. They are described in detail in Table 9-1.
7. If you want to add text to one of the events, you should click the Script button.
8. When you are finished, click the OK button.

You can customize the way your SingleLineEdit control looks and performs with the attributes listed in Table 9-1.

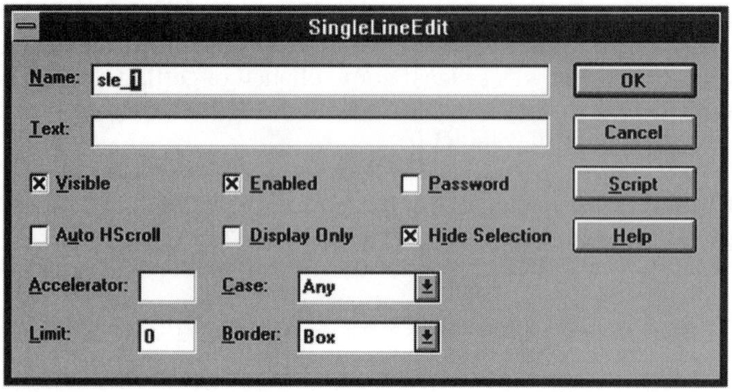

Figure 9-2: Customize your Single-LineEdit to make it perform just the way you want.

Table 9-1: SingleLineEdit attributes

Attribute	*Use*
Visible	Choose whether your SingleLineEdit is visible or invisible. You can change this attribute at run time to have controls appear and disappear.
Enabled	If a control is enabled, you can give it focus by clicking on it or tabbing to it. When it is not enabled, this control is read-only; it cannot send or receive messages.
Password	Use this SingleLineEdit to obtain a password. All text entered appears as asterisks.
Auto HScroll	Determine if automatic left and right scrolling is enabled.
Display Only	Choose whether or not the user can change the text in a SingleLineEdit.
Hide Selection	When deselected, this attribute causes highlighted text to stay highlighted, even when the control no longer has focus.
Accelerator	An integer equaling the ASCII value of a key you want as an accelerator.
Case	Choose whether you want text entered in the control to be upper- or lowercase, or converted to either all upper- or all lowercase.
Limit	This is an integer equaling the maximum number of characters a user can enter into the SingleLineEdit control.
Border	When selected, the SingleLineEdit appears with a border, as in Figure 9-1.

SingleLineEdit controls are normally used with StaticText controls. These controls place text on a window. For the SingleLineEdit control to make sense to anyone, there should be some clue to what should be entered into the control; see Figure 9-3 for an example. ■

Enter Name

First Name Last Name

Figure 9-3: Use StaticText controls to let users know what to do with the SingleLineEdit controls.

We mentioned earlier that you can click with the right mouse button on your control. This is true of any visual object, not just controls. For example, you can also right-click on windows. This brings up the menu shown in Figure 9-4. This popup menu allows you to do everything you could do by double-clicking on the object, and more.

Script...
Border
Color
Drag and Drop
Name...
Pointer...
Style
Bring to Front
Send to Back
Clear
Duplicate

Figure 9-4: This popup lets you define all the attributes of an object.

The popup menu is different for each object. The menu shown in Figure 9-4 is for a SingleLineEdit control. You can see that there are options, such as changing colors, that were not available in the SingleLineEdit dialog box. Think of that as a "quick configure" dialog, with full configuration capabilities in the popup menu. Figure 9-5 shows how easy it is to change both background and text colors.

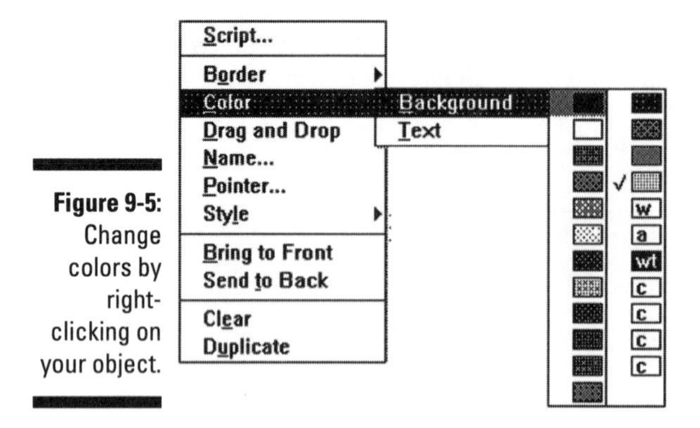

Figure 9-5: Change colors by right-clicking on your object.

Adding special effects, such as different border styles, can make an application appear more professional, and more fun. Figure 9-6 shows the choices for border styles. Figure 9-7 shows the SingleLineEdit controls with some of the different styles.

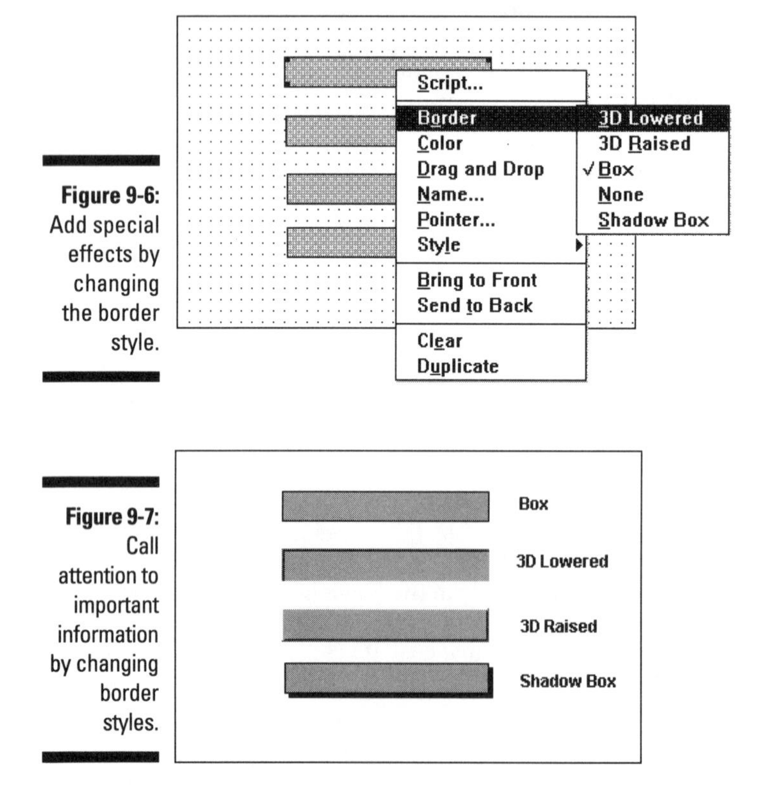

Figure 9-6: Add special effects by changing the border style.

Figure 9-7: Call attention to important information by changing border styles.

Be careful not to get too carried away changing colors and border styles. Most applications are more pleasant when they use only a few colors and styles. Otherwise, they become busy, intense, and hard to look at for more than a few minutes.

One additional feature is the ability to move objects to the front or back. This is important if you are using one object on top of another. For example, you can have a SingleLineEdit appear above a picture object used as a background. This type of data-entry screen can be artistic and powerful (see Figure 9-8). Use the popup menu to move controls to the front or to the back when they are on top of one another.

Figure 9-8: Be creative with your use of controls.

For the textually verbose...

The next level up in entering text is the MultiLineEdit control. There are always places in applications where you need to enter notes, comments, or text of some undetermined length.

Figure 9-9 shows a MultiLineEdit control being used in a window. MultiLineEdit controls have some of the same features as some text editors or low-end word processors. You can configure this control to fit most of your needs.

You can add and configure the MultiLineEdit using the same steps for adding and configuring a SingleLineEdit. There are a few differences from the SingleLineEdit, such as the fact that its default name is mle_1 instead of sle_1. A MultiLineEdit control does not have a Password attribute. The rest of the attributes are described in Table 9-2.

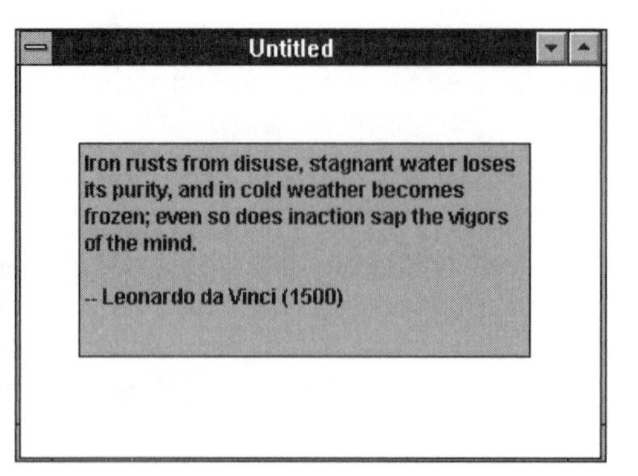

Figure 9-9: You can write anything you want using a MultiLineEdit.

Table 9-2: Additional MultiLineEdit attributes

Attribute	*Use*
HScrollBar	Displays a horizontal scroll bar beneath the MultiLineEdit control. Don't confuse this with the HScrollBar control. This attribute allows you to scroll left and right in the MultiLineEdit control.
VScrollBar	Displays a vertical scroll bar on the right side of the Multi-LineEdit control. Again, don't confuse this with the VScrollBar control. This attribute allows you to scroll up and down, or between pages in the MultiLineEdit control.
Auto VScroll	Determines if the MultiLineEdit can scroll up or down automatically as the user enters data.
Alignment	Determines the text alignment in the MultiLineEdit — left-, center-, or right-aligned.
Tab Stop	One or more integers, separated with a space, that define the position of each tab stop in the MultiLineEdit. The integer value is in number of characters.

Remember that you can click on the MultiLineEdit with the right mouse button and set all of its attributes. You can refer to the description of this popup menu in the section on SingleLineEdit controls. ■

The text in the MultiLineEdit is stored as one continuous character string. It's stored in the text attribute of the MultiLineEdit. You can use this attribute as you would a variable. You can either store values to this attribute directly, or use the value stored there. Make sure you precede the text attribute with the name of the MultiLineEdit, like this: mle_1.text

Santa's little ListBox

The famous Ray Kroc, founder of McDonald's, was responsible for changing the way people think. He saw that he would sell more product by giving us a greater choice of sizes. He invented the medium-sized drink. Here we are, all these years later, and now we demand choices. PowerBuilder hasn't let us down. The ListBox control lets users select from a list by clicking on a selection with their mouse.

When creating applications, use ListBoxes to give users choices to select from rather than having to type information. This will reduce typos and speed up data entry. ListBoxes can also inform users about what the different data-entry choices might be. This is excellent when the options change. It's a little like a restaurant where they slip a piece of paper in the menu to inform customers of the daily specials.

Putting a ListBox on your window is as easy as clicking the ListBox icon in the Painter Bar and then clicking on the window. Once it's there, you need to add the choices that will appear in the ListBox. There are two ways to do this:

- Double-clicking the ListBox control will bring up a dialog where you can enter the choices (see Figure 9-10)
- Using PowerScript, you can add the choices by using the AddItem( ) function

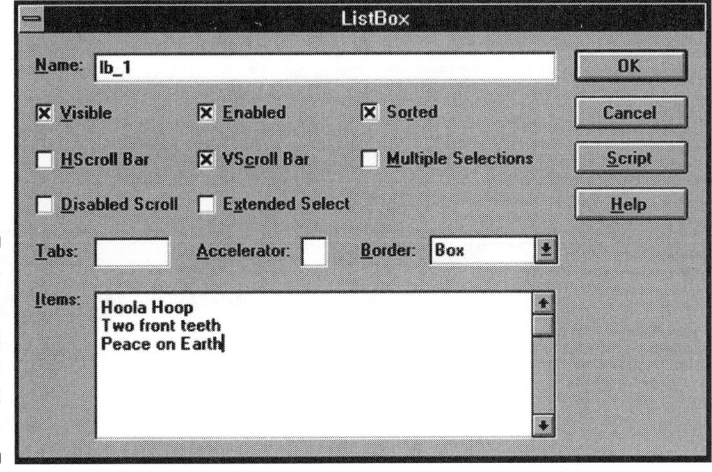

Figure 9-10: Add items to a ListBox in the ListBox dialog.

The other way to add items to a ListBox is to use the ListBox function, AddItem( ), like this:

```
lb_1.AddItem( "Hoola Hoop")
lb_1.AddItem( "Two front teeth")
lb_1.AddItem( "Peace on Earth")
```

In the preceding example, lb_1 is the default name for the ListBox control, and AddItem( ) is the ListBox function. The text in quotes is the text to add to the ListBox control. By the way, the AddItem( ) function will accept only string values.

The first method, adding items to the ListBox when it's created, is fine if the items are not likely to change. Defining them here keeps you from having to write any PowerScript code.

On the other hand, adding PowerScript code that initializes the ListBox items allows you to create item lists dynamically. These items can come from many places; the database, calculations, or controls, for example. ListBoxes are great ways to display dynamic lists in a data-entry screen.

An example for a human resources program could include a ListBox that would allow the user to select health benefit plans. The plans available to the employee might depend on benefit elections, employee status, dependents, and length of employment. All of these factors could be taken into account when the list of choices is created. Then, only appropriate choices are given to the user. This way, the program assumes responsibility for certain information, and does not leave it to the user to figure out what the choices should be.

Once you have a ListBox on the screen you may want to change its attributes. Double-clicking the ListBox will bring up the dialog shown in Figure 9-10. Most of the attributes should be familiar by now. There are a few that are unique to ListBoxes. They are explained in Table 9-3.

Table 9-3: Additional ListBox attributes

Attribute	*Use*
Sort	When selected, the ListBox items are sorted alphabetically.
Multiple Selections	Lets the user make several selections from the ListBox instead of just one.
Disabled Scroll	When selected, the ScrollBar always appears, needed or not; when not selected, the ScrollBar appears only when needed.
Extended Select	When selected, advanced selection capabilities exist for multiple selection.
Items	This is a character array that contains the items that will appear as choices in the ListBox.

You can use the same methods as the SingleLineEdit for changing the appearance of your ListBox. Remember to keep your colors and styles consistent among the different controls for a sense of continuity. Too many colors and styles gives an application the look of a collage or a "Where's Waldo" poster.

Finding out what choice a user makes is done using PowerScript. Here is an example of a ListBox in which a single choice is allowed:

```
String TheChoice

TheChoice = lb_1.SelectedItem()
```

In this example, TheChoice is a string variable that will hold the result of the user's selection from the ListBox lb_1. The SelectedItem( ) function returns the text of the selected choice. You can also use the SelectedIndex( ) function to return the index number of the item selected. Each of the choices in the ListBox has a corresponding index number representing the item's position in the list.

If your ListBox allows for multiple selections, you can find out how many items have been selected by using the TotalSelected( ) function. To find out which items have been selected, you will have to cruise through the ListBox checking the state of each item. Here is an example:

```
integer i, totalitems

totalitems = lb_1.TotalItems()
FOR i = 1 to totalitems
   IF lb_1.State(i) = 1 THEN
      // This item is selected. Do something here.
   END IF
NEXT
```

The FOR loop will loop for the total number of items in the listbox lb_1. While it is looping, each item is checked using the state( ) function. This function returns 1 if selected, and 0 if not selected. You can do anything you want when a selected item is located. Bounce them, float them, wait, this sounds like my checkbook. Speaking of checks...

Czech boxes are finely crafted in the Slovak Republic

CheckBoxes are a great way to make choices in a data-entry screen. They are like switches — either they're checked or unchecked. Whenever simple choices between two opposing possibilities must be made, this is a slick way to do it. For those old enough to vote, you may recall checking squares on a ballot next to the name of the person you were hoping to put into office.

Now that we have explained that CheckBoxes are good when there are two possibilities, it's time to jump in and let you know that PowerBuilder has a special option for CheckBoxes. It's called the *third state*. You know that period of time somewhere between sound asleep and sucking down a cup of java? That's the third state. It's a third possibility. It's not checked; it's not unchecked. In fact, it's gray. You might use the third state in an application where you are taking a poll. Checked could mean, "Yes, I love it." Unchecked could be, "No, I hate it." The third state could mean, "I couldn't care less."

Using CheckBoxes can:

- Save valuable room on the screen, answering three possible questions with a single check
- Simplify data entry by saving keystrokes
- Make an application look very snazzy

Putting a CheckBox on the window is the same as any other control. There are a few attributes you should know about, though. They are listed in Table 9-4.

Table 9-4: Additional CheckBox attributes

Attribute	*Use*
Automatic	Allows the X to appear or disappear automatically when you click the CheckBox; it's the default.
Checked	When this is selected, the CheckBox contains an X. This attribute changes as you click on the control; setting this during application development sets the initial value.
Three State	Allows the CheckBox to have a third state.
Third State	Shows whether or not the CheckBox is currently in the third state; this changes as the control is clicked. Setting this during application development sets the CheckBox initial value to the third state. It is not possible to select both third state and checked. If you're bored, try it.
Left Text	When selected, any text accompanying the CheckBox appears on the left side, instead of on the default right side of the little box.

You can use two attributes to get information from a CheckBox. The checked attribute lets you know if the item is checked or unchecked. It returns TRUE if checked. Use the other attribute, ThirdState, when your CheckBox can have three states. When this returns TRUE, the CheckBox is in the third state.

The checked attribute had better return FALSE if ThirdState returns TRUE. Here are a couple of examples:

```
Boolean IsPregnant

IsPregnant = cb_1.checked
```

In this example, IsPregnant is a boolean type variable that stores the setting of the checked attribute of the CheckBox named cb_1.

This next example sets three different variables depending on the state of the three state CheckBox, cb_2. Your child might use this type of CheckBox to rate babysitters.

```
Boolean IsNice, IsMean, IsOK

IF cb_2.checked
  IsNice = TRUE
ELSE
  IF cb_2.ThirdState
    IsOK = TRUE
  ELSE
    IsMean = TRUE
  END IF
END IF
```

You will find numerous uses for this control. Whenever you catch yourself having someone enter a single character, or a Yes or No answer, think about CheckBoxes.

Don't touch that dial!

Many years ago, some clever person decided to add buttons to car radios. These allow the driver to pay attention to driving and select between five or six favorite radio stations. That same logic applies to RadioButton controls. Your user can choose among five or six options during data entry. RadioButtons are so named because of their similarity in behavior to actual car radio buttons. Even though it is possible, it makes no sense to use only one radio button in an application. This would be like having one button on the car radio. I suppose you could always tune in your favorite station, but this would not be much of a selling feature.

RadioButtons are grouped. When one button is clicked and becomes selected, the other RadioButtons in the group are deselected. Yep, just like the car. Each RadioButton in a window is part of a group unless you create separate groups by placing them within a GroupBox, as we did in Figure 9-11.

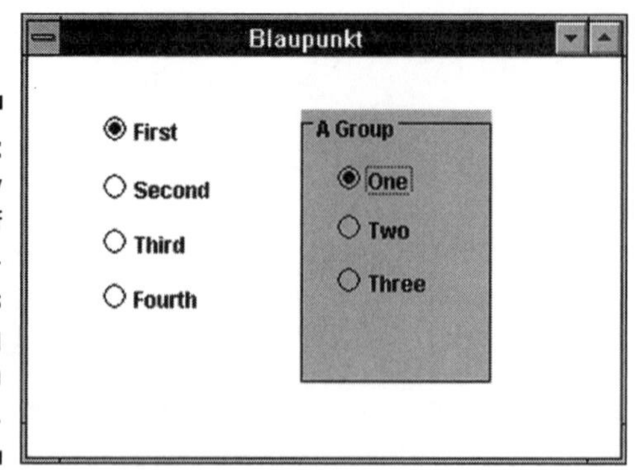

Figure 9-11: Create many groups of Radio-Buttons by putting them in GroupBoxes.

You can configure RadioButtons and get data from them in the same manner as you would a CheckBox. Simply check the value of the checked attribute. Remember that only one RadioButton in a group can be checked.

Drop down and give me twenty, soldier!

Here's a ListBox that would make Penn and Teller proud. (They are the magicians who made the Space Shuttle disappear, or was that Congress?) When you are pressed for space, the *DropDownListBox* is really handy. This control is sometimes known as a ComboBox because it is a combination of a Single-LineEdit and a ListBox (Figure 9-12).

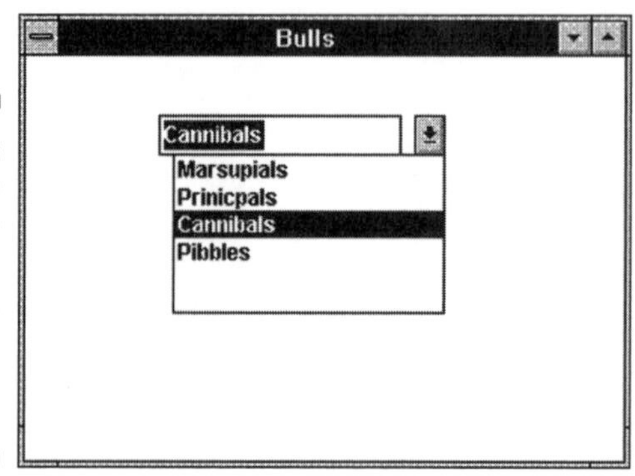

Figure 9-12: The Drop-DownList-Box is a combination Single-LineEdit and ListBox.

Use it like a SingleLineEdit. Use it like a ListBox. Use it in the dark. Use it on a train, and in a car, and in a tree, they are so good, so good, you see.

The DropDownListBox is often preferred to the ListBox on a data-entry screen because the choices remain visible in the edit portion of the control. Another reason it is sometimes preferred is that a user doesn't have to stop typing and grab the mouse in order to select an entry, as he would with a simple ListBox.

The DropDownListBox has only one attribute we haven't talked about before, Always Show List. This attribute, as its name implies, always forces the DropDownListBox to appear in the dropped-down condition. This is as opposed to the default, when only the edit portion appears with an arrow; click the arrow, and the list appears.

Adding items to the list is exactly the same as adding items to a ListBox. You can add them during application development or during run time using PowerScript.

Getting data from a DropDownListBox is much easier than from a ListBox. The selected or typed entry appears in the text attribute of the control.

Because your selection in a DropDownListBox appears in the text field of the control, you cannot select multiple items from the list. Selecting different items changes what appears in the text field. If you want to select multiple items from a DropDownListBox type control you will have to read ahead to the section on DropDownDataWindows. ■

Using the Data that God Gave You

You now have a good idea of the different elements of a data-entry screen. You can get user input, respond to it, and supply information to the user in the form of lists. Only one question remains. What do you do with all the information stored in the attributes of all these controls?

Several *Green Eggs and Ham* references come to mind. Seriously though, most often you'll use data-entry controls to accept simple input from the user. This input could be anything from words to search for in the database to which employee record to access. Using data-entry controls and PowerScript branching and decision-making, your applications can become more flexible and more useful.

Summary

Deciding how to collect the information, what controls to use, and how to format them can be a very creative and rewarding challenge. Our recommendation is that you don't take the easy way out by making everything a SingleLineEdit. In fact, Chapter 12 shows you how you can build the same type of data-entry screen with one DataWindow control.

Sometimes it is easier to create different windows from which users can select information. These are called *Popup windows* and that's what's coming next.

Chapter 10

Creating Response Windows

In This Chapter

- Building response windows
- Understanding modal versus non-modal windows
- Passing information to a window
- Returning information from a window

In a business, when you need a very specific bit of information or function performed, you bring in a consultant or a specialist. In a computer application, there are times when you need to bring in specialists. You already know that Windows applications usually have certain windows for opening files, saving files, and printing files. Each of these windows has a specialty. The Open File window specializes in opening files; the Print File window knows only about printing files.

This type of "specialist" window is called a *response* window. This chapter covers the important things about building response windows. More importantly, it also covers passing information to and from windows in PowerBuilder.

R.S.V.P.

Chapter 7 showed you how to build a window and configure it to look and act exactly the way you want. When you build a window, one of the attributes you set is the window type.

The different types of windows are:

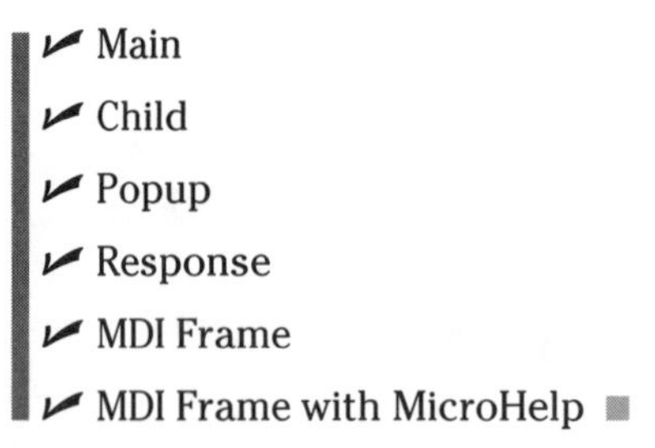

- Main
- Child
- Popup
- Response
- MDI Frame
- MDI Frame with MicroHelp

We are detailing the response window type because, used effectively, it can be a powerful tool. Using response windows also fits in well with Responsibility Oriented Software Engineering. A data-entry window should not be concerned with opening, closing, or printing files. The responsibility of a data-entry window should be data entry, but it still needs to perform these other tasks.

The philosophy behind building a response window should be to make it do one thing and do it well. Keep the functionality of a response window very specific. This doesn't always mean simple, however. For example, in a telecommunications software program, a response window may be responsible for setting all of the communication parameters. Figure 10-1 shows a response window from the Windows Terminal program.

Figure 10-1: Response windows are specific, but not always simple.

Motile is moving, modal is not

You may remember that in Chapter 7 we described the response window as a stubborn brute. This window type is known as a *modal* window. A modal window is one that waits for a user response before it will close and return control to your program. Modal windows are not only stubborn and brutish, they are egocentric — you cannot click on any other window or menu outside of this window; while it is open, it is the only active window. Response windows are modal so that your application will stop and wait for a response before continuing. This stubborn streak exists only in your application. The user can switch to other applications and return back to this patiently waiting response window.

All other window types are considered non-modal. If more than one window is open, you can switch between them or choose menu options from the application menu.

Creating the response window

You create response windows as you would any other window type, by using the Window Painter. Begin by starting the Window Painter:

1. Click the Window Painter icon in the PowerBar. This will start the Window Painter.
2. Double-click the new window to bring up the Window Style dialog. (By the way, the Window Style dialog is a response type window. Try clicking outside the window.)
3. Click the Response radio button in the Window Type box. Notice that many of the options become disabled.
4. Give your response window a name. Response windows normally have names that relate to their function, such as Open File or View File. This name will appear in the title bar of the window.
5. Modify any of the other options. It's a good idea to keep the control menu, and you are forced to keep the border.
6. Click the OK button when you are finished setting the Window Style options.

It isn't a hard and fast rule, but response windows are normally smaller in size than the windows from which they're called. You can resize a window by grabbing any side with the mouse and stretching or shrinking it. ■

Here's something to go on

Many response windows don't need information passed from the application. Windows such as File Open simply accept user input. But windows like File Save really should know ahead of time what file you are thinking about saving. This information is passed to the window when it is opened.

In Chapter 7 you learned that opening a window is accomplished using the Open( ) function. When you need to pass information to the window when you open it, there is a special function just for that purpose — the OpenWith-Parm( ) function. This is short for Open With Parameter.

Here is the syntax for OpenWithParm( ):

```
OpenWithParm( windowname, parameter, parent )
```

- *windowname* is the name of the window you want to open. This can also be a variable of type window.
- *parameter* is the information or object you want passed to the window.
- *parent* is an optional parameter that allows you to designate which window you want to have as the parent of the window you are opening.

The OpenWithParm( ) function not only opens the window, it also passes a parameter to the window being opened. This way, File Save windows can know ahead of time which file to save.

You can pass any data or object type as a parameter. The next section goes into how to receive the passed parameter. Basically, parameters are sent and received as one of three basic types:

- String — sent as a string and received as a StringParm
- Number — sent as one of the numeric data types and received as a LongParm
- Object — sent as an object and received as a PowerObjectParm

The creative gears in your mind are already cranking. Now you want to know how many parameters you can pass to the window. The answer is one. One what? you ask. In Chapter 8 you learned about structures. Here is the perfect opportunity to use a structure. You can create a structure to hold all of the variables or objects you want passed to the new window, and then pass the structure as the one variable. That's like the genie coming out of the lamp and telling you that you have only one wish. "I wish for a genie that will give me ten wishes!" ■

Here is an example script that could be found in the clicked event of a button that brings up a response window:

```
// This stores communication parameters in a structure, Paramstruct
MyStruct Paramstruct
```

```
Paramstruct.Baud = 9600
Paramstruct.Parity = "N"
Paramstruct.Databits = 8
Paramstruct.Stopbits = 1

// Open the window, CommSet and pass the structure as a parameter
OpenWithParm( CommSet, Paramstruct )
```

Remember that you can include comments in your PowerScript code by preceding the comment with a double forward slash (//).

The first line in the button script creates a structure of type ParamStruct. See Chapter 8 to learn how to create a structure. Then, values are stored in each of the structure's predefined elements. Finally, the OpenWithParm( ) function is used to open the window CommSet, while passing the structure as a parameter.

Receiving passed parameters

Learning how to pass parameters and not having a way to receive them is like inventing a radio that only transmits. Somehow, knowing your voice is out there somewhere isn't quite as satisfying as having someone else be able to hear it. Passing parameters to a window is the same kind of thing. This section will cover the way windows receive passed parameters.

PowerBuilder has a special object for receiving messages called the message object. You can think of it as the window's in-box. The message object can receive three types of messages.

- Numbers
- PowerBuilder objects
- Character strings

To retrieve messages from the message object, you can refer to them as you would elements of a structure called message. The three elements are:

- message.DoubleParm
- message.PowerObjectParm
- message.StringParm

Using message.PowerObjectParm

We are going to cover the PowerObjectParm first since it has the greatest utility. You can pass many types of objects and structures using this message object variable. Here is an example of script in the Open event of the response window we previously opened using OpenWithParm( ):

```
MyStruct CommParams          // Create a structure of type MyStruct

CommParams = message.PowerObjectParm

em_1.text = String(CommParams.Baud,"####")
em_2.text = CommParams.Parity
em_3.text = String(CommParams.Databits,"#")
em_4.text = String(CommParams.Stopbits,"#")
```

The structure, CommParams, receives the passed structure from the message object. The EditMask controls are now used to display and edit that information on the window. The String( ) function is used to convert the numeric type variables to string.

Using message.StringParam

Strings are passed to the window in the same manner structures are passed, using the OpenWithParm( ) function. The window receives them with message.StringParm rather than the message.PowerObjectParm it uses to accept structures.

Here is an example of receiving a string passed to a window using message.StringParm:

```
st_1.text = message.StringParm
```

In this example, the text received in message.StringParm is stored directly into the text attribute of a SingleLineEdit.

Using message.DoubleParm

Numbers are received in the same manner as strings except that the values are received in message.DoubleParm. Here is an example of receiving a number passed to a window:

```
Integer x, y, z       // Set up three integer variables

x = 23        // Store the number 23 in x
y = message.DoubleParm        // Store the passed parameter in y
z = x / y     // z is x divided by y
```

There are certainly other ways to access the information in other windows. One such temptation is to use global variables. Even though it's true that there is less programming involved — passing, receiving, and so on — it isn't the best way to develop applications. There are not many real needs for a global variable. When you find yourself using one, ask yourself if it isn't better defined as an instance or local variable.

He's Going Long for the Pass, but It's a Hand-Off

Response windows would be pretty useless if they kept their responses to themselves. That would be like going to a tax preparer with a year's worth of receipts and then never hearing from this person again.

Passing the results of a response window back to the parent window is like opening a window with a parameter, but in reverse. The values are passed using the CloseWithReturn( ) function. Information in the response window is handed back to the parent, or calling, window.

The CloseWithReturn function has only two parameters:

```
CloseWithReturn( WindowName, ReturnValue )
```

- *WindowName* is the name of the response window you are closing.
- *ReturnValue* is the parameter you are returning to the calling, or parent, window.

The CloseWithReturn( ) function is normally placed in the clicked event of either an OK or a Cancel button. When you click the OK button, the response window closes and the information is returned. In the Cancel button, you may choose to use the Close( ) function or CloseWithReturn( ), passing a value that tells your calling window that the user exited with the Cancel button. The latter makes it easier for the calling window to figure out what happened.

Just as in OpenWithParm( ), you can pass strings, numbers, and objects using CloseWithReturn( ). Here is an example in which the communication parameters of our earlier examples are being sent back to the calling program as a formatted string. This example is in the clicked event of the OK button:

```
String ReturnVal

ReturnVal = em_1.text + ", " + em_2.text + ", " + em_3.text +&
        em_4.text

CloseWithReturn( CommSet, ReturnVal )
```

The first thing to notice in this example is that PowerScript command lines can be continued on the next line by ending the line to be continued with an ampersand. ■

It would have been possible to return all four values as a structure — the same way they were passed to the response window. We thought we would pass a formatted string back instead. The text values of the four EditMasks are concatenated with commas separating the values. The resulting string, ReturnVal, is then sent back in the CloseWithReturn( ) function.

The Cancel button might have a one-line script that looks like this:

```
CloseWithReturn( CommSet, "Canceled" )
```

The calling window, or parent window, can receive the return value using the message object. Here is the example we started earlier, where we passed the values to the response window. We will now add the script necessary to receive the returned values:

```
// This stores communication parameters in a structure, Paramstruct
MyStruct Paramstruct
String CommString

Paramstruct.Baud = 9600
Paramstruct.Parity = "N"
Paramstruct.Databits = 8
Paramstruct.Stopbits = 1

// Open the window, CommSet and pass the structure as a parameter
OpenWithParm( CommSet, Paramstruct )
CommString = message.StringParm
IF CommString = "Canceled" THEN
   // the response window was closed with the cancel button
ELSE
   // CommString contains the formatted communication string
END IF
```

You can see from this example that you can check the returned value to find out if the response window was canceled or if the OK button was pressed. If no value is returned, the message object will contain Null values. Instead of passing back the word "Canceled," you could check for Null values, but why the values are Null is not always evident. If there is an error in your program, and the values are not returned as they should be, there would be no way of telling this.

Summary

Response windows are an essential tool. They are the specialists in your application. You have seen how to pass information to a window and then return values to the parent, or calling, window.

Response windows can simplify your application; with them you can perform the same specialized function from anywhere in the application without writing redundant code. You can also simplify window design by pulling complex data entry into separate windows.

The next chapter will teach you how use menus to tie your application together and simplify tasks.

Chapter 11

Menus

In This Chapter

- Using the Menu Painter to create a menu
- Enhancing your menus with accelerators and shortcuts
- Creating cascading menus
- Making your menu do something
- Constructing popup menus

In this world of gadgetry, a popular little device is the universal remote control. This little gizmo controls the TV, the VCR, the stereo, and if you're lucky, the kids. It gives you a common tool to control all of those expensive goodies, right from your armchair.

Windows in PowerBuilder are a little like the consumer electronics crowding your family room. They all do something special and each has its own user interface stuck on the front of it. To call your consumer electronics an "entertainment system" you need the universal remote. To call the windows you build an application, you need a *menu.* A menu acts like that universal remote — it provides a common interface.

Menus, once they are created using the Menu Painter, are attached to windows by clicking the Menu option in the Windows Style dialog. Double-click the window and you will see a Menu: checkbox. If the checkbox is enabled (not gray) you will be able to attach a menu. All window types, with the exception of popup and response type windows, can have menus attached.

Creating a Menu

A common mistake, even in some of the finest restaurants, is skimping on the creative energy put into menus. After all, the menu is many people's first impression of the duck à l'orange (or of a software application). Which sounds better:

- Duck in an orange sauce
- Wild ranging foul deliciously smothered in tangy citrus marmalade

How selections are described is not the only test of a good menu. Have you ever been out to eat and tried to find the beverage section of the menu? Try it at Denny's — impossible! In most Windows applications, a standard format for menus has evolved. This book is not a standards guide. But it isn't too hard to take a look at a few applications to see that they normally start with a File menu and end with a Help menu. Study how other applications' menus are designed to see how you might design yours.

It really helps users, especially new users, feel comfortable with a program if it seems similar to other programs they use regularly. The menu, above all else, can give that comfort. People no longer feel mystified by new software if they at least know how to get help and quit the program.

Menus are created using the Menu Painter. To start the Menu Painter click the Green Menu icon in the PowerBar. This will start the Menu Painter, as shown in Figure 11-1. When the Select Menu dialog appears, choose New.

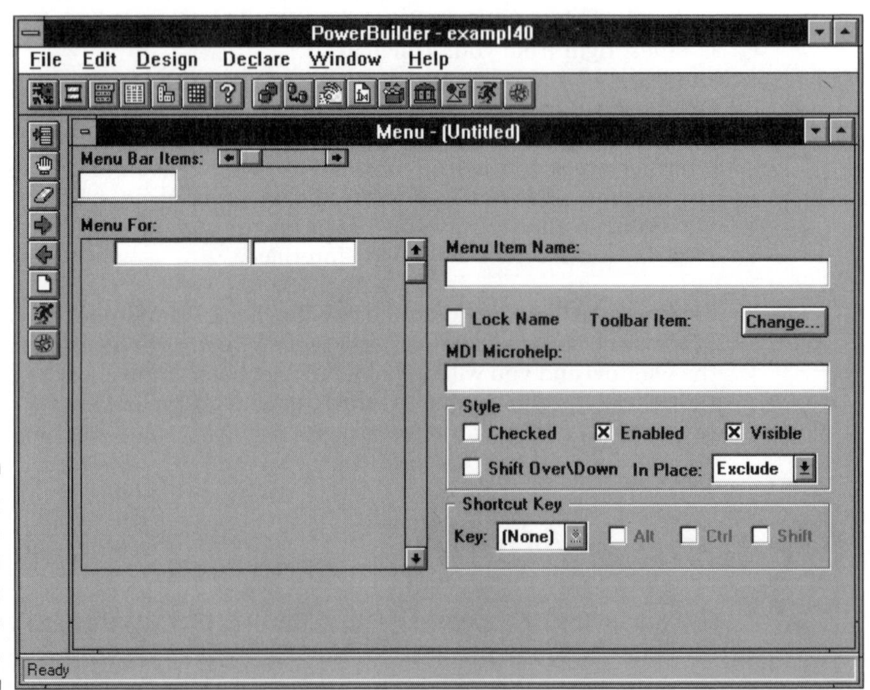

Figure 11-1: Use the Menu Painter to create menus.

May I have the menu please?

There are two types of menus in PowerBuilder. The *window* menu appears in a bar on the top of the window and has choices that drop down; a *popup* menu can appear anywhere on the screen. To begin, we will learn how to create a window menu. First we'll create its File menu:

1. Start the Menu Painter by clicking the Menu Painter icon in the PowerBar.
2. Click the New button in the Select Menu dialog.
3. We will now add the menu bar items, the ones that are visible all the time across the top of the window. Don't worry about the little underlines yet. Add a menu choice to the box below Menu Bar Items: by adding the word File.
4. Beneath the word File, the Menu Painter now says Menu For: File. This is where we will add the menu items that will drop down when File is selected. Add the word New. A default Menu Item Name appears, m_new. You can change this if you want.
5. Ignore the empty box next to the word New, and hit the Tab key. An empty box appears beneath the first menu item. Add the word Open. Continue adding menu items. Be sure to add the words Close and Exit to the menu items. Your screen should look something like Figure 11-2.

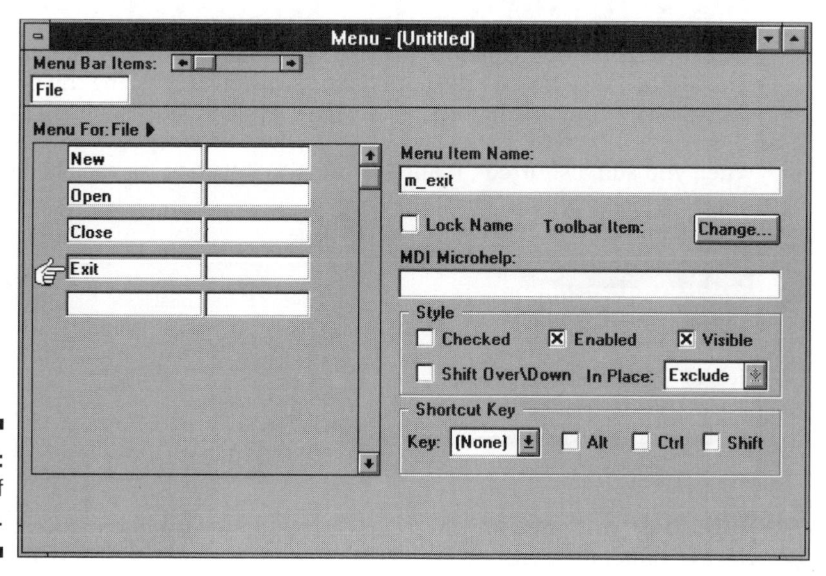

Figure 11-2: The birth of a menu.

To go, press the accelerator

You have just built the first set of menu choices. Now let's enhance these choices a bit and make them do something. Hah! You thought you were done, and that you love menu building because it's so easy! Well, it is easy. Now we get to add those little underlines you see in everyone else's menu. These single-character underlines are called *accelerator keys*. An accelerator key allows the user to select a menu item by pressing the underlined character rather than using the mouse to select it.

When using the keyboard instead of the mouse to operate menus, use the Alt key to access the menu. You can then use a combination of the arrow keys and accelerator keys to make a selection. These keys may be different on your Macintosh or UNIX machine. ■

An accelerator key is created by adding an ampersand (&) in front of the letter you want to be an accelerator key. The ampersand will not appear as part of the menu item. Instead, the character following the ampersand will appear underlined. For example, &File will appear as File. You can embed accelerator keys within words; for example, &Format will appear as Format. You can add accelerator keys to either the menu bar items or to the menu items that drop down below them.

The wolf knew a shortcut Little Red didn't

Shortcut keys allow the user to press a key combination that activates a menu choice from anywhere in the application, without accessing the menu. A shortcut key combination might be Ctrl + N to activate the menu item New.

When you add a shortcut, it appears next to its menu item, as in Figure 11-3.

File
New... Ctrl+N
Open... Ctrl+O
Close

Figure 11-3: Using shortcuts keeps your hands on the keyboard and off your mouse.

By the way, you can't add shortcuts to the top-level menu bar items because they wouldn't do anything except bring up more choices. There are already shortcuts to do that — the accelerator keys. ■

To add a shortcut key:

1. Select the menu item for which you want a shortcut key by clicking on it in the Menu Painter.
2. In the Shortcut Key section of the painter, first select either the Alt, Ctrl, or Shift key by clicking the checkbox next to your choice.
3. From the list box labeled Key:, select the character or function key. The new shortcut key combination will appear in the box next to its menu item. It will also appear there when the menu displays (Figure 11-3).

PowerBuilder has a weird interface misbehavior. If you check Alt or Control before you pick the key, the check will not appear to be checked. When you select the key, the check miraculously appears. If you choose the key first, though, the check for Alt or Ctrl appears when clicked.

Adding separators to your menu

When menus have several different types or categories of selections, it can look slick to separate them into sections. Adding separators is quite simple. While adding menu items, add a dash (-) instead of text where you want the separator to appear. Menu items that follow the dash will appear in a separate section, as in Figure 11-4. If this is starting to look like menu selections from a very popular word processor, it isn't.

File Edit View Insert
New... Ctrl+N
Open... Ctrl+O
Close
Find File...
Summary Info...
Templates...

Figure 11-4: Separate menu items according to function.

A preview of what's to come

There's a little tidbit you should know about adding menu items. A menu item followed by an ellipsis (three dots...) designates that a dialog box will appear on the screen if you select this menu choice. Some menu choices do a task and then return. If the user is going to see a dialog box when they make a menu selection, add the three dots to the end of the text, like this:

```
&Sort...
```

Another clue about what is to come is the little arrow that lets users know that there is an additional drop-down menu.

Falling for cascading menus

An additional drop-down menu allows users to make further selections. This type of attention-getting menu is called a *cascading* menu. For example, the New menu item might have an additional menu that allows users to select the type of file they want to create. Take a look at Figure 11-5 — a picture is worth a thousand words.

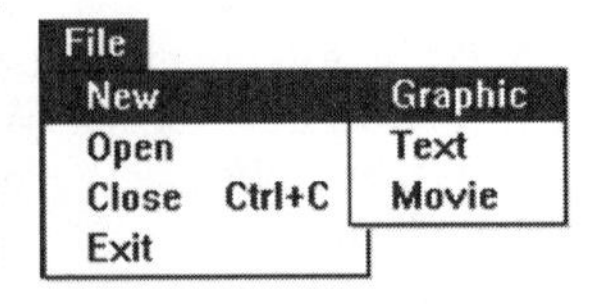

Figure 11-5: Allow additional menu choices with a cascading menu.

Since a cascading menu cascades from a particular menu item, to create one, click the menu item in the painter and then click the right arrow. See Figure 11-6.

Figure 11-6: Click the right arrow to enter a cascading menu.

You will notice that a new area for entering menu items appears in the painter. If the menu bar item is File and the menu item beneath that is New, you will see: You can build more than one layer of cascading menus. Move back and forth between them using the pink left and right arrow buttons. (Figure 11-6)

Moving Mountains

You can see the menu you have created so far by selecting Preview from the Design menu. You can click different choices with the mouse or navigate through the menu using the keyboard. As fun as it is to see your menu pop open and close, and the highlight bar move up and down or back and forth, the fact is, this menu doesn't do anything yet.

You attach a script to each menu item to make it do something. To add a script to a menu item:

1. In the Menu Painter, click on the menu item to which you want to add a script. A finger pointer appears next to the selected menu item.
2. Click on the Script icon in the Painter Bar. It is the icon that looks like a dog-eared piece of paper. The Script Painter will appear. The default event is the Clicked event.
3. When you have finished adding your script, click the Green Menu icon to return to the Menu Painter.

Add a script to each of your menu choices. Here is an example of a script in a menu choice called Cyberspace. This is selected from a cascading menu beneath the Open menu, which is selected from the File menu:

```
// This script opens the window Cyberspace

OPEN(Cyberspace)
```

To add comments to your program, as we have in the last example, precede them with a double slash (//). The PowerBuilder compiler ignores any program statements that follow the double slash. ■

Menus are popping up everywhere

A popup menu can appear anywhere on the screen, anytime you need it. Popup menus appear in response to an event in a window or control.

Building a popup menu is a little trickier than creating a window menu and attaching it to a window. Here are the steps for creating and using a popup menu:

1. Create a menu in the Menu Painter with only one MenuBar item, for example, File.
2. Write an event script for each menu item.
3. Save your new menu.
4. To use your new menu, create an instance of the menu. (See the following example.)
5. In some event, include the PopMenu function.

When you create a menu using the Menu Painter, you create a definition for a menu, not the actual menu. It's like creating a blueprint for a menu. Now, we must actually create the menu. Do this by creating a variable. Then, create the menu object, saving it to the new variable.

For this example you need to have created a menu and saved it as MyMenu. We will create an instance of MyMenu and call it ThePopMenu. This is a two-step process:

1. Create a variable of type MyMenu by typing MyMenu followed by the new variable.
2. Create a MyMenu object with the CREATE command and store it in the new variable.

Here is how it looks:

```
MyMenu MyPopMenu
MyPopMenu = CREATE MyMenu
```

Now there is a menu object called ThePopMenu. The next step is to use the PopMenu( ) function to bring up the popup menu. There are two parameters to the PopMenu( ) function:

```
Menu.MenuItemName.PopMenu(x position, y position )
```

- *Menu* is the name of the menu object. In our example it is ThePopMenu.
- *MenuItemName* is the top menu item. In our example this is m_file.
- *x position* is the x-axis screen coordinate of the popup menu.
- *y position* is the y-axis screen coordinate of the popup menu.

Include the PopMenu( ) function in an event such as the Open event of the window. Here is how our example might look:

```
MyPopMenu.m_file.PopMenu(250, 500)
```

Another thing you can do is have the popup menu appear wherever you click the mouse. (There are two functions that return the mouse cursor position.) Here is how you would do that:

```
MyMenu MyPopMenu
MyPopMenu = CREATE MyMenu

MyPopMenu.m_file.PopMenu(PointerX(), PointerY() )
```

Figure 11-7 shows what a popup menu might look like.

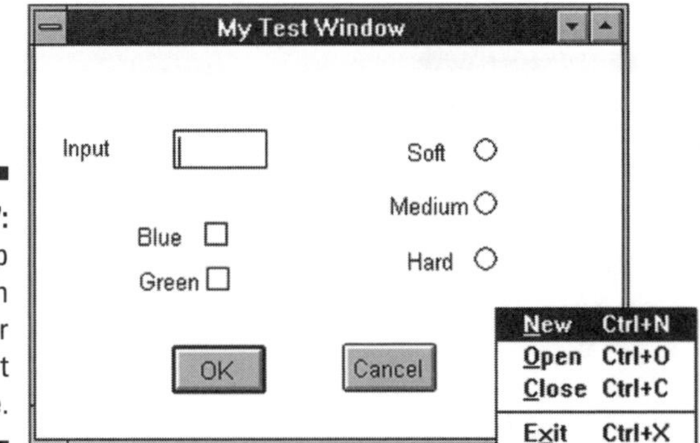

Figure 11-7: Popup menus can appear almost anywhere.

These examples assume that you do not want to use the menu that is already attached to the window. If you do, it is not necessary to create an instance of the menu using the CREATE command. It is not necessary to precede the MenuItemName with the menu, either. All you have to do is use the PopMenu( ) function like this:

```
MenuItemName.PopMenu(x position, y position )
```

MenuItemName must be one of the top-level menu bar items. You can use popup menus as a quick access to your window menu. One way to use this is to put the popup menu in the rbuttondown event, the event called when the right mouse button is pressed. (This is shift-click on the Macintosh.)

Summary

A menu can make an application easy to navigate. Taking care to plan menus carefully will make users much happier. You can also take advantage of accelerator keys and shortcut key combinations to limit use of the mouse.

Popup menus can give your application a very professional look and feel. Give your users many ways of doing the same thing. This gives them the option of following the approach they feel most comfortable with. This will give the greatest pleasure to the largest numbers.

In the next chapter you will begin learning about PowerBuilder's most powerful tool, the DataWindow. Remember back in grade school when the teacher would fill the board with all kinds of numeric equations, procedures, and other cryptic formulas? Then, after you spent the whole night memorizing it, the next morning she would smile and then show you the one-line shortcut. Well, here's the shortcut!

Part IV

DataWindows

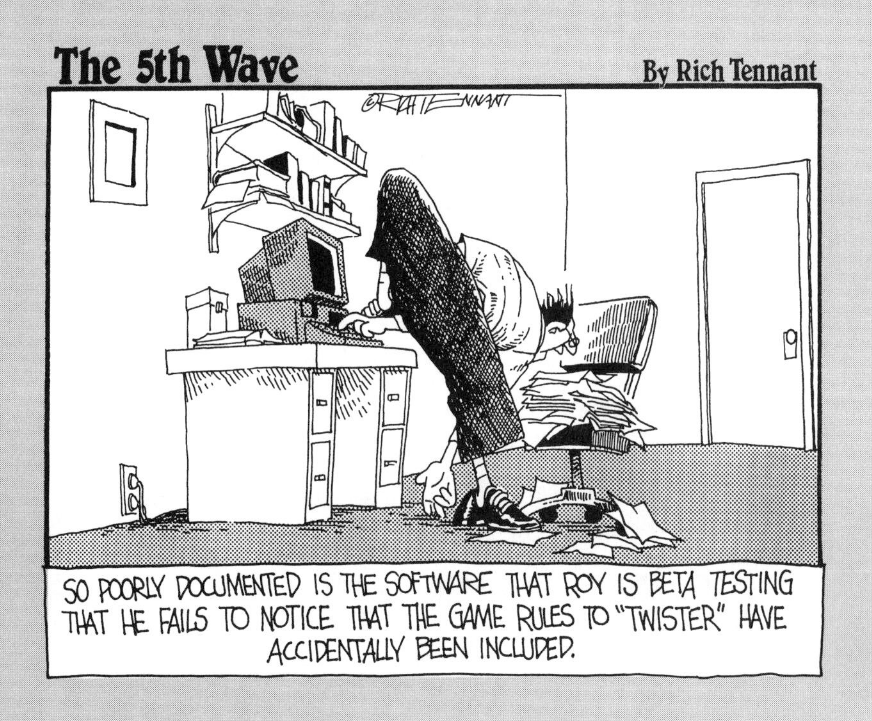

In This Part...

A DataWindow is a little like a table, a little like a window, and a lot like a powerful data management tool. DataWindows can be used to do many things, such as:

- Display and print reports and graphs
- Perform queries and display the results
- Create complete data-entry screens
- Process data and perform calculations

DataWindows have two parts. First, there's the *DataWindow definition*. A DataWindow definition describes the DataWindow and determines where its data comes from. Second, there's the *DataWindow control*. A DataWindow control lets you use the DataWindow definition as a user interface element on a window or as a data manipulation tool for your PowerScript code.

This part covers both the DataWindow definition and the DataWindow control. It shows you the most important aspects of each, and provides a solid foundation for the use of DataWindow technology in your PowerBuilder applications.

Chapter 12

Building and Using a DataWindow Definition

In This Chapter

- Using the DataWindow Painter
- Selecting a data source and a presentation style
- Configuring a DataWindow definition
- Applying a DataWindow definition in your program

DataWindow definitions are complete descriptions of the DataWindow. They're created using the DataWindow Painter. To access the DataWindow Painter, click on the DataWindow icon in the PainterBar. The window shown in Figure 12-1 appears on the screen, allowing you to select a DataWindow to modify. Click on the New button to create a new DataWindow definition.

Describing the DataWindow

All DataWindows have two things in common:

- They obtain data from somewhere.
- They present data in some way.

The origin of data in a DataWindow is known as its *data source*. Your parents are a bit like your data source. The way that a DataWindow presents its data is known as a *presentation style*.

When you create a new DataWindow definition, the first thing you do is choose a data source and a presentation style. The window shown in Figure 12-2 appears on the screen to allow you to do just that.

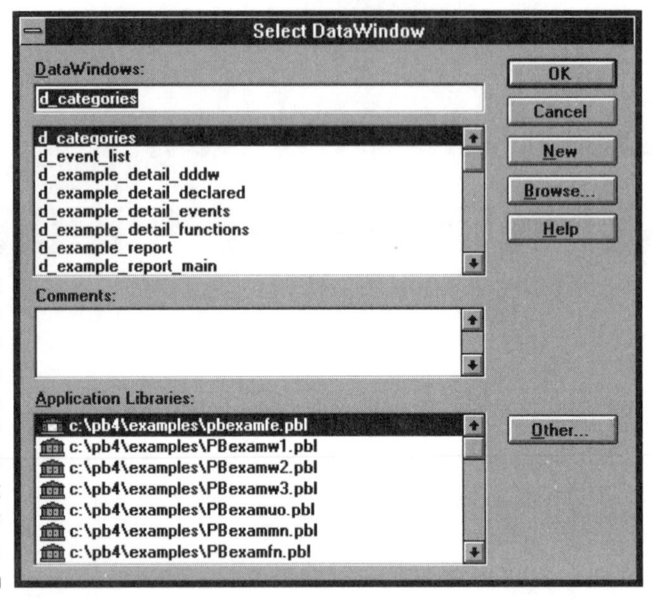

Figure 12-1: Select the DataWindow definition you want to modify using the Select DataWindow window.

You can preview your new DataWindow automatically after you're done defining its data source by clicking on the Preview When Built checkbox. Previewing a new DataWindow in this way shows you what the DataWindow will look like if you accept the default configuration for the presentation style you select. ■

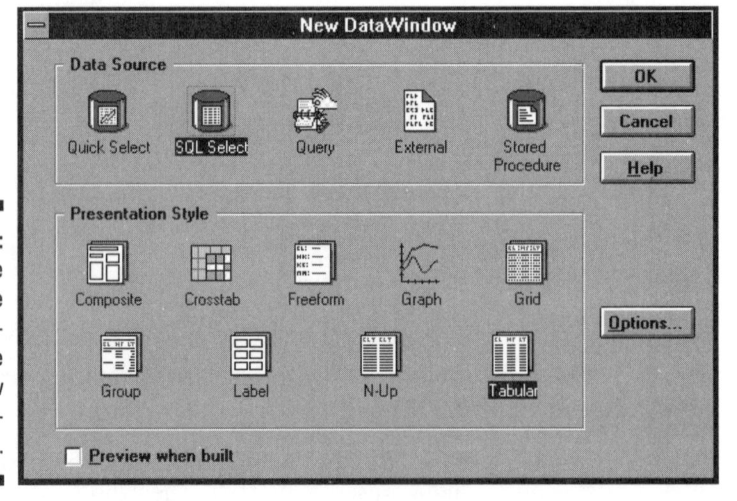

Figure 12-2: Choose the data source and presentation style of your new DataWindow.

Enterprising people can find Data in many places

If you were the captain of the starship *Enterprise*, you'd let other people find Data, and define data sources too. Since you're probably not, you'll have to do this yourself for now. (If you *are* the captain of the *Enterprise*, will you please send us your autograph?)

Do the following to select a data source and a presentation style for your DataWindow definition:

1. Click on the SQL Select Data Source icon.
2. Click on the Tabular presentation style.
3. Click on the OK button.

The full potential of DataWindow definitions are explored in Chapters 14 and 15, as we delve deeper into the use of data sources and presentation styles. For now, let's create a simple DataWindow definition that gets data from one database table. When the SQL Painter appears on the screen, do the following:

1. Click on the customer table in the Select Tables window. If there isn't a customer table, click on another one instead.
2. Click on the Open button to display the columns in the table, as shown in Figure 12-3.
3. Click on the fname, lname, and phone columns. These columns become highlighted to indicate that they're selected, and the SQL Select syntax on the bottom of the screen changes to include these columns.
4. Switch to the DataWindow Painter by clicking on the Design icon in the PainterBar. (The Design icon looks like a triangle and a t-square.)

The DataWindow Painter now appears on your screen (see Figure 12-4). As you can see, the three columns you selected in the SQL Painter are presented in a table-like layout, and headings appear just above each column. This is the Tabular presentation style.

To return to the SQL Painter, click on the SQL icon in the PainterBar. You can also choose Edit Data Source... from the Design menu. The DataWindow definition's data source can be edited at any time, even after you save the DataWindow definition. ■

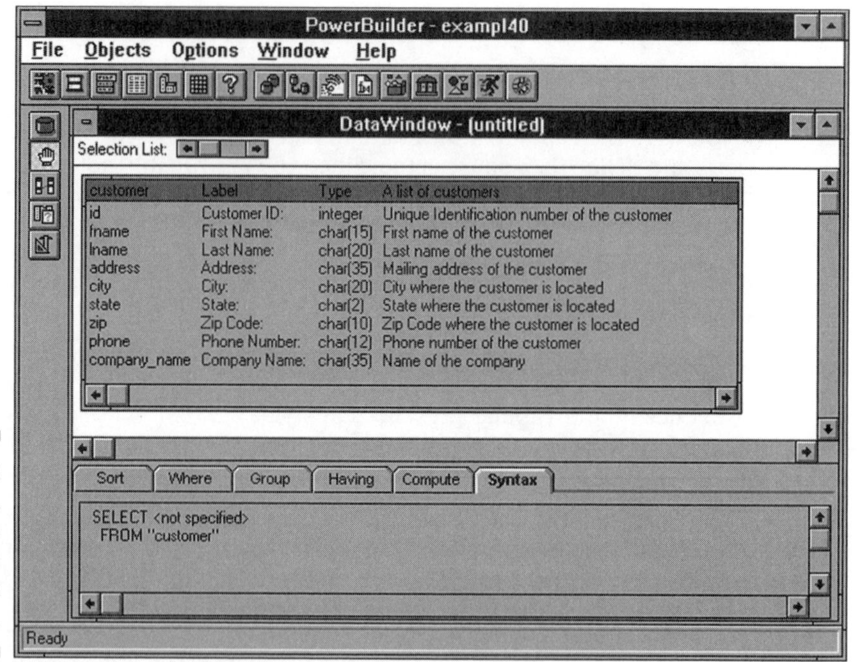

Figure 12-3: Use the SQL Painter to define an SQL Select data source.

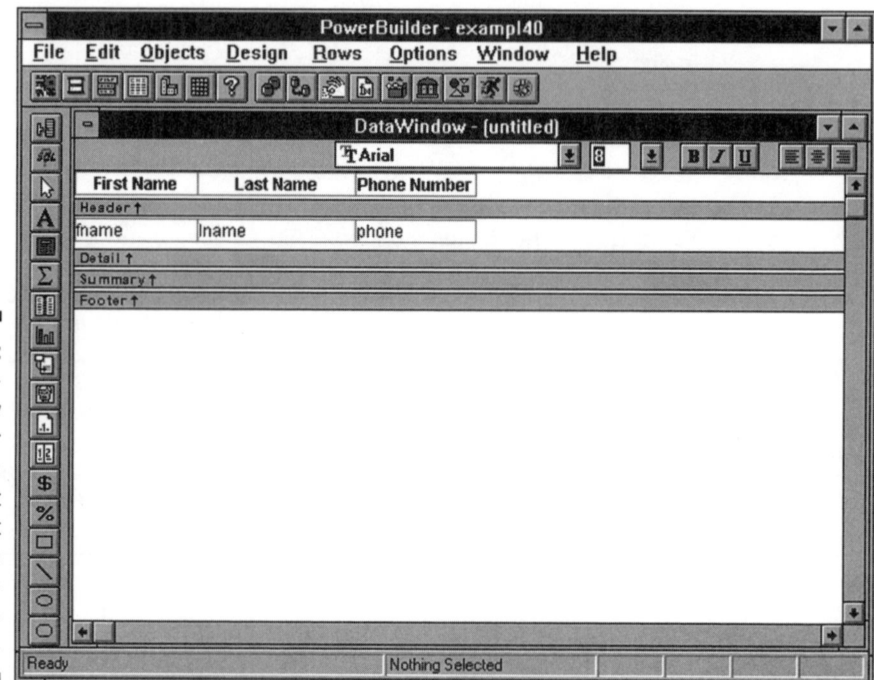

Figure 12-4: The DataWindow Painter presents a default layout based on the presentation style you select.

Once you've reached this point in creating a DataWindow definition, the only thing left to do is configure it. Everything you can possibly imagine is configurable in the DataWindow Painter. Do you want a column to display in a specific font or color? No problem. Do you want to add special columns that summarize other columns? No problem. Do you want your DataWindow definition to talk to you and swirl around the screen in blazing psychedelic color? Well, that would be a problem.

You can also stop right here and accept the default DataWindow configuration. The choice is yours. The next few sections describe the most important concepts and options to consider when configuring a DataWindow definition.

Changing the visual stimuli provided by a DataWindow definition

Appearance is everything. The way that you appear to your peers, your family, and your friends is most often determined by things that are tangible. Whether or not you take the time to talk to people and get to know them, for example, gives people a tangible way to determine how serious you are about your relationship with them. Conversely, if you scowl a lot and talk down to people, it might lead them to decide that you're a jerk.

The appearance of a DataWindow definition is determined in the same way. Tangible attributes are configured to produce just the right appearance. You can even add pictures and draw happy faces (or scowling faces if you prefer) to attain the appearance you're after.

To see what your DataWindow will look like, preview the DataWindow definition by choosing Preview... from the Design menu. You can also click on the Preview icon in the PainterBar or press Ctrl+W. ■

Selecting items in the DataWindow definition

Selecting items in the DataWindow definition is exactly like selecting controls on a window. To select a single item, click on it. To select multiple items, do one of the following:

- Click and drag, forming a box around the objects to be selected.
- Click on one object, then hold down the Control key while clicking on additional objects.

There are a few things that can't be done until you've selected items in the DataWindow definition. For example, before you can delete items, you have to select them. Once you've selected the items to be deleted, press the Delete key or choose Clear from the Edit menu.

You can also size, space, and align objects in the DataWindow definition as you would controls on a window. Select the objects to adjust and choose Align Objects, Space Objects, or Size Objects from the Edit menu.

Adding text objects to a DataWindow definition

Text objects can be added to your DataWindow definition to display text. Click on the Text Object icon in the PainterBar, the icon with the large A, then click on the DataWindow in the location you want to add a text object.

Begin typing to replace the contents of the text object. Text you enter appears both in the text object and in the upper-left corner of the DataWindow Painter. You'll also notice that the text object automatically resizes as you type.

Computed fields make cents

Sometimes it makes sense to perform calculations using the values in a DataWindow column. For example, it's often useful to summarize the contents of a numeric DataWindow column. Using a *computed field*, the DataWindow definition can handle this type of task for you automatically.

To create a computed field that summarizes the values in a numeric DataWindow column, do the following:

1. Click on the Compute icon in the PainterBar. The Compute icon looks like a small calculator; the kind you'd use to balance your checkbook but that wouldn't be much help in predicting the flight trajectory of two swallows carrying a coconut to England.
2. Click on the DataWindow definition in the location you'd like to add a new computed field. The Computed Field Definition window appears next (see Figure 12-5). This window is actually the *Expression Painter* in disguise. You'll see more of the Expression Painter later — it likes to appear in obscure places and never calls itself the Expression Painter.
3. Type a name for your new computed field in the Name: entryfield and press the Tab key.
4. Find the sum(#x for all) function in the Functions: list box by scrolling down the list. Click on it to paste it into the expression workspace. Notice that the #x is automatically highlighted.

5. Click, in the Columns: list box, on the name of the numeric DataWindow column you want to summarize. Character columns can't be summarized, so be sure to click on a numeric column. Since the #x was highlighted, it's replaced with the name of the column to summarize. You can also just type the column name; the Expression Painter is smart enough to figure out what you mean.

6. Click on the OK button to accept your new computed field.

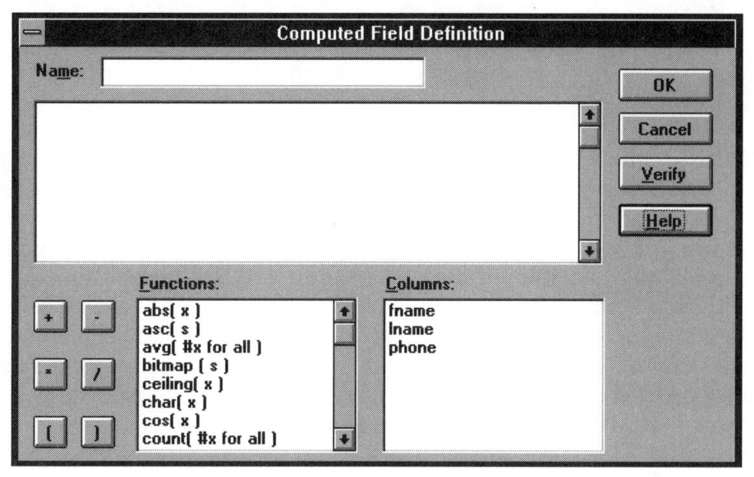

Figure 12-5: Create computed fields in your DataWindow definition by using the Expression Painter.

Another way to create a computed field that summarizes a numeric DataWindow column is to click on the numeric column you want to summarize, then click on the Sum icon in the PainterBar. A new computed field is created containing a sum() expression like the one you just built.

Computed fields can do a lot more than just summarize numeric DataWindow columns. You aren't limited to calculations based on DataWindow columns. You don't even need to use a DataWindow column to create a valid computed field. The PainterBar has two good examples of this:

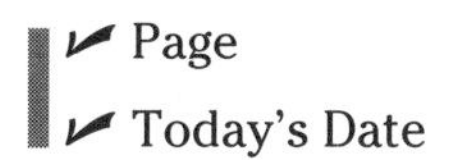

- Page
- Today's Date

The Page computed field displays the current page number and the total number of pages. This is most useful when printing a DataWindow. The computed field for Today's Date does what you might think — it displays the current date. To add either of these computed fields to your DataWindow definition, click on either the Page Computed Field icon or the Today's Date icon and then click on the DataWindow definition in the location you'd like the computed column to appear.

Should I go west, old man?

Deciding where to direct the objects in a DataWindow definition is key to creating an effective layout. Each DataWindow presentation style is slightly different, but all of them, with the exception of the graph style, contain the following sections:

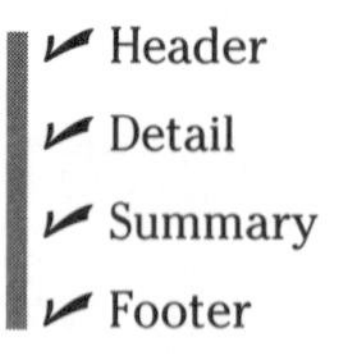

- Header
- Detail
- Summary
- Footer

The Header section appears at the top of the DataWindow and remains stationary. The Detail section appears once for each row of data in the DataWindow and can be scrolled up or down, left or right. The Summary section appears once as the very last row in the DataWindow. The Footer section appears at the bottom of the DataWindow and remains stationary.

All items placed in a particular section of the DataWindow become part of that section. To see how this works in the DataWindow you created earlier, click on the Preview icon in the PainterBar. Figure 12-6 shows what the previewed DataWindow definition looks like.

Figure 12-6: Preview the DataWindow definition to see how each section displays.

As you can see, the contents of the Header section display as fixed column headings. When you scroll down through the DataWindow using the vertical scrollbar, the header stays in one place. The data in the Detail section, however, scrolls by as you move through the DataWindow using the vertical scrollbar. This is because the Detail section defines the way that each row displays in the DataWindow.

The two sections that you don't see in the DataWindow preview are Summary and Footer. This is because there's nothing in them. An empty section doesn't display when the DataWindow definition is used.

Click on the Design icon in the PainterBar to return to the DataWindow Painter, and try the following:

1. Move the mouse pointer over the Footer bar.
2. When the mouse pointer changes to a double-ended arrow, click on the Footer bar and drag it down toward the bottom of the screen.
3. You've just enlarged the Footer section. Now click on the Text Object icon in the PainterBar.
4. Click in the Footer section to create a new text object.
5. Change the text displayed in the new text object by typing the following:

   ```
   Our customers are the best!
   ```

6. Click on the Preview icon again to see how this changes the DataWindow layout.

As you can see in Figure 12-7, a footer now appears at the bottom of the DataWindow. When you scroll through the rows in the DataWindow using the vertical scrollbar, both the Header section and the Footer section stay on the screen while the data scrolls by. Try one more example by doing the following:

1. Click on the Design icon in the PainterBar to return to the DataWindow Painter.
2. Add another text object to the DataWindow definition. This time place the text object inside the Detail section.
3. Type something in the text object and then click on the Preview icon again. You may be surprised at the result.

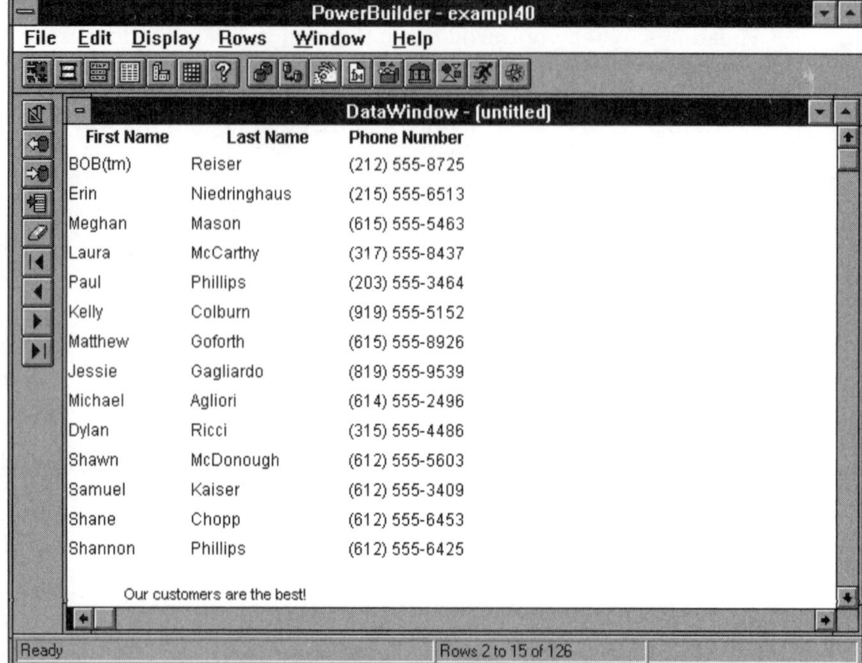

Figure 12-7: Preview the DataWindow definition again to see how your changes affected things.

Call 'em what you will, they're still columns

Columns come in many shapes and sizes, from ancient Greek columns to post-modern industrial columns. Some columns are meant to be decorative; others keep Bill in Accounting from crashing through the floor and landing on your head.

The appearance and purpose of DataWindow columns can be equally diverse. To change the visual characteristics of a DataWindow column, do the following:

1. If you're still in Preview mode, click on the Design icon in the PainterBar to return to the DataWindow Painter.
2. Click with the right mouse button the column you want to change. The popup menu shown in Figure 12-8 appears on the screen.
3. Choose a visual characteristic, such as Border, Color, or Font..., from the popup menu and select a new setting for the characteristic.

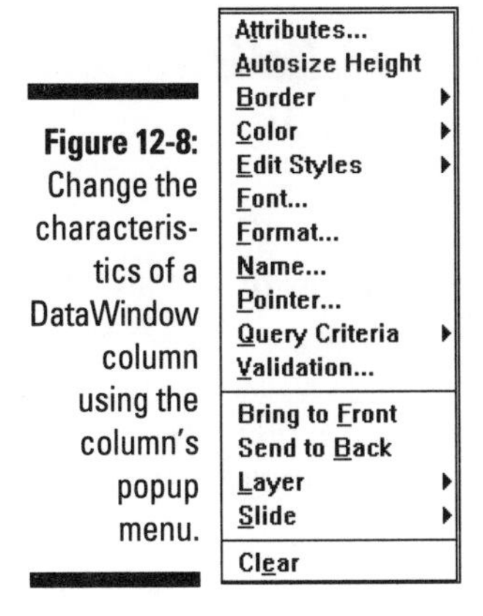

Figure 12-8: Change the characteristics of a DataWindow column using the column's popup menu.

As you can see in Figure 12-8, the popup menu for a column allows you to change many characteristics of a column, including visual characteristics such as border, color, and font.

Saving the DataWindow definition

To save your new DataWindow definition, choose Save from the File menu. When the window titled Save DataWindow appears, choose a PowerBuilder library for the new DataWindow definition, give the DataWindow a name, and enter any comments in the Comments: area. Then click on the OK button to save the DataWindow definition.

Using the DataWindow Definition

There are several ways to use a DataWindow definition once you've created and saved it. The most common use for a DataWindow definition is in the creation of a DataWindow control.

A DataWindow control is similar to other window controls. For example, events occur in a DataWindow control as they do in other controls, and you can write event scripts for a DataWindow control just as you can for other controls. Chapter 13 covers setting up and using a DataWindow control. The remaining sections of this chapter give you a glimpse of using a DataWindow definition in a DataWindow control.

Creating a DataWindow control and selecting a DataWindow definition

Do the following to create a DataWindow control:

1. Start the Window Painter and either create a new window or edit an existing one.
2. Click on the DataWindow icon in the PainterBar, which looks just like the DataWindow icon in the PowerBar. The difference is that the icon in the PainterBar is used to create a DataWindow control; the icon in the PowerBar is used to open the DataWindow Painter.
3. Click on the window in the location you'd like to add a new DataWindow control.

Now select a DataWindow definition to use in the DataWindow control by clicking with the right mouse button on the blank DataWindow control and choosing Change DataWindow... from the control popup menu. The window shown in Figure 12-9 appears, allowing you to select an existing DataWindow definition. Click on the definition you want to use and then click OK.

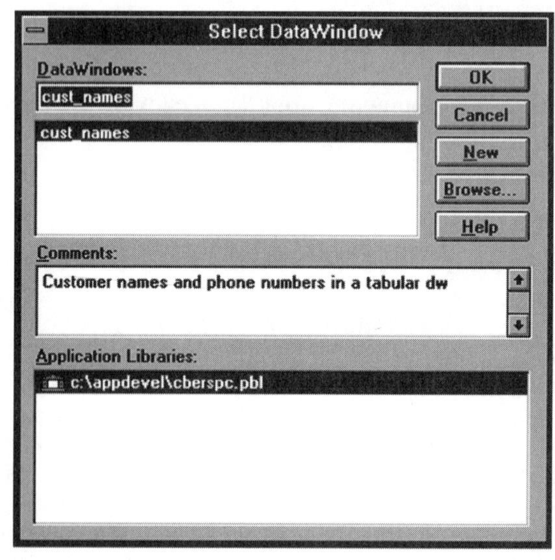

Figure 12-9: Select a DataWindow definition to use in the new DataWindow control.

The blank DataWindow control now displays the DataWindow definition you selected.

If you can't see the whole definition, change the size of the DataWindow control by clicking on the corner of the control and dragging to a new size. ■

Now give the DataWindow control a new name by doing the following:

1. Double-click on the DataWindow control with the left mouse button.
2. Type dw_test in the Name: field.
3. Click on the OK button to accept the new name.

Setting up the database transaction for a DataWindow

Once you create a DataWindow control and select a DataWindow definition, you're almost ready to see the DataWindow in action. Before your DataWindow control can talk to the database, however, you must first set up a new database transaction for the DataWindow control. Do the following:

1. Double-click on the window to open the Window Style window.
2. Click on the Script button to access the PowerScript Painter.
3. Choose the open event from the Select Event drop-down list box.
4. Type the following in the open event script:

```
dw_test.SetTransObject(SQLCA)
```

5. Click on the Window icon in the PowerScript PainterBar to return to the Window Painter.

The function SetTransObject() tells the DataWindow control named dw_test which transaction object to use when accessing the database. Whenever the window opens, the transaction object is set for the DataWindow control. This makes it possible for the DataWindow control to communicate with the database engine.

Retrieving data into a DataWindow control

The last step is for the DataWindow control to tell the database that it would like to retrieve data. Do the following to add to the window a new CommandButton that will tell the DataWindow control when to send this message to the database:

1. Click on the CommandButton icon in the PainterBar.
2. Click on the window in the location you'd like to add a new CommandButton.

3. Type the word Retrieve to change the text displayed on the new CommandButton.
4. Double-click on the CommandButton to access the CommandButton window. Type cb_retrieve in the Name: field to give a new name to the CommandButton.
5. Click on the OK button to accept the new name.
6. Click on the Retrieve CommandButton with the right mouse button and choose the Script... option from the popup menu.
7. In the clicked event script, type the following:

```
dw_test.Retrieve()
```

8. Click on the Window icon in the PainterBar to return to the Window Painter.
9. Save the changes to the window by choosing Save from the File menu. Give the window a name if you haven't already.

Now the application object must be told to open the window and connect to the database.

Connecting to the database in the application object

When your application is executed, the first thing it should normally do is connect to the database. This makes it possible for the DataWindows, PowerScript scripts, and other elements in your application to communicate with the database engine. The next thing that your application will normally do is open a window. Do the following to tell your application object to connect to the database and then open the window that you just created:

1. Click on the Application icon in the PowerBar to start the Application Painter.
2. Click on the Script icon in the PainterBar to access the PowerScript Painter.
3. Choose the open event from the Select Event drop-down list box.
4. Type the following at the beginning of the open event script to tell the application to connect to the database engine using the PowerSoft demo database:

```
sqlca.DBMS = "ODBC"
sqlca.database = "psdemodb.db"
```

```
sqlca.userid = "dba"
sqlca.dbpass = "sql"
sqlca.dbparm="ConnectString='DSN=Powersoft Demo
      DB;UID=dba;PWD=sql'"
connect using sqlca;
```

5. Add the following to the end of the open event script. If there's already an open() function call in the open event script, change it to this. Replace *WindowName* with the name of your window:

```
open(WindowName)
```

6. Click on the Application icon in the PainterBar to return to the Application Painter.
7. Choose Save from the File menu to save the changes to the application object.
8. Click on the Run icon in the PowerBar to run the application.

When the window appears, click on the Retrieve button. Figure 12-10 shows what happens.

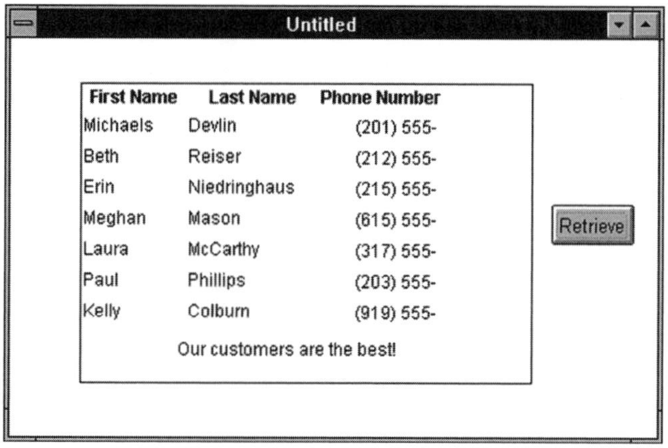

Untitled

First Name	Last Name	Phone Number
Michaels	Devlin	(201) 555-
Beth	Reiser	(212) 555-
Erin	Niedringhaus	(215) 555-
Meghan	Mason	(615) 555-
Laura	McCarthy	(317) 555-
Paul	Phillips	(203) 555-
Kelly	Colburn	(919) 555-

Our customers are the best!

Retrieve

Figure 12-10: Use event scripts to tell a DataWindow control when to retrieve data from the database.

Summary

In this chapter you learned how to use the DataWindow Painter to create powerful DataWindow definitions. You also saw how to put a DataWindow definition to use by creating a DataWindow control. The next chapter covers the DataWindow control in more detail and shows you how to get more out of your DataWindows.

Chapter 13

The DataWindow Control

In This Chapter

- Creating the custom DataWindow control
- Setting the DataWindow control attributes
- Adding PowerScript to the DataWindow control

The DataWindow is PowerBuilder's "magic wand." This control is the most powerful tool in PowerBuilder. In Chapter 12 you learned how to create a DataWindow definition. You also saw briefly how the definition is used in a control.

This chapter will guide you through the adventure of actually making the DataWindow control work for you. Accessing this control's real power will make your application simpler to create, easier to debug, more robust.

It's a window, it's a control, it's a DataWindow control. This control is actually a window with special abilities. You will see in this chapter that you can customize this control in very much the same way as you would a window. It can also be customized to act less like a window and more like a data-handling control.

Customizing the DataWindow Control

Begin by putting a DataWindow control on a window. This is very similar to adding any other type of control. To add a DataWindow control to a window, do the following:

1. Start the Window Painter and either create a new Window or edit an existing one.
2. Click on the DataWindow Control icon in the PainterBar.
3. Click on the window where you'd like to add a new DataWindow control.

The new DataWindow control appears as a blank white rectangle. It looks very much like a MultiLineEdit control when you first place it on the window, but that's where the similarity ends. The blank white square in Figure 13-1 is the DataWindow control after it is first placed on a window.

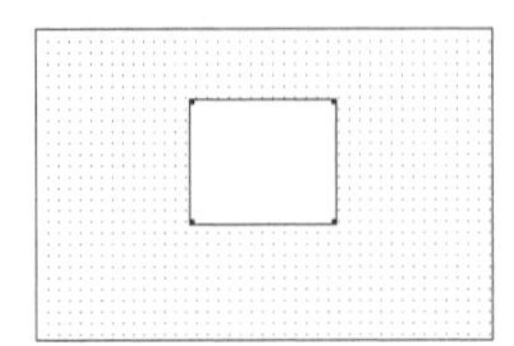

Figure 13-1: There is nothing more powerful than a DataWindow whose time has come.

There are many things about a DataWindow that are customizable and there isn't a particular order in which it must be done. We recommend, however, that you begin by attaching the DataWindow definition to the control.

You can place a DataWindow control on a window without having given it a definition. However, making sure the DataWindow control is the right size may be a little difficult without seeing how the definition will appear.

Once the DataWindow control has been placed on the window, double-click the control. The Select DataWindow dialog will appear (Figure 13-2.) From this dialog you can choose a definition that already exists or create a new one. By the way, you can use the same DataWindow definition in more than one control.

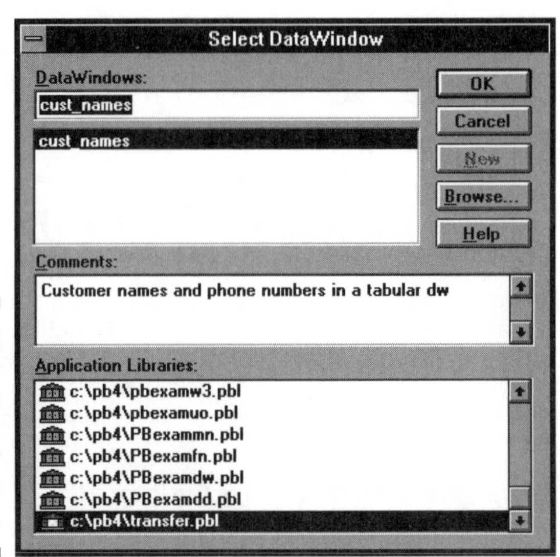

Figure 13-2: Select the DataWindow definition for your control from this list.

To use a DataWindow definition that already exists, select one from the list and click the OK button. If the DataWindow definition you want is not in the current PBL, you can change PBLs by selecting a new PBL from the list in the window at the bottom of this dialog, as shown in Figure 13-2.

This is a good time, once again, to point out the usefulness of adding comments to all of your controls. The list in Figure 13-2 was compiled from the PowerBuilder example application. You will notice that some of the names are cryptic. If comments had been added, it would be much easier to identify the correct definition. This is especially true if you are working with a group of programmers and someone else has to use the definition you've created. ■

To add a new definition, click the New button. Follow the instructions in Chapter 11 for building a new definition. Whether you are adding a new definition or selecting a definition that already exists, a definition must be attached to the control for it to be useful. It's sort of like a two-part epoxy. If you don't add part A to part B, before trying to glue something together, you end up with a useless, sticky mess.

Once you have either created or selected a definition, the DataWindow dialog appears. Notice in Figure 13-3 that the title of the dialog window shows which definition was selected.

Figure 13-3: Use the DataWindow dialog to customize some of the DataWindow control attributes.

What's in a name?

All controls are given a default name when they are placed on a window. This sounds like the beginning to Caesar's *Gallic Wars*, "All Gaul is divided into three parts." Anyway, it's important to note that this is another opportunity for making your application a little easier to work with. Leaving the default name as dw_1, or dw_2, or whatever it ends up being, is satisfactory but not exceptional.

Giving your DataWindow control a meaningful name will make referring to it in other parts of the application much more useful. This is why children get a name instead of a number. Imagine if your name was Smith_1 or Smith_2 or whatever else your birth order dictated. The only useful tidbit of information contained in names like these is the chronology of creation. Unless you are creating a pecking order, this is pretty unimportant. A name like dw_client_list or dw_insurance_entry gives you a little better understanding of what that control is all about.

As unimportant as naming the DataWindow seems to be in the grand scheme of things, it can help you create a better application. The more you can do to make the elements of your application clear and precise, the easier it will be for you and anyone else to create with it.

The Marquis DataWindow

A title for your DataWindow is optional. If you choose to title the DataWindow, the title will appear as a window title, or, as in this section heading, as a marquee.

Creating a title for your DataWindow depends on how you want the DataWindow to appear. A DataWindow can take on many appearances. It's sort of a "master of disguises." You can make a DataWindow look like a ListBox, a SingleLineEdit, a DropDownList, or an entire data-entry screen.

It is useful to give your DataWindow a title when an explanation of the information shown is necessary. This can be true especially when your DataWindow is a graph or a report.

To add a title, you must first click the Title Bar checkbox. With this selected, you can add a title in the Title: box (Figure 13-4). The title will appear automatically centered in a box at the top of the DataWindow control (Figure 13-5).

Figure 13-4 Add a title bar to your DataWindow control by checking Title Bar and typing in a title.

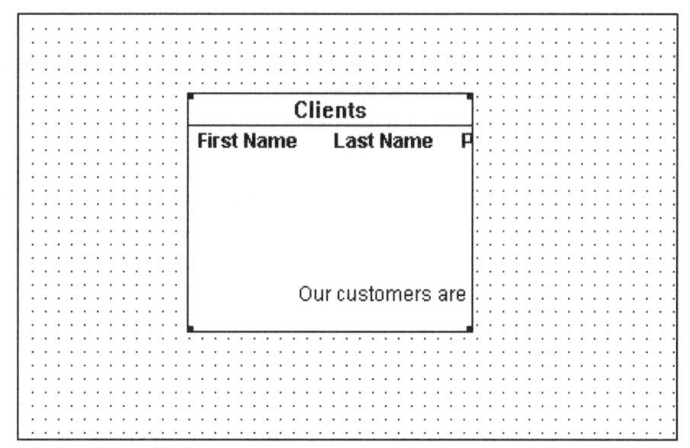

Figure 13-5: Your DataWindow title appears centered at the top of the DataWindow control.

The invisible man had a good side

The Visible checkbox is one of the first attributes that appears in the list of checkboxes used to customize your DataWindow. You may be wondering why, after all that trouble creating this beautiful control, you would want to make it invisible. Here are some reasons why:

- You're not very artistic and you don't want anyone to see the embarrassing mess you've created.
- You want your creation to make a grand entrance.
- The user of your application doesn't need to see the DataWindow all of the time.
- It is being used as a work space and never needs to be seen by the user of your application.

The last two choices are the more likely reasons for making a DataWindow control invisible. Use the visible attribute when you need to make a DataWindow appear and disappear in an application. The visible checkbox determines whether the DataWindow is initially visible or invisible. Then use PowerScript to change this attribute at a later time. To make a DataWindow called client_list visible in a CommandButton script, type the following:

```
client_list.visible = TRUE
```

Separate the DataWindow name from the attribute or method with a dot. The dot operator can be thought of as a possessive, like hers or his, or the attribute that belongs to this DataWindow.

You can see that this attribute is boolean. This means that it has a value of either TRUE or FALSE. Of course, a TRUE value means that the DataWindow is visible; FALSE, that it is there but invisible.

Invisible DataWindows can still be manipulated using PowerScript. In particularly complex windows, invisible DataWindows can be used as work areas. Information can be compiled in these work areas, formatted, stored temporarily, or stored with the idea of updating the database. We'd love to show you a picture of a DataWindow used in this manner, but none of our screen-capture utilities would allow us to capture an invisible DataWindow.

Setting up the control window

The DataWindow control has characteristics of a window as well as a control such as a CommandButton or a SingleLineEdit. You can customize a DataWindow so that it appears more like a window, or less like a window, and more like other controls.

One of a window's features is the ability to have a control menu in its upper-left corner. A control menu has menu choices that depend on the type of window and what capabilities you have given the window. Figure 13-6 shows you what the control menu for client_list DataWindow looks like.

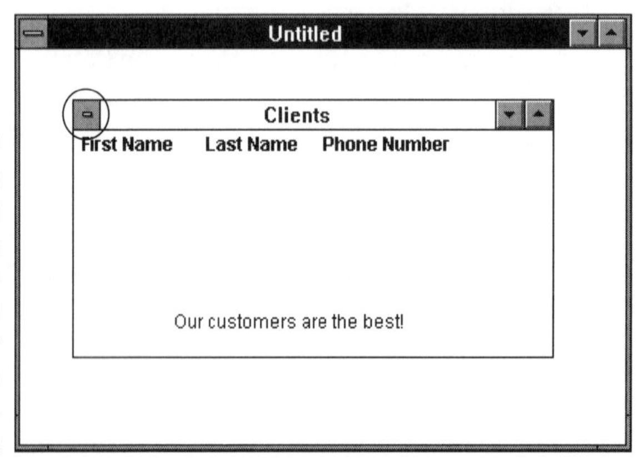

Figure 13-6: The control menu allows you to control the DataWindow like a window.

Figure 13-6 shows you that not all the menu choices are available. You can make these available by changing the DataWindow attributes. We will continue to cover these different abilities throughout the rest of this chapter. As you can see, the DataWindow control can have many of the characteristics of a separate popup window. The main difference is that the DataWindow control belongs to the window it is placed on in the same manner as a CommandButton or any other control.

The size and shape of things to come

The DataWindow control has other window features. It has:

- A maximize box
- A minimize box
- Resizeability
- A HScrollBar
- A VScrollBar

The Maximize and Minimize boxes are the up and down arrows in the right corner of a window that cause the window to maximize (fill the entire screen) or minimize (turn into an icon). With these grow and shrink capabilities comes the ability to restore, or return the window to its normal state. The normal state is neither maximized nor minimized; it's some other size.

You can add either or both the Maximize or Minimize boxes by clicking the Maximize or Minimize checkboxes.

A window is resizeable when it has the ability to expand or shrink both vertically and horizontally. This is done by grabbing the sides or corners of the window and dragging them to a new position.

Windows are resized by grabbing any border side or corner and dragging it with the mouse. Grabbing a side allows you to change one dimension while leaving the others alone. Grabbing a corner allows you to change the window both vertically and horizontally at the same time. The corner opposite from the one you are dragging remains fixed.

The border on a resizeable window appears "hollow" rather than solid and thick, like the border of a non-resizeable window (see Figure 13-7).

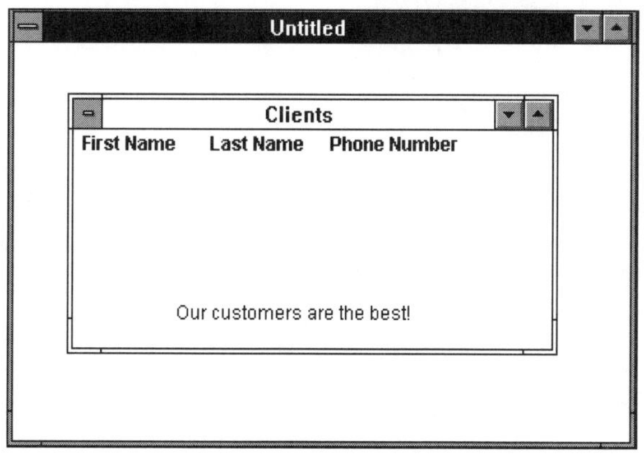

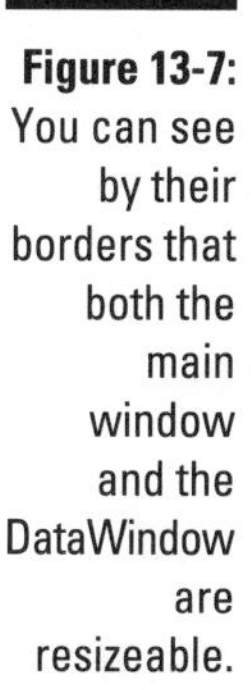

Figure 13-7: You can see by their borders that both the main window and the DataWindow are resizeable.

Scrolling through the park one day

Have you ever wanted to scroll left and right or up and down in a DataWindow? You can add horizontal and vertical scroll bars to your DataWindow. The horizontal scroll bar will appear with left and right arrows along the bottom of your DataWindow. The vertical scroll bar appears with up and down arrows on the right side of the DataWindow.

What goes up must come down

Use horizontal scroll bars by selecting the HScrollBar attribute and use vertical scroll bars by selecting the VScrollBar attribute.

Don't confuse horizontal and vertical scroll bars with HScrollBar and VScrollBar controls. The horizontal and vertical scroll bars used on your DataWindow control allow you to scroll to parts of the DataWindow that are not currently on the screen. For example, your DataWindow might have one hundred and forty-four rows. Perhaps only sixteen will fit on the screen at any one time; you can use the vertical scroll bar to scroll up and down between the rows.

To add scroll bars to the DataWindow, select either the HScrollBar, VScrollBar checkboxes, or both. The DataWindow will then look like Figure 13-8.

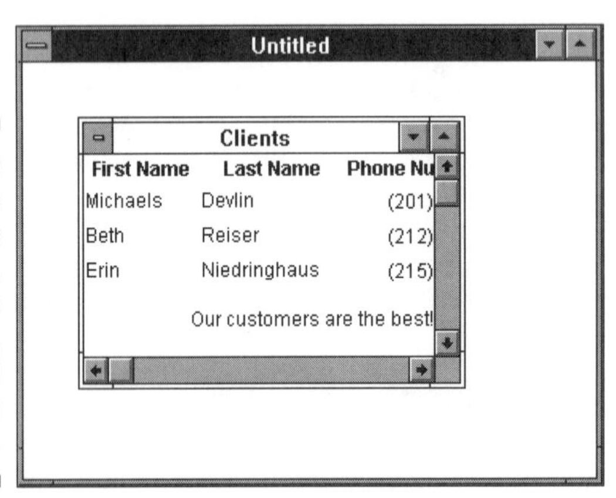

Figure 13-8: Scroll to the left, scroll to the right, scroll up and down, scroll through the night.

We're live and it's Saturday Night!

When the Live Scrolling attribute is set to TRUE, the rows in a DataWindow scroll by when the vertical scroll bar's scrollbox is moved. When live scrolling is FALSE, the rows in a DataWindow don't scroll as the scrollbox is moved. Instead, the DataWindow changes its display only when the user is done moving the scrollbox. DataWindows that have many columns or rows can sometimes take a long time to scroll. Turning off live scrolling lets the user move directly to rows or columns without watching (and waiting for) everything in between scroll by.

Creating a split view

You can separate your DataWindow into two separate views of the same information. When the view is split, using the H Split Scrolling attribute, two separate sets of horizontal scroll bars appear, one in each view. This allows you to look at one column of data while scrolling to another column that may not normally be visible at the same time.

Another use for horizontal split scrolling is to view one column next to another. This allows you to compare the values in columns that do not normally appear next to one another.

When the H Split Scrolling attribute is selected, a small black bar appears to the left of the horizontal scroll bar. Click and drag this bar within the DataWindow to create a second view. Figure 13-9 shows a DataWindow with a horizontal split view. Notice that the views are separated with a heavy dark line. Our example has only three columns. Therefore, we have two identical views of the same data.

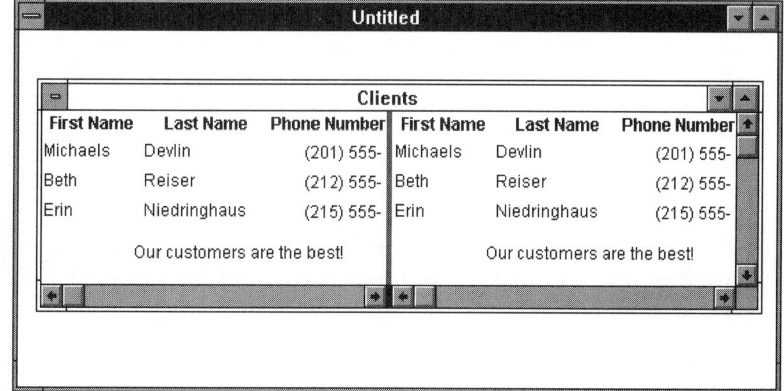

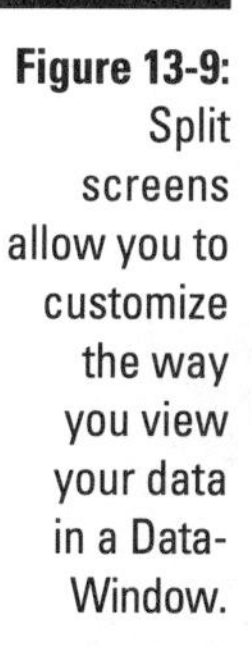

Figure 13-9: Split screens allow you to customize the way you view your data in a DataWindow.

Programming with DataWindow Controls

Programming with a DataWindow control is like fishing with a submarine. It gets the job done faster, it's high-tech, and you only use a small portion of its abilities at once. DataWindows have so many features and possible uses that you may never try them all. The following sections describe some of the more common DataWindow programming techniques.

Chasing rabbits in the clicked event

One of the most useful scripts you can add to a DataWindow control is a clicked-event script that figures out which row the user clicked on and highlights that row. Two DataWindow control functions make this possible:

- GetClickedRow( )
- SelectRow( )

You'll usually retrieve data from the database into the DataWindow control to give the user rows to click. Be sure to use the SetTransObject( ) and Retrieve( ) functions to fill in the DataWindow control. The last chapter showed you how to do this.

Put the following script in the clicked event of a DataWindow control to highlight the row that the user clicks:

```
SelectRow(0,FALSE)
SelectRow(GetClickedRow(),TRUE)
```

The first line of this event script deselects all of the rows in the DataWindow control. The next line selects the row that the user clicked. The GetClickedRow( ) function returns the number of the clicked row in the DataWindow control; the SelectRow( ) function selects the row returned by the GetClickedRow( ) function.

The second parameter passed to SelectRow( ), TRUE or FALSE, determines whether rows are selected (TRUE) or deselected (FALSE). The first parameter specifies the row to select or deselect. If a zero (0) is passed, then every row in the DataWindow is selected or deselected.

Use the following script in the clicked event to let the user select multiple rows in a DataWindow control. The IsSelected( ) function returns TRUE if the specified row is already selected. If the clicked row is already selected, this script deselects it. This creates a toggle effect, allowing the user to switch between selected and deselected simply by clicking on a row.

```
long lClickedRow

lClickedRow = GetClickedRow()
IF lClickedRow > 0 THEN
     IF IsSelected(lClickedRow) = TRUE THEN
          SelectRow(lClickedRow,FALSE)
```

```
      ELSE
           SelectRow(lClickedRow,TRUE)
      END IF
END IF
```

Two more functions let you find out what the user clicked on in the DataWindow control:

- GetClickedColumn()
- GetObjectAtPointer()

The GetClickedColumn() function returns the number of the column that the user clicked. For example, the following clicked event script displays a message box indicating the number of the clicked column:

```
MessageBox("Message","The clicked column is number " + &
            String(GetClickedColumn()))
```

The MessageBox() function displays a message window on the screen; the String() function converts the number returned by GetClickedColumn() to a string so that it can be added to the message. If no column is clicked, for example, the DataWindow header or footer is clicked instead of a column, then the GetClickedColumn() function returns 0.

GetObjectAtPointer() can be used to determine which object the user clicked. The return value of the GetObjectAtPointer() function is a bit strange; it's a string that contains the name of the object in the DataWindow that's under the mouse pointer, followed by a ~t, and then the row number. For example, a return value of text~t7 means that the object beneath the mouse pointer is named text and the row beneath the pointer is number 7. The following example shows how you can use this return value in the clicked event of a DataWindow control:

```
string sClickedObject, sObjectAtPointer
integer iPos

sObjectAtPointer = GetObjectAtPointer()

iPos = Pos(sObjectAtPointer,"~t")
iPos = iPos - 1
sClickedObject = Left(sObjectAtPointer,iPos)

IF sClickedObject = "text" THEN
     MessageBox("Hurray!","The text object was clicked!")
END IF
```

In this example, sObjectAtPointer is set to the return value of the GetObjectAtPointer() function. Next, the variable iPos is set to the position of the ~t within sObjectAtPointer. Then, so that iPos will contain the position of the last letter in the name of the object, 1 is subtracted. The Left( ) function is used to return just the name of the object from sObjectAtPointer without the ~t or the row number, and this return value is stored in the sClickedObject variable. Now sClickedObject contains the name of the object that was clicked in the DataWindow control. This value is compared to the string "text". When it matches, a message is displayed indicating that the text object was clicked.

Manipulating data in a DataWindow control

You probably don't like being manipulated, but since DataWindows do, do the following:

1. Click on the DataWindow Painter icon in the PowerBar.
2. Click on the New button to create a new DataWindow definition.
3. Choose External Data Source and Tabular presentation style, then click OK.
4. In the Result Set Description window, type BAND in the Name column and change the Length to 20.
5. Click on the Add button and type RATING in the Name column.
6. Select number from the Type drop-down list box.
7. Click on the OK button to accept the new DataWindow Result Set.
8. Save the new DataWindow definition as dw_bands.

Now create a new DataWindow control on a window of your choice. Double-click on the DataWindow control and choose dw_bands from the list, then click OK. When the window titled *DataWindow - dw_bands* appears, change the Name: field to dw_bands and click OK.

The next few sections use this dw_bands DataWindow control to demonstrate data manipulation in a DataWindow control. This DataWindow doesn't retrieve anything from the database, so rows need to be added to the DataWindow control before data can be manipulated.

Inserting and deleting rows

To add a new row to the end of the DataWindow control, use the InsertRow( ) function, like this:

```
dw_bands.InsertRow(0)
```

The 0 tells InsertRow( ) to add a new row to the end of the DataWindow. The InsertRow( ) function can also be used to insert a new row before an existing row by specifying the existing row number. For example, the following will insert a new row before row 8:

```
dw_bands.InsertRow(8)
```

The InsertRow( ) function returns the number of the row that it inserts. After inserting a row, you can use the SetItem( ) function to store values in each column. The syntax for the SetItem( ) function is:

```
dw_bands.SetItem(TheRow,TheColumn,TheValue)
```

TheRow and *TheColumn* identify the row and column in which to store *The-Value*. The data type of *TheValue* must match the data type of the column it's stored in or you'll get an error. After you insert a new row, it's a good idea to capture the return value of the InsertRow( ) function so that you'll know the number of the row that was just inserted. For example, the following stores the number of the new row in the variable lRow:

```
long lRow
lRow = dw_bands.InsertRow(0)
```

Add the following script to the constructor event of the DataWindow control to insert rows and data in the DataWindow when it first appears on the screen:

```
long lRow

lRow = InsertRow(0)
SetItem(lRow,1,"Pearl Jam")
SetItem(lRow,2,8)

lRow = InsertRow(0)
SetItem(lRow,1,"REM")
SetItem(lRow,2,9)

lRow = InsertRow(0)
SetItem(lRow,1,"Bad Religion")
SetItem(lRow,2,7)

lRow = InsertRow(0)
SetItem(lRow,1,"Pink Floyd")
SetItem(lRow,2,10)
```

This script simply inserts a new row and sets the column values in the new row four times.

This script is placed in the constructor event of the DataWindow control instead of in the open event of the window because it makes more sense for the DataWindow control to fill itself with data than it does for the window to do it. This is the essence of Responsibility Oriented Software Engineering — asking yourself which method makes the most sense; asking whether a window should populate a DataWindow control or whether the DataWindow control should populate itself. The other advantage is that because the DataWindow control functions are being called from an event script within the DataWindow instead of from an event script in the window, the functions don't need to be preceded with the DataWindow name, as in:

```
dw_bands. SetItem(lRow,1,"Pearl Jam")
```

Now the dw_bands DataWindow contains data that can be manipulated. To delete a row that contains a band that you don't like, use the DataWindow control function DeleteRow( ), like this:

```
dw_bands.DeleteRow(3)
```

This example deletes row 3 in the DataWindow dw_bands.

Reading, searching, sorting, and salivating

There are six functions for reading data from a DataWindow control:

- GetItemDate( )
- GetItemDateTime( )
- GetItemDecimal( )
- GetItemNumber( )
- GetItemString( )
- GetItemTime( )

As the names suggest, each of these six functions is designed to get a particular type of data out of a DataWindow control. When one of these GetItem functions is used, it returns the value from the specified row and column. For example, the following will return the string located in row 2 column 1:

```
dw_bands.GetItemString(2,1)
```

Sometimes you'll only be interested in reading data out of a row that has been selected by the user. To find a selected row, use GetSelectedRow( ). The GetSelectedRow( ) function accepts a single parameter — the row after which to begin searching for a selected row. To begin searching for a selected row at the beginning, pass a zero (0) to the function, like this:

```
GetSelectedRow(0)
```

The GetSelectedRow( ) function returns the number of the first selected row after the row specified. ■

To search through the contents of a DataWindow, use the Find( ) function. Find( )accepts three parameters:

- An expression that tells Find( ) what to search for
- The number of the row at which to begin the search
- The number of the row at which to end the search

For example, the following will search for the string 'Pink Floyd' in the band column:

```
Find("band = 'Pink Floyd' ", 1, RowCount())
```

The expression "band = 'Pink Floyd' " tells Find( ) what to search for; the number 1 says begin searching in the first row; the function RowCount( ) returns the number of rows in the DataWindow control, which causes Find( ) to search every row in the DataWindow control. Find( ) returns the row of the first match that it locates for the given expression. If no matches are found, Find( ) returns zero (0).

To sort the data in a DataWindow control, first set the sort criteria using SetSort( ) like this:

```
dw_bands.SetSort("rating A")
```

Sort criteria can also be specified in the DataWindow definition. This example sets the sort criteria in dw_bands to ascending order, and sorts using the rating column as the sort key. To sort by multiple columns, separate the sort criteria for each column with a comma:

```
dw_bands.SetSort("rating A, bands A")
```

To specify a sort column with the column's number instead of its name, use the following:

```
dw_bands.SetSort("#2 A")
```

And to sort in descending order instead of ascending, replace the A with a D. Use the Sort( ) function to perform the actual sorting. For example, the following sorts the dw_bands DataWindow:

```
dw_bands.Sort()
```

A DataWindow control can be reset, which clears all of the rows and columns out of the control using the Reset( ) function. For example, the following resets the dw_bands DataWindow control:

```
dw_bands.Reset()
```

Printing the contents of a DataWindow control

To print a DataWindow, use the Print function:

```
dw_bands.Print()
```

By default, a dialog box appears, allowing the user to cancel printing by clicking on a Cancel button. If you don't want this dialog box to appear, pass FALSE to the Print function, like this:

```
dw_bands.Print(FALSE)
```

Summary

This chapter has shown how you can format a DataWindow to look like a control or a window, depending on how you intend to use it. You have also seen that PowerScript can make your DataWindow control come alive. The next four chapters are dedicated to DataWindows. The better you understand these tools, the more powerful your program will be and the simpler it will be to create. Remember, work hard to work smart!

Chapter 14

Determining the Source of Your Data

In This Chapter

- Grasping DataSources
- Choosing just the right DataSource
- Specifying retrieval arguments

Everything comes from somewhere. This simple law of thermodynamics is true even in PowerBuilder. In the last two chapters you have been learning about DataWindows. You have learned to create DataWindow definitions and how to use those definitions in a DataWindow control. The primary purpose of a DataWindow is to handle data. Where this data comes from is the subject of this chapter.

May the Source Be with You

Information in a computer application can come from many different places. You might think that in a database application all the data must come from the database. Not so; it can have several sources:

- The application's user
- Program calculations
- External sources, such as ASCII files
- Database tables
- Microprocessors that didn't pass third-grade math

It's important to know where all your data comes from in order to create a strategy for handling it. Don't get stuck on the idea that all data comes from and goes to the database. In that case, your application becomes nothing more than a data funnel, to and from the database.

Also, take into account all the different ways information is processed.

- Users process information, making decisions, doing calculations, and providing many needed information variables not contained in the program code.
- Programs process information. They perform calculations, query users for additional information, query the database to provide information, and used stored procedures and algorithms to derive new information.
- Databases process information. Databases store information; database indexes sort information; and stored procedures can process information.

It's a good idea to analyze the overall data requirements of your application. With a clear understanding of your program's data needs, you can be more versatile in your programming. Part of DataWindows' versatility is that they have many different possible data sources. Choosing one is known as choosing the DataWindow's *DataSource*.

If the Source Fits, Wear It

Defining a DataSource for a DataWindow does two things. First, it determines the structure of the DataWindow columns; second, it determines one possible way to receive data. There are two basic places from which a DataWindow can receive data:

1. The database
2. An external source

Most of the DataSources you can define for a DataWindow use an SQL Select statement to retrieve data from the database. The only DataSource that does not involve the database is an external one.

When defining a DataSource using an SQL Select statement, the columns of the DataWindow are automatically defined to match the columns defined in the Select statement. When you choose an external DataSource, you are required to define the columns manually.

Table 14-1: DataSources

DataSource	*Description*
Quick Select	Simple-to-use SQL generator. Select related tables, columns, and set criteria.
SQL Select	Graphic SQL generator. Select tables, set SQL criteria. This requires some knowledge of how SQL works.
Query	Developed the same way as the SQL Select, but saved in a separate file as a query.
External	Define the columns manually with no database interface.
Stored Procedure	Use a database stored procedure as a DataSource (where databases can use stored procedures).

Using Quick Select

The Quick Select DataSource helps people with little or no SQL experience build database queries that will be used as the source of data for their DataWindows.

To use the Quick Select DataSource:

1. Start the DataWindow Painter by clicking on the DataWindow Painter icon from the PowerBar.
2. From the Select DataWindow dialog, click the New button. This will bring up the New DataWindow dialog.
3. In the Data Source group of icons at the top of the New DataWindow dialog, click the Quick Select icon. See Figure 14-1.
4. Select a Presentation Style from the icons in the lower portion of this dialog. Then click the OK button.
5. Select a table from the Tables: list by clicking on one with your mouse. It will become highlighted. If the table has others related to it, an arrow will appear indicating whether this table is a parent or child table. If they exist, other related tables will appear in the list. You may continue selecting tables until all related tables have been selected (Figure 14-2).
6. Select columns from the Columns: list. These are the columns from the selected tables, not Corinthian or Doric columns. Notice that selected columns appear in the box at the bottom (Figure 14-3).
7. As shown in Figure 14-3, fill in the criteria box with any selection criteria required to return your desired result set.

8. Fill in sort criteria by clicking the sort box and selecting sort criteria from the list that appears.

9. Fill in any relational operators and data values in the Criteria: field. You don't need to enter an equal sign if the values are meant to match. See Figure 14-4.

10. When you have finished adding criteria, click the OK button. This will take you into the DataWindow Painter with the correct columns selected (Figure 14-5).

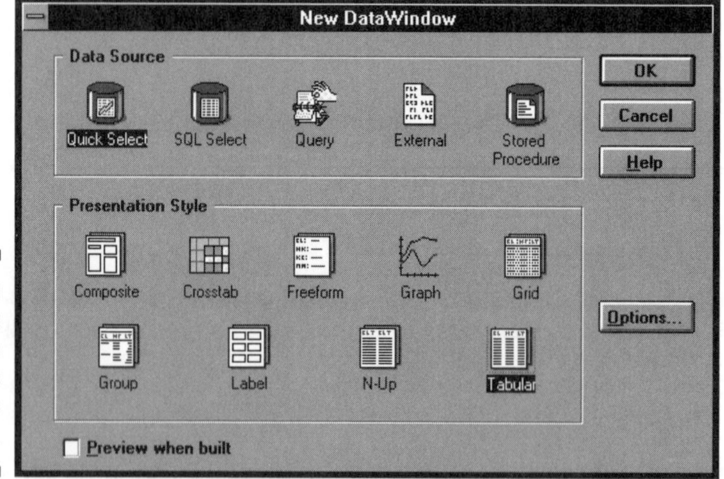

Figure 14-1: Select the DataSource from this group of icons.

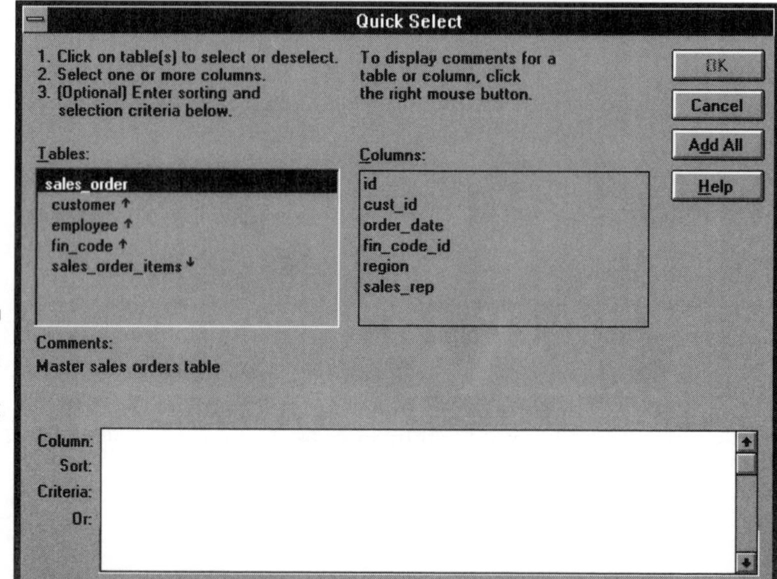

Figure 14-2: Select the tables that contain the columns you want in your DataWindow.

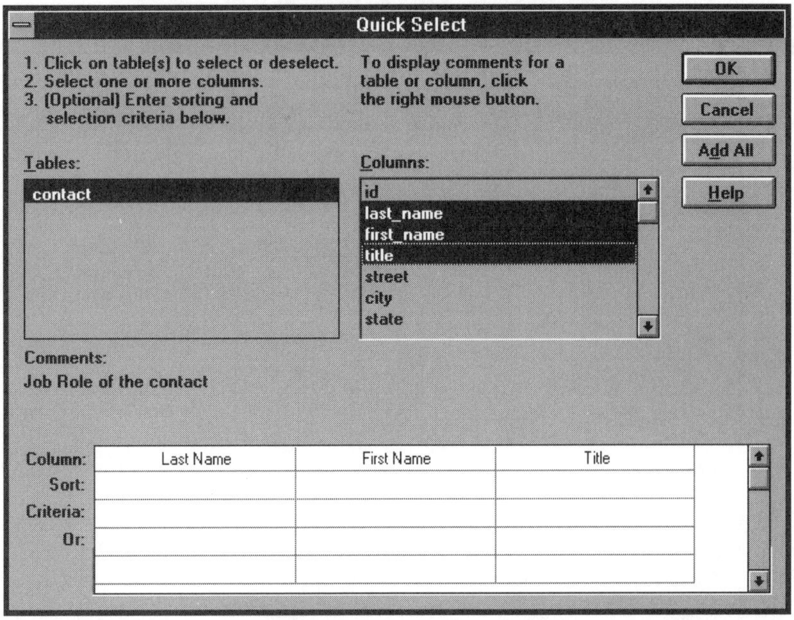

Quick Select

1. Click on table(s) to select or deselect.
2. Select one or more columns.
3. (Optional) Enter sorting and selection criteria below.

To display comments for a table or column, click the right mouse button.

OK | Cancel | Add All | Help

Tables: contact

Columns: id, last_name, first_name, title, street, city, state

Comments:
Job Role of the contact

Column:	Last Name	First Name	Title
Sort:			
Criteria:			
Or:			

Figure 14-3: Selected columns appear in the criteria box at the bottom of the Quick Select dialog.

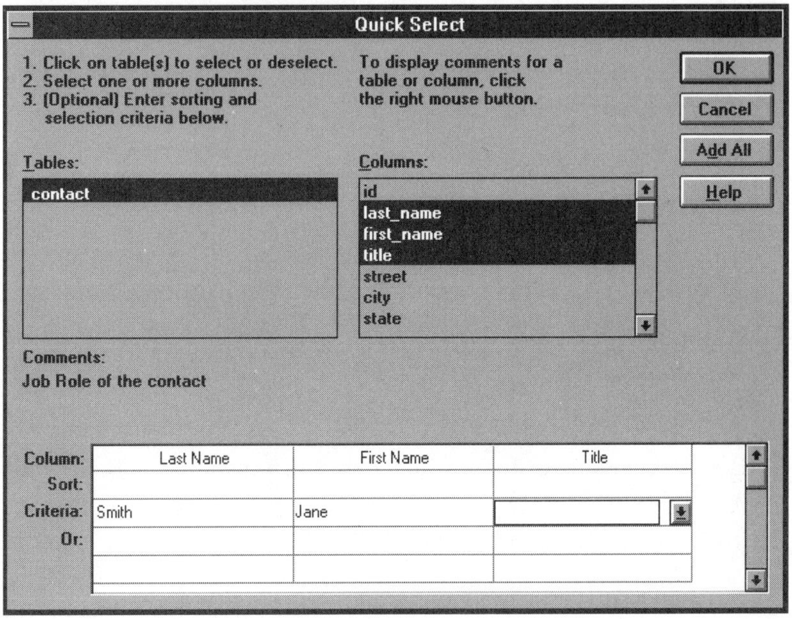

Quick Select

1. Click on table(s) to select or deselect.
2. Select one or more columns.
3. (Optional) Enter sorting and selection criteria below.

To display comments for a table or column, click the right mouse button.

OK | Cancel | Add All | Help

Tables: contact

Columns: id, last_name, first_name, title, street, city, state

Comments:
Job Role of the contact

Column:	Last Name	First Name	Title
Sort:			
Criteria:	Smith	Jane	
Or:			

Figure 14-4: Fill in criteria beneath the column titles.

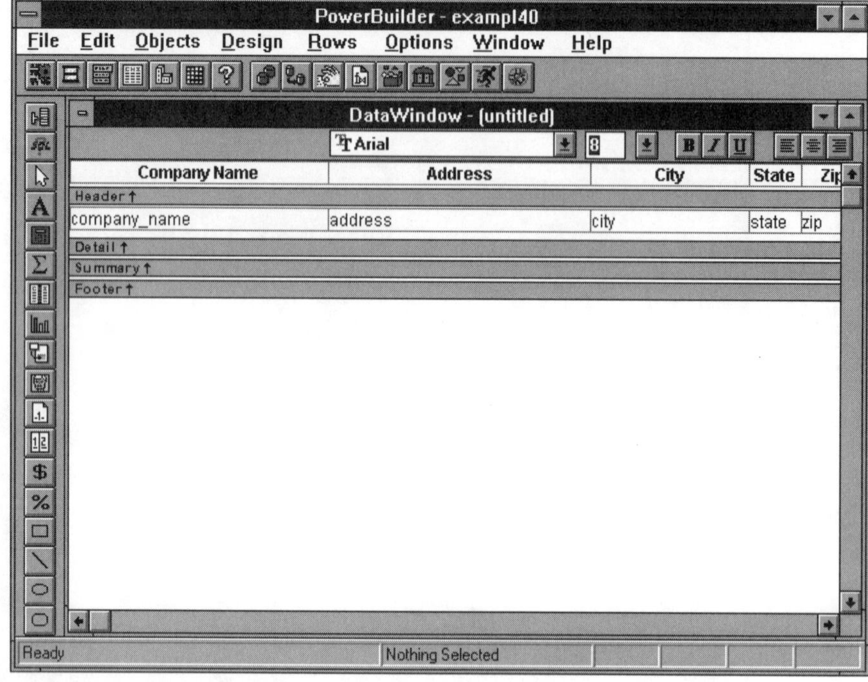

Figure 14-5: The DataWindow Painter displays the selected columns.

The Quick Select DataSource builds SQL syntax in the same manner as the SQL Select DataSource.

Using SQL Select

The SQL Select DataSource is created by using the SQL Painter. This is described in detail in Chapter 3. To review, the process involves:

- Selecting a table or tables that contain the columns you want to use in your DataWindow
- Selecting columns that contain the data you want in your DataWindow
- Defining the order in which data will appear in the DataWindow by setting Sort criteria
- Limiting the number of rows that will be retrieved into the result set by setting the Where clause
- Creating groups with the Group clause and limiting the information in the group with the Having clause
- Creating and adding computed fields

Figure 14-6 shows how SQL syntax is created with the SQL Select DataSource.

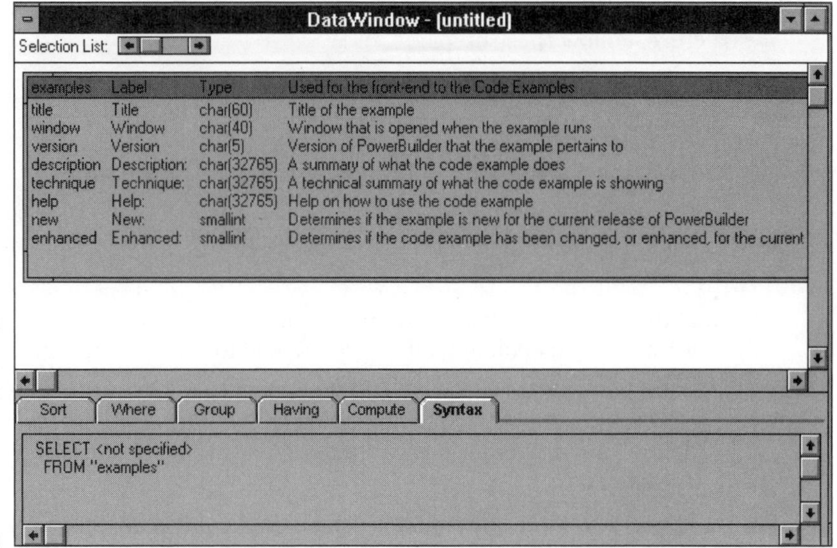

Figure 14-6: Construct DataWindows using the SQL Painter.

The predefined query

In Chapter 5 you learned how to create a query and save it to a query file. Now is an opportunity to use that query. Queries can be used as DataSources. Because it is essentially no more than a saved SQL Select statement, a query will define the columns and selection criteria as if you had used the SQL Select DataSource.

An advantage to using a query rather than the SQL Select as a DataSource is that you can create the query, and optimize it as a separate process from creating the DataWindow definition. Also, this same optimized query can be used in multiple places.

Going out for some data

DataWindows don't have to receive their data from or have their columns defined by the database. You can create the column definitions manually by using the External DataSource. Then, to add data to the DataWindow you can:

- Use PowerScript functions to add data
- Import data from strings or files
- Add data manually using PowerScript to add new rows

Creating an External DataSource is fairly simple. It is a little like creating a structure. Follow these steps:

1. Start the DataWindow Painter by clicking the DataWindow Painter icon on the PowerBar.
2. From the Select DataWindow dialog click the New button.
3. In the Data Sources group of icons, select the External DataSource and click the OK button. This brings up the Result Set Description dialog, shown in Figure 14-7.
4. In the Name field, type a column name. You can use the same guidelines for creating a column name as you would for creating a column in a table.
5. Define a Type for your column. You can either accept the default type or click on the drop-down list box to select a different type. Make sure you define your column types carefully. This is not a situation where opposites attract.
6. Just as in a table, you must set the column width in some types that require it.
7. To continue adding columns you must use the Add button. (Clicking this button with your mouse will not give you Attention Deficit Disorder. However, if you've already forgotten why you pushed the Add button you might need help with ADD.)
8. When you are finished adding columns, click the OK button.

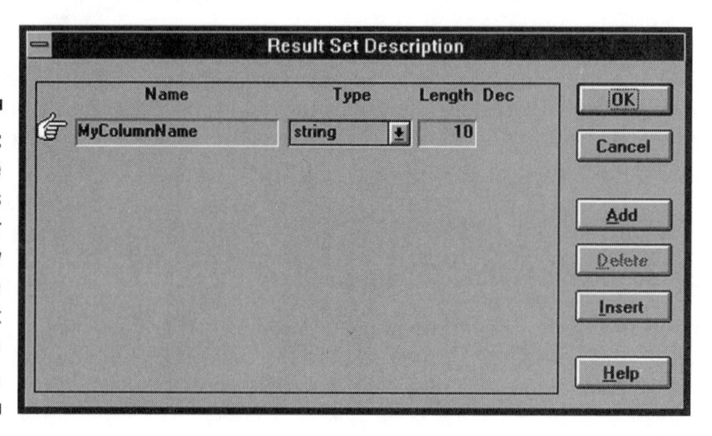

Figure 14-7: Define columns for your DataWindow using the Result Set Description dialog.

The External DataSource is an extremely useful tool for building DataWindows that may have nothing to do with the database. There are so many different uses for DataWindows that you may find yourself using this DataSource quite often.

Using the Stored Procedure

Not all databases support Stored Procedures. If your database supports these, you can use them as a DataSource. To use them:

1. Start the DataWindow Painter by clicking the DataWindow Painter icon on the PowerBar.
2. From the Select DataWindow icon click the New button.
3. In the Data Sources group of icons, select the Stored Procedure DataSource and click the OK button.
4. Choose a Stored Procedure from the Select Stored Procedure dialog, as shown in Figure 14-8, and then click OK.

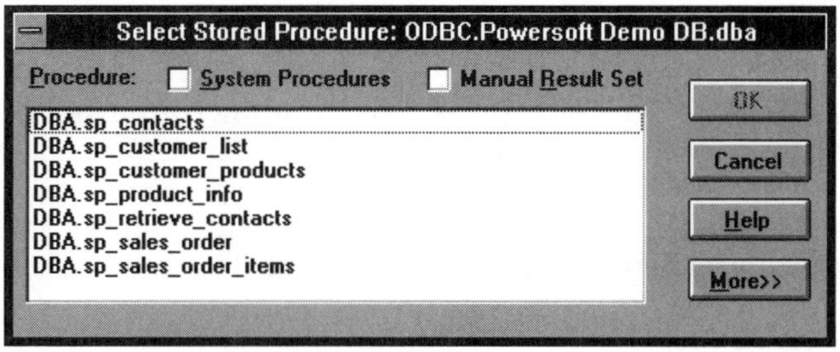

Select Stored Procedure: ODBC.Powersoft Demo DB.dba
Procedure: System Procedures Manual Result Set
DBA.sp_contacts
DBA.sp_customer_list
DBA.sp_customer_products
DBA.sp_product_info
DBA.sp_retrieve_contacts
DBA.sp_sales_order
DBA.sp_sales_order_items
OK
Cancel
Help
More>>

Figure 14-8: Pick a Stored Procedure, any Stored Procedure.

Checking the Manual Result Set checkbox allows you to build a DataWindow Data Source structure similar to an External DataSource. Leaving this checkbox unchecked tells PowerBuilder to determine the DataSource structure automatically by using the result of the Stored Procedure.

Who's Gonna Get It? Not Me. Yes, You Are. No, I'm Not!

Retrieval arguments allow you to pass parameters to the SQL Select statement. This allows you to narrow your selection criteria at run time.

These arguments can be used only when retrieving data from the database, otherwise there's no one to argue with. To set up these retrieval arguments, you must have selected the SQL Select DataSource. The Quick Select is more like the express checkout at the supermarket. You know, no checks, no ATM, no retrieval arguments.

You can also define retrieval arguments when creating queries. You can't modify the query in the DataWindow Painter to add retrieval arguments — you have to exit and start the Query Painter to add retrieval arguments to a query. ■

Once you have selected the SQL Select DataSource, the SQL Painter will appear on the screen. In the SQL Painter do the following:

1. Select Retrieval Arguments... from the Objects menu. This will bring up the Specify Retrieval Arguments dialog.
2. Create a name for your retrieval argument. This can be a unique name. It doesn't have to match any other program variables. When you pass a value as a retrieval argument, this is what it will be called.
3. Set the data type of the argument you are going to pass by choosing one from the drop-down list box.
4. Modify the Where clause of the SQL statement to use the retrieval argument. To do this, click on the Where tab at the bottom of the screen. Then fill in the Column field by clicking on a blank row beneath the Column heading and typing the name of a column. You can also choose a column from the drop-down list. Next, select an Operator such as equal (=). Finally, enter a colon (:) in the Value field followed by the name of your retrieval argument.

Now your SQL Select DataSource includes a retrieval argument and a Where clause that uses the retrieval argument. To add additional retrieval arguments, first define them by choosing Retrieval Arguments... from the Objects menu then add them to the Where clause. You can add as many arguments as needed. Remember that at run time you will have to supply these values to the Retrieve( ) DataWindow function.

Summary

Choosing DataSources is just one of the components in building DataWindows. We will continue our adventure into DataWindows in the next chapter when we cover Presentation Styles.

Chapter 15

DataWindow Presentation Styles

In This Chapter

- Adding style to your DataWindows
- Graphing in a DataWindow
- Creating mailing labels

The Smell of Grease Paint, the Roar of the Crowd

An actor can portray many characters without changing who he really is as a person. Makeup, special effects, accents, costumes, and elevator shoes can all contribute meaning to the audience. DataWindows have a similar ability to appear in many different disguises, or *presentation styles*.

Information can be interpreted differently depending on how it is displayed. A DataWindow full of numbers may have more impact as a graph. Another presentation style may add pizzazz to a sales report or highlight critical information in a result set.

Give your presentation with style

PowerBuilder allows you to present data in a DataWindow using a number of different presentation styles. The presentation style is independent of the DataSource you have chosen.

Choosing a presentation style is like choosing the right clothes to wear in the morning. They should be functional, practical, stylish but not pretentious, comfortable, and meet the expectations of those who have to look at you. If you choose a graph when someone expects a list, confusion is often the result. Good design requires a careful choice of display mediums. You wouldn't paint a mural on a building with watercolors (unless you're a graffiti artist). It's important to choose the right medium for your message.

The rest of this chapter will discuss each presentation style. Some of them, such as graphing, are covered in more detail in other parts of this book. This chapter is more about using presentation styles as an overall application-design strategy than it is a step-by-step attempt to tell you how to use each feature.

To get started, each of the examples in this chapter use the Quick Select DataSource and the fin_data table.

Here are the steps to get those loaded:

1. Begin by starting the DataWindow Painter — click the DataWindow Painter icon in the PowerBar.
2. Select the Quick Select DataSource.
3. Choose the presentation style appropriate to each example and click the OK button.
4. Select the fin_data table from the list of tables.
5. From the list of columns, select all the columns.

This should get you started. Refer back to these instructions before each example if necessary.

Totally Tabular

Perhaps the most widely used presentation style for DataWindows is the *Tabular* format. This is the typical row and column seen so often in the world of data. It looks like a spreadsheet, it can act like a spreadsheet, and, like a spreadsheet, will capture the attention of almost no one. Tabular formats are certainly one of the most useful and functional of all the formats. Just realize that using this format carries the side-effect of boredom. It is up to you to add features and style to jazz it up.

You can use the Tabular presentation style to:

- Display information in a row and column format.
- Edit or add information directly in the DataWindow *fields*.
- Find and select information as though the DataWindow were a multi-column list box.

Here are some basic terms used in referring to the parts of a Tabular presentation style. Field, in a DataWindow, refers to the box, or cell, located at the intersection of each row and column. Columns in a Tabular format represent either the columns in a table or user-defined columns from the External Data-Source. Rows represent individual rows in a database table or user-entered rows of information.

The Tabular-style DataWindow is discussed in detail in different places throughout this book:

- Building a Tabular-style DataWindow definition from the ground up — Chapter 12.
- Retrieving data into a Tabular-style DataWindow — Chapter 12.
- Modifying the DataWindow control when using a Tabular presentation style — Chapter 13.
- Using the Tabular-style DataWindow as a multi-column list box — the end of Chapter 13.
- Using the Tabular presentation style for data entry — Chapter 17.

Because this presentation style is covered in so much detail in other chapters, we direct you there for detailed information on creating, using, and customizing this DataWindow style.

Crosstab is not a kind of cat

The *Crosstab* DataWindow presentation style is used when you need to cross-tabulate information from your table. That is, the table is tabulated, or summed, based on the values in two different columns. This makes the Crosstab presentation style perfect for summarizing financial data.

In our financial data example we use the Crosstab presentation style to show the tabulated amounts for the quarters of each year. One of the fields in the fin_data table is the year, another is the quarter, and a third column in the table has an amount.

In our Crosstab DataWindow, the year acts as the column heading, the quarter acts as the row heading, and the tabulated amount appears at the intersection of the row and column.

The Crosstab presentation style cannot be used for data entry. The Crosstab is used only as a summary report. The Crosstab presentation style automatically creates a computed field that represents the tabulation of values, and computed fields can't be edited. ■

If you have been following along, you have already done these steps; if not, do this:

1. Start the DataWindow Painter and click on the New button to create a new DataWindow.
2. Select Quick Select from the DataSource, Crosstab from the Presentation Styles, and click OK.
3. Click on the fin_data table and select all its columns, then click OK.

Your screen should now look like the dialog in Figure 15-1.

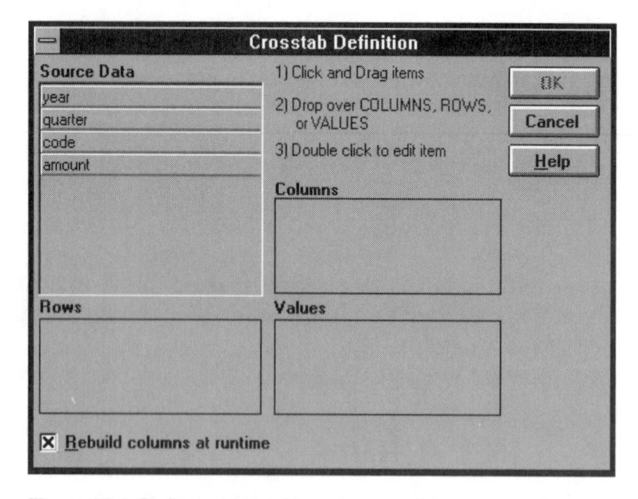

Figure 15-1: Define which table columns will represent the DataWindow columns, rows, and data values in the Crosstab Definition dialog.

To set up the Crosstab definition do the following:

1. With your mouse, click and drag the year column from the Source Data list to the box labeled Columns.
2. Click and drag the quarter column from the Source Data list to the box labeled Rows.
3. Click and drag the amount column from the Source Data list to the box labeled Values. Notice that this column changes when it appears in the Values box. The formula sum (amount for crosstab) appears.
4. Click the OK button.

When you have finished creating the Crosstab definition, the Design section of the DataWindow Painter will be displayed. See Figure 15-2.

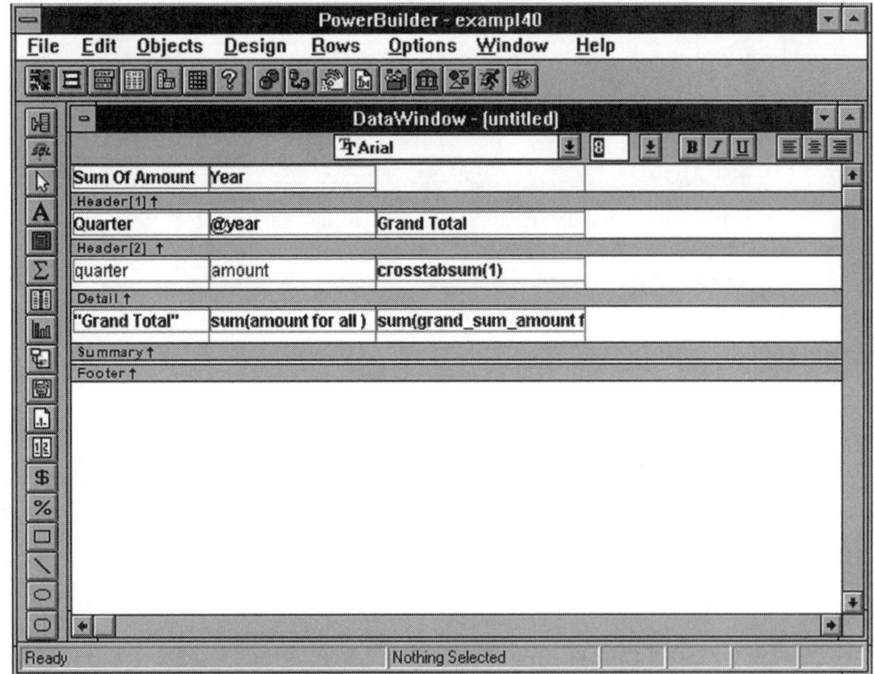

Figure 15-2: The Crosstab presentation style is so intelligent that it has two headers instead of one.

If you want to view or modify the computation used in the computed fields, double-click on the fields and a Computed Field Definition dialog box appears. ■

In the design section of the DataWindow Painter you can change any of the default headings created in the Crosstab presentation. You can change colors, titles, and fonts. Unless the computations are wrong, it's probably not a good idea to change the expressions in the computed fields.

The Crosstab design can appear a bit confusing. We recommend that you try previewing how the DataWindow will look by selecting Preview... from the Design menu. It should resemble Figure 15-3.

You can refer back and forth between Figures 15-2 and 15-3 to see how each of the headers and computed fields are used to create the Crosstab presentation style.

Sum Of Amount	Year			
Quarter	1992	1993	1994	Grand Total
Q1	4202	8954	18501	**31657**
Q2	6263	10934	21133	**38330**
Q3	7789	15166	24589	**47544**
Q4	8390	15963	28300	**52653**
Grand Total	**26644**	**51017**	**92523**	**170184**

Figure 15-3: The Crosstab presentation style summarizes table information but does not change it.

Freeform is another word for art

There are many ways to display and edit information. Two of them stand out among the rest. The Tabular style, where information is displayed in row and column format, and the *Freeform* style. The Freeform presentation style allows you to arrange DataWindow columns and labels in just about any format you want.

To create a DataWindow with the Freeform presentation style:

1. Start the DataWindow Painter, select the DataSource and Freeform presentation style as described in the beginning of this chapter.
2. When you have finished selecting columns in the Quick Select DataSource, the DataWindow Painter should look like Figure 15-4.

The DataWindow Painter senses your desire to be stylish. The data fields appear with shadow box borders (Figure 15-4). You are certainly welcome to change this by clicking on the field with the right mouse button and selecting Border from the popup menu.

Here are a few things you can do to customize the way your DataWindow looks and behaves:

- Change the border styles of the labels and fields.
- Change the foreground and background colors of the DataWindow, labels, and fields.
- Move the labels and fields to new positions on the window.
- Change the tab order of the fields to change data-entry order or make certain fields view-only.

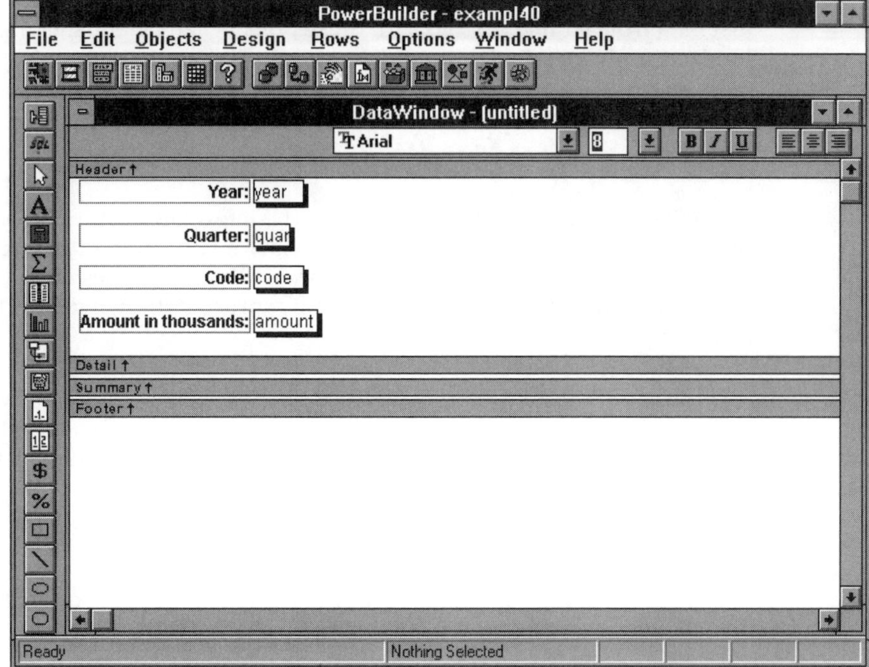

Figure 15-4: Use the Freeform presentation style to create flexible DataWindow layouts.

Chapter 12 has gone into considerable detail on changing the appearance of your DataWindow. You can also change the way your DataWindow behaves. Setting the *tab order* changes the behavior of your DataWindow. The tab order is the order in which fields and controls are accessed when the Tab key on your keyboard is pressed. Change the tab order by selecting Tab Order from the Design menu in the DataWindow Painter. Modify the red numbers that appear next to each item. The order of the numbers determines the order in which it is accessed by the Tab key. The user can't edit an item that is not in the tab order. So, changing the number to 0 (zero) removes it from the tab order and makes it read-only.

Be creative when using the Freeform presentation style. Select objects from the Objects menu to enhance your DataWindow, including:

- Drawing objects, such as rectangles, ovals, and lines
- Graphs, pictures, and OLE objects
- New columns, computed columns, and nested reports (for adding more data)
- Text objects (for adding additional text or creating new labels)
- Special fields that display today's date or automatically calculate the page numbers and displays them

As you can see, there are many things to add to your DataWindow other than just data from a table. Each one of these objects can be enhanced, customized, and beautified, but not folded, spindled, or mutilated.

The Graph shows all

DataWindows can graphically represent the information stored in your tables by using the Graph presentation style. This is a fancy way of saying that you can use your data to create pretty pictures. Chapter 16 goes into considerable detail, describing how this graphical representation of data is useful and how each style is configured.

To use the Graph presentation style do the following:

1. Start the DataWindow Painter, select the DataSource and the Graph presentation style, as described in the beginning of this chapter.
2. After selecting the columns in the Quick Select DataSource, the Graph Data dialog box appears.
3. Select quarter from the drop-down list box in the Category field. The item in the category field determines what is displayed along the category axis of the graph.
4. Choose sum (amount for graph) from the drop-down list box in the Value field. This will set the values that display along the value axis of the graph.
5. Click on the Series checkbox to activate the series feature. The sample graph now shows three bars for each category instead of just one. This illustrates the difference between a graph that uses a single series and one that uses multiple series. With one series, this graph would show one value for each quarter. By adding series, you can make the graph display separate bars for each quarter of different years. To do this, choose year from the drop-down list in the Series field.

Your Graph Data dialog box should now look like Figure 15-5. To see the graph that this configuration produces, click on the OK button then choose Preview... from the Design menu.

Grid your teeth

The Grid presentation style presents information in a row-and-column format in a fashion similar to the Tabular presentation style. Some of the basic features of the Grid presentation style are:

- You can reorder your columns at run time.
- You can vertically resize your columns at run time.
- Data displays in a grid.
- You can't add titles or special header information as you can in a Tabular presentation style.
- Data entered into a field is truncated to fit the width of the field.

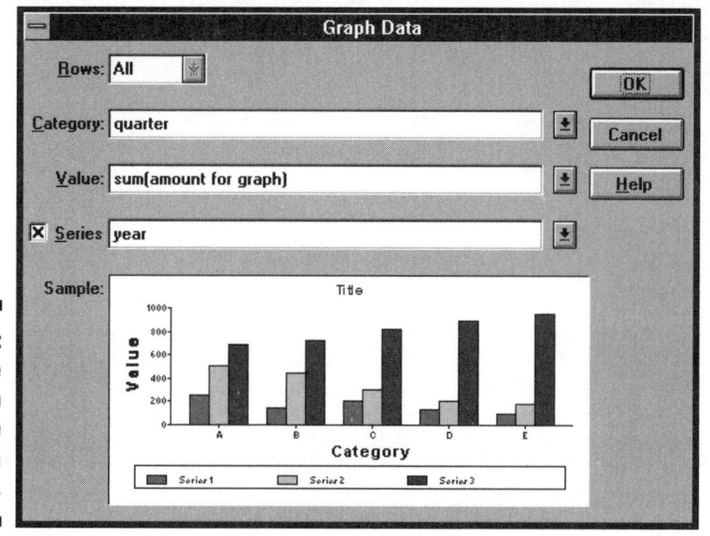

Figure 15-5: Configure your graph in the Graph Data dialog box.

To create a DataWindow with the Grid presentation style, follow these steps:

1. Start the DataWindow Painter, select the DataSource and the Grid presentation style, then click the OK button.
2. Select the columns in the Quick Select DataSource and click the OK button. The columns will appear in the DataWindow Painter's Designer window (Figure 15-6).
3. Click with the right mouse button on either the header or detail information to customize the appearance of the grid display.

You can preview your DataWindow by clicking the Preview icon in the PainterBar. While you are previewing the DataWindow, you can try some of the features of a Grid presentation style. Clicking on the column header will highlight all the rows in that column (see Figure 15-7). With all the rows highlighted, you can then drag a column either left or right to a new position. The user can do the same thing at run time. Be aware that changes made in the column order during preview are reflected back in design mode.

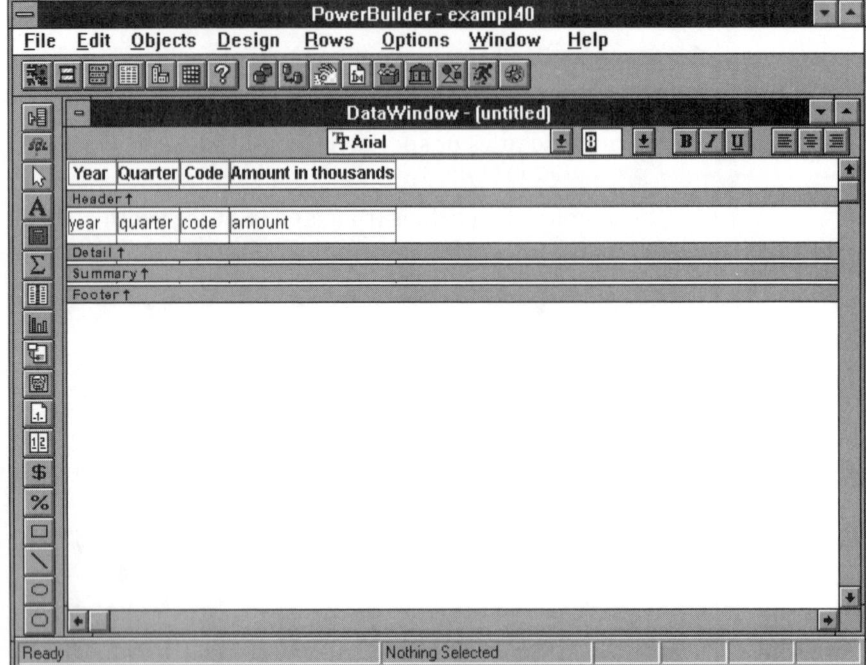

Figure 15-6: The Grid presentation style is similar to the Tabular presentation style, but with some major differences.

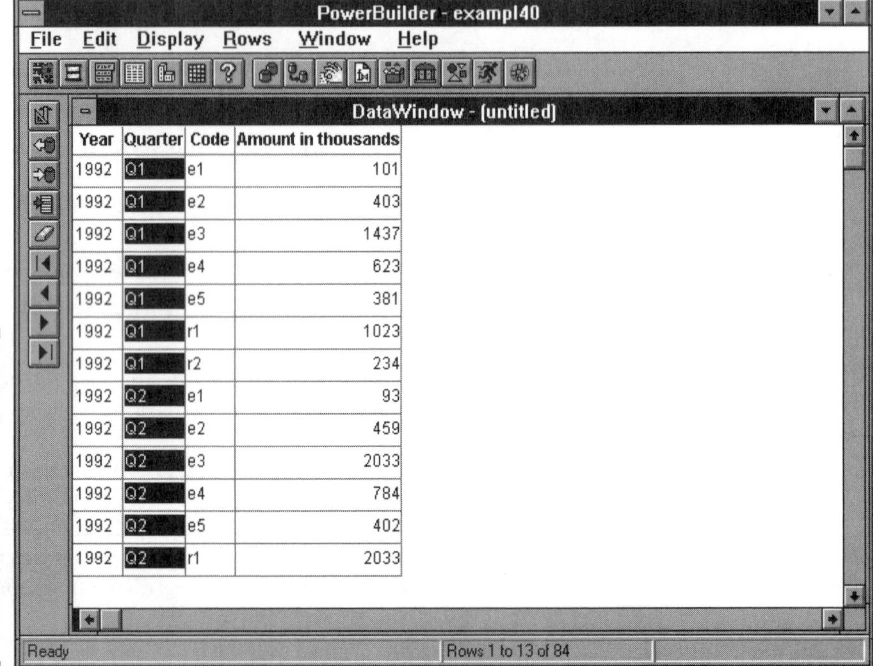

Year	Quarter	Code	Amount in thousands
1992	Q1	e1	101
1992	Q1	e2	403
1992	Q1	e3	1437
1992	Q1	e4	623
1992	Q1	e5	381
1992	Q1	r1	1023
1992	Q1	r2	234
1992	Q2	e1	93
1992	Q2	e2	459
1992	Q2	e3	2033
1992	Q2	e4	784
1992	Q2	e5	402
1992	Q2	r1	2033

Figure 15-7: One of the highlights of the Grid presentation style is its unique user interface abilities.

You can resize the column width. Dragging the vertical column bar to a new position resizes the column. The rows must not be highlighted when you do this or PowerBuilder will think you are trying to move the column, not resize it.

Group DataWindows are fun

Group DataWindows are fun because they are so simple. The Group presentation style is designed to display groups of data. To create the Group presentation style, follow these steps:

1. Start the DataWindow Painter and select the Quick Select DataSource.
2. Select the Group presentation style and click the OK button.
3. When the Specify Page Header dialog appears on the screen (Figure 15-8), enter a meaningful page header or accept the default, Fin Data Report.
4. The Specify Group dialog appears on the screen after you specify the page header (see Figure 15-9). Click and drag the quarter column from the Source Data box to the Columns box on the right. The DataWindow will now be set up to display data grouped by quarter.
5. You can optionally set the DataWindow to start a new page every time a new group is formed by clicking the New Page on Group Break checkbox at the bottom of the dialog box.
6. You can choose to reset the page number on group break by selecting the Reset Page Number on Group Break checkbox.
7. When you are finished in the Select Group dialog, click the OK button.

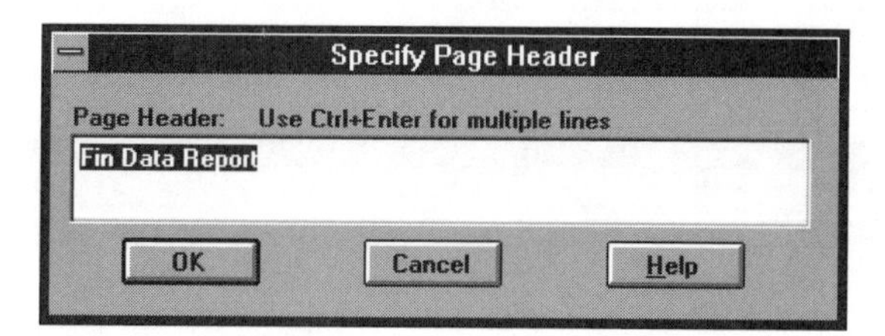

Figure 15-8: The Group presentation style automatically puts the header you enter here on the top of the page.

Figure 15-10 shows the Design window of the DataWindow Painter. You can modify this in the same manner you would a Tabular DataWindow.

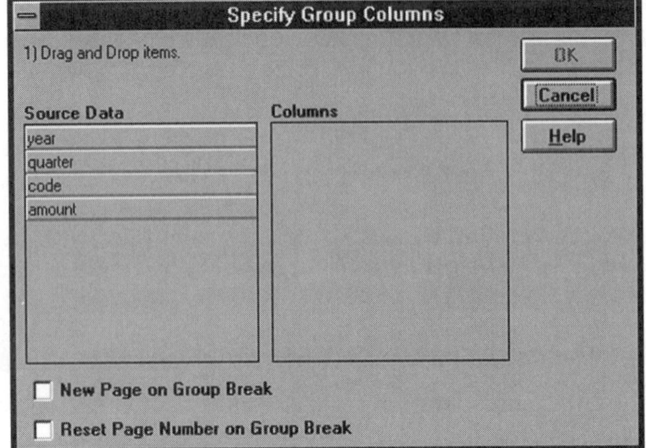

Figure 15-9: Choose the columns to group by using this window.

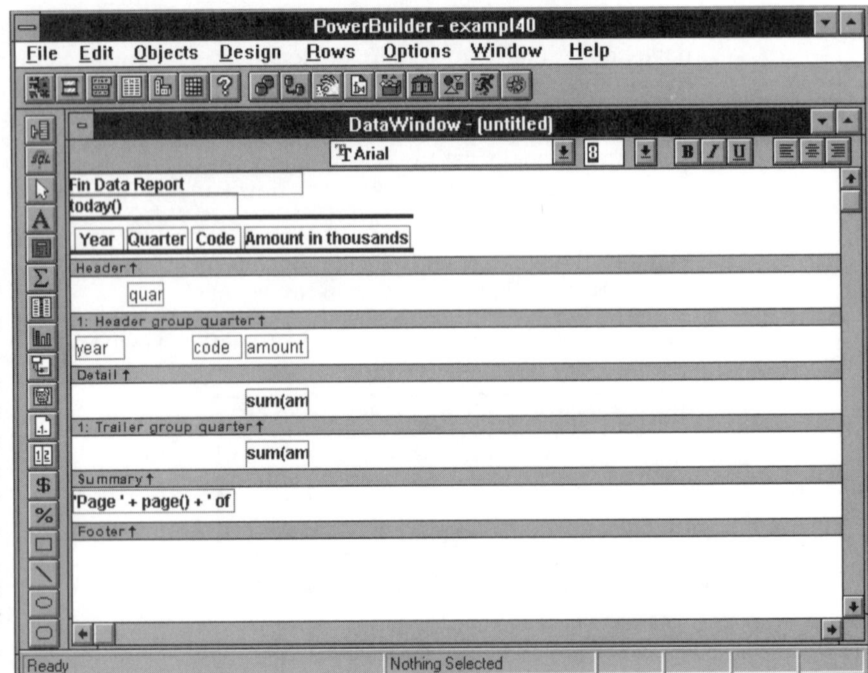

Figure 15-10: Design a Group DataWindow as you would a Tabular Data-Window, using the DataWindow Painter.

Labels are OK

The Label presentation style is used to create a format that can be used to print labels. Here are some of the label types you can print:

- Address labels
- Audio- and video-cassette labels
- Business cards
- Diskette labels
- Index cards
- Postcards
- Name badges

There are an incredible number of predefined label formats for both laser printers and pin-fed impact printers. If you can't find just the right format in this list, you probably just overlooked it. If you really can't find one, you can create your own custom format. Figure 15-11 shows the Specify Label Specifications dialog.

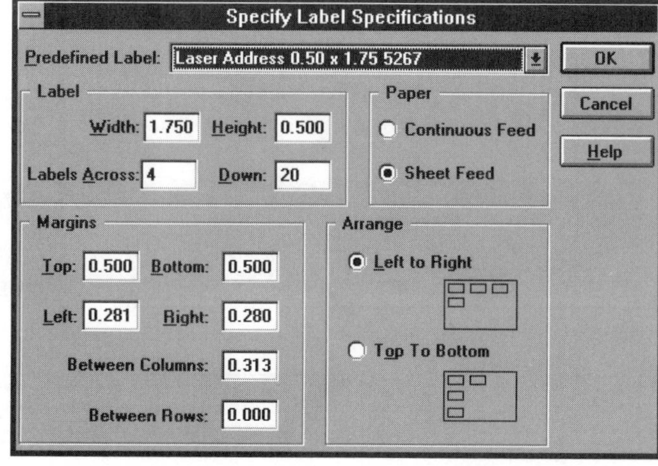

Figure 15-11: Select a predefined format or create your own custom label format.

To use the Label presentation style, do the following:

1. Start the DataWindow Painter, select the DataSource and the Label presentation style. For this example, choose the Customer table.
2. Select the fname, lname, address, city, state, and zip columns in the Quick Select DataSource and then click the OK button. The DataWindow Painter then presents the Specify Label Specifications dialog, as shown in Figure 15-11.

3. Either select a predefined format from the Predefined Label drop-down list box or define your own format by setting values in the Label, Paper, Margins, and Arrange sections of the dialog box.

4. In the DataWindow Painter, move the fields to their correct place on the label and set the font size so that all the information will fit, as in Figure 15-12.

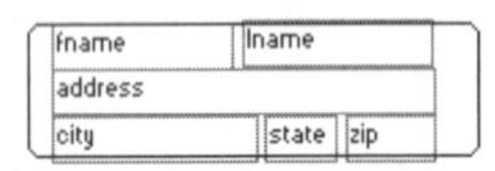

Figure 15-12: Arrange fields on the label in the format you want them to print.

When you preview the DataWindow, the results should look similar to Figure 15-13, depending on the label style you selected. Remember, never put a label in a place you can't reach.

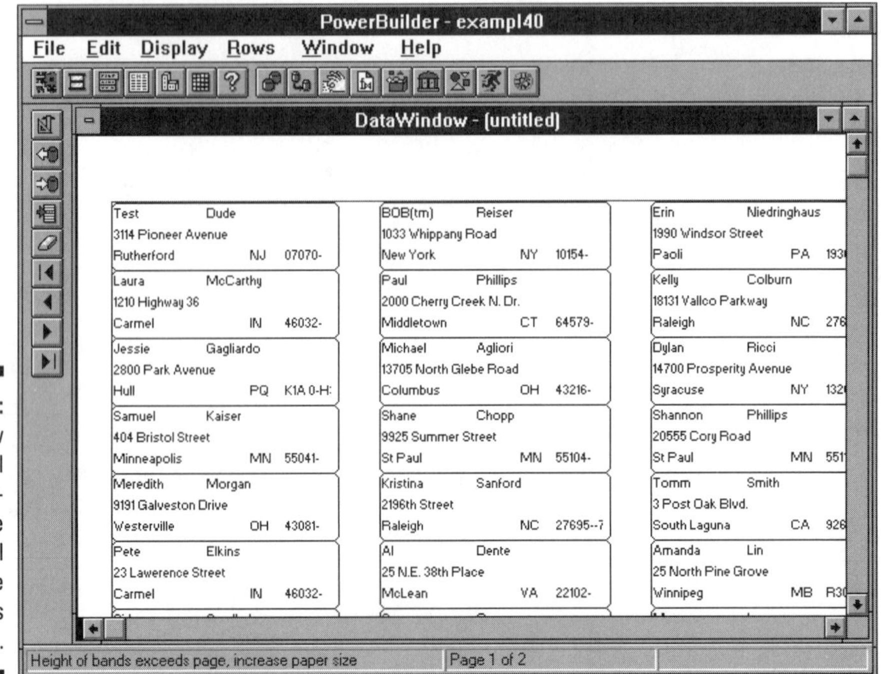

Figure 15-13: Preview your Label DataWindow to see what it will look like when it's printed.

N-Up, could be more or less than 7

7-Up would be a lot of columns. The N-Up presentation style allows you to present multiple columns next to one another, similar to newspaper columns. This can make better use of the space on either your screen or printed page.

We find that the concepts in this DataWindow are simple. The terms to describe it are confusing. Therefore, a group of columns, the fname and lname in our example, is called a detail row. Two detail rows are two columns of first and last names. Three detail rows are three columns of first and last names, and so on.

You can get similar results by using the Label presentation style. The only difference is how sorted information appears in the columns. You can experiment between the two presentation styles to get exactly the format you are looking for. ■

To create an N-Up presentation style DataWindow, do this:

1. Start the DataWindow Painter and select a DataSource. In our example, we are using the Quick Select DataSource and the N-Up presentation style.
2. Select a table or tables. In this example, we select the Customer table and the fname and lname columns; then click the OK button.
3. Specify the number of rows in the Detail Band. This is where you determine the number of detail rows as described earlier. In our example, this means that we must specify the number of columns of first and last names.

Once you have specified the rows in the detail band, the DataWindow Painter will present the DataWindow Painter. Previewing the results will look like Figure 15-14.

Act 1: the Composite DataWindow

For your viewing enjoyment we present the Composite DataWindow. Now, composite plastics are really hard, composite metals are extremely hard, but fortunately, composite DataWindows are not hard at all. This special DataWindow allows you to combine several DataWindow reports into one. You may be wondering what advantages this holds for you. Well, here are a few:

- Printing is easier. Issue only one print command and get all the reports at the same time.
- Use the same Header, Footer, and Summary information for all the reports.
- Page numbers will continue from the first to the last page without starting over when a new report begins.
- Your efficiency and use of alternative strategies will impress everyone so much that you are promoted to senior analyst, where you never have to develop another application for the rest of your life.

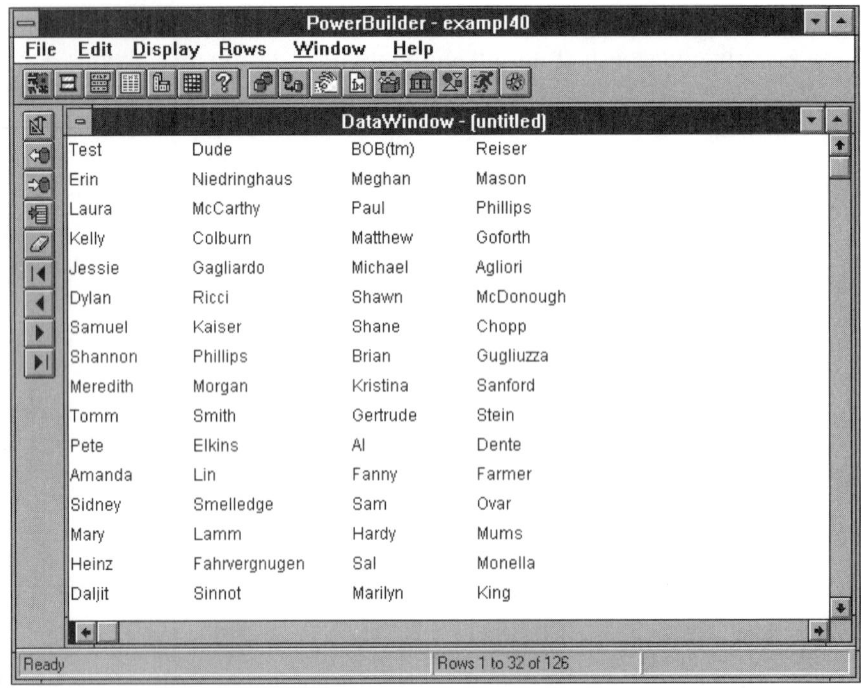

Figure 15-14: The N-Up presentation style formats its data like the columns of a newspaper.

Creating a Composite DataWindow is quite simple. The first thing to know is that a Composite DataWindow does not use a DataSource. Since the Composite DataWindow is made up solely of other DataWindows, each has its own DataSource. So begin the steps one step later than you are used to:

1. Start the DataWindow Painter and select Composite as the presentation style. Don't worry that all the DataSources no longer have names. That's PowerBuilder's way of saying, "Out of sight, out of mind."
2. Click the OK button; the Select Reports dialog appears on the screen.

3. From the list box in the Select Reports dialog, select as many reports (DataWindows) as you would like displayed, then click the OK button.
4. Each report will appear as a rectangle in the Detail Section of the Composite DataWindow. You can arrange them in any fashion you want.

Add headers, footers, and summary information as you would in other DataWindow presentation styles. You can even add objects from the Objects menu to enhance your report. Add the date or page numbers to add continuity to your Composite report.

Summary

The DataWindow is, without a doubt, the most incredible data-manipulation object ever conceived: If you can't do it in a DataWindow, maybe it can't be done. As you become more familiar with the presentation styles available in DataWindows, your PowerBuilder programming will take on new depth as you discover more flexibility in the ways that you design your applications.

The next chapter will take you deeper into the Graph presentation style. Just when you thought you'd seen everything, you find that we have just begun.

Chapter 16

Displaying Data with Graphs

In This Chapter

- Learn graph basics
- Configure your graph display
- Select just the right graph type
- Choose between 3D and 2D graph types

DataWindows have many different presentation styles to display information. Chapter 15 explains how to use each of them. In the last chapter you also learned that one of those presentation styles is the Graph. Most presentation styles arrange the actual text information in different configurations. This chapter shows how to represent that same information graphically, where you can:

- Create more impact with your information
- Simplify complex information
- See trends that might not be evident from looking at the values
- Look at the same information in many different graphical representations

This chapter will teach you some of the basics of graphing and a little about how each graph type might be used.

One Who Likes Graphing Is not a Graphite (a Lead In)

Graphs are an illustrated representation of information. To be displayed visually, information must have value that can be represented. A statement such as "that football stadium is big" can't be graphed. However, saying that it seats 50,000 people gives it a displayable value. In a list of the major football stadiums telling how many people each seats, it might take a moment find the stadium with the largest capacity. A graph, on the other hand, gives information instantly. The largest stadium would be immediately obvious. This is what graphing does for us — it gives us another way to look at information. It provides a visual format that makes the information we seek evident from the first glance.

Not only do graphs make information easier to analyze, pictures are easier to remember than words. Information then has more impact, staying in the minds of people who see it for a longer period of time.

A Picture Is Worth a Million Bytes

There are a couple of terms that need to be defined when talking about graphs. It's important to understand the difference between the *dependent* value and the *independent* value. The independent value is used to plot a value that affects equally all items being graphed. Its value is independent of any other forces. The dependent value depends on the value of the independent variable. For example, if you were graphing the pulse rates of mice in a pressure chamber where the pressure was gradually climbing, the independent variable would be the pressure, and the dependent variable, the one you can't control unless you're a mouse, is the pulse rate.

There are some other basic terms used to describe the different parts of a graph. Table 16-1 defines some of them so that you can refer to them as needed as you go through the chapter.

Table 16-1: The major parts of a graph

Graph Part	*Description*
Title	This is the optional title you can give your graph. This normally tells the user briefly what this graph is all about, such as "Annual Productivity Increase."
Value axis	The axis along which the dependent variables are plotted.
Category axis	The axis along which the independent variables are plotted.
Series	A group of data points.
Series axis	This is the axis along which the data points (series) are plotted. Graphs with more than one series can be 2D or 3D; a 2D column graph shows multiple columns next to each other — one for each category. A 3D column graph has multiple rows of 3D towers.
Legend	This optional feature identifies the series. In graphs with more than one series, you need to specify a legend to tell the series apart.

Graph types

In PowerBuilder there are two basic ways to create graphs. One of them is using the Graph style DataWindow; the other is by defining a graph object on a window through the Window Painter. You may want to create a graph using a graph object on your window so that you can view the data used to create the graph and the graph itself at the same time. This chapter primarily covers creating a graph style DataWindow, although many of the principles apply to graphs in general.

When creating a graph type DataWindow, entering the design mode of the DataWindow Painter brings up the dialog window shown in Figure 16-1. The Graph Data dialog is where you assign the various graph variables to their axes. Assign the independent variable to the category and the dependent variable to the series. If you have more than one dependent variable, you can create multiple series.

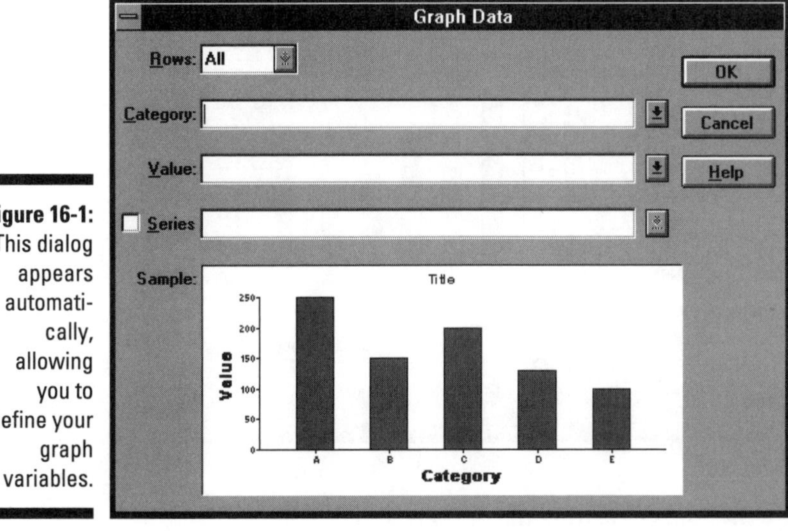

Figure 16-1: This dialog appears automatically, allowing you to define your graph variables.

Choosing the Right Graph

How information is represented is an art. As in art, you want to portray more than a sense of beauty; you sometimes want to send a message or convey a feeling. Numbers in a list can sometimes give you a feeling, especially when they turn from black to red. Seeing these numbers change in a graphed representation can help you see patterns that may have been hidden within the data. This is especially true when there are hundreds or thousands of data points.

A matter of style

PowerBuilder allows you to display information in several different graph styles. Read the description of each graph type and decide which graph will best represent your information. Still, a good deal of experimentation may be in order to find just the right graph style.

Setting graph options

Once you have selected the columns for your DataSource, the DataWindow Painter displays a default column graph. Double-click the graph to bring up the Graph dialog window shown in Figure 16-2.

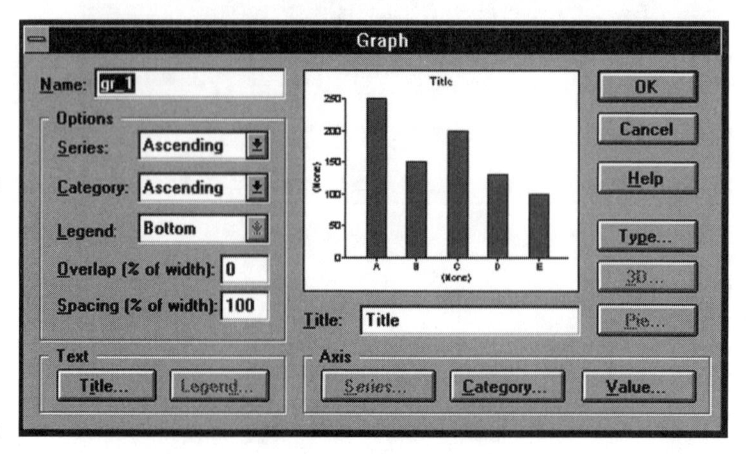

Figure 16-2: Set options and graph type in the Graph dialog window.

Here are the steps to setting the options for a graph:

1. Give your graph a name. Graphs normally have the default name of gr_?, where ? is some number. It is a good idea to give your graph a meaningful name. This will make it much easier to refer to in the event you want to update its attributes using PowerScript.
2. Your graph can have a title. This is not a must, but it can sometimes help the user grasp immediately what they are looking at.
3. You can change the location of the graph legend from its default position at the bottom to either the left, right, or top of the graph.

4. You can have the objects, such as bars in a bar graph, overlap. To change the default (no overlap), enter an integer that represents the percentage of overlap you would like.
5. The default spacing for objects such as the bars in a bar graph is that the space is the same width as the bar. You can change this spacing by entering an integer that represents the percentage of the bar's width you would like to see as a space.
6. You can add an optional title to your graph by entering it into the Title: field. You can further modify how that title appears on your graph by clicking the Title... button and modifying the display or font characteristics.
7. You can modify the characteristics of the Series, Category, and Value displays by clicking the corresponding button in the Axis group of buttons.
8. Most importantly, you can select your graph type by clicking the Type... button.

Some of the options are not selectable until you have selected a graph type that allows those options to be set. For example, when a 3D graph is selected, you will be able to set some of the positioning options of 3D graphs by clicking the 3D... button.

Configuring the axis

The Series, Category, and Value buttons all bring up similar configuration dialogs. You can customize how each axis of your graph is displayed by changing the label, tick marks, vertical and horizontal grid lines, the scale, and how the text appears.

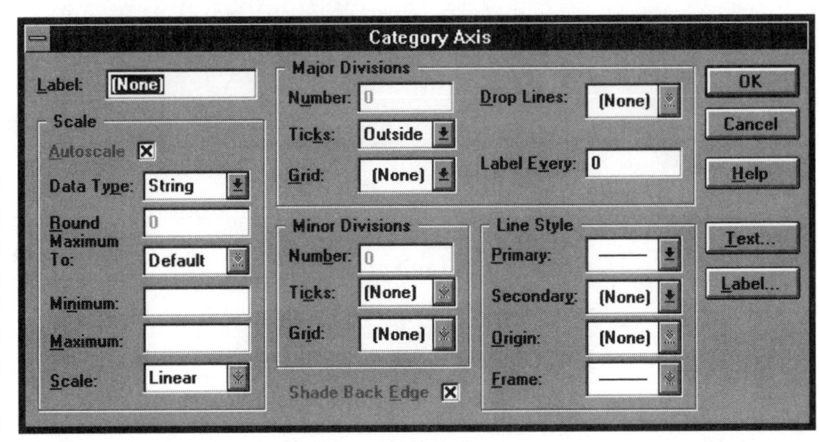

Figure 16-3: Configure the Category Axis to enhance the bottom line.

Figure 16-3 shows that you can set:

- The Axis label
- The Scale parameters
- How the major divisions are shown
- How the minor divisions are displayed
- The line style

Changing each of these parameters changes how your graph appears. There are way too many possible configurations to walk you through every one of them. They are very straightforward. We suggest that you experiment with each one to see how it affects the look or shape of your graph.

Selecting the graph type

To select the type of graph you would like to display your data, click the Type... button in the Graph dialog (which was shown in Figure 16-2). The Graph Type dialog appears, as shown in Figure 16-4.

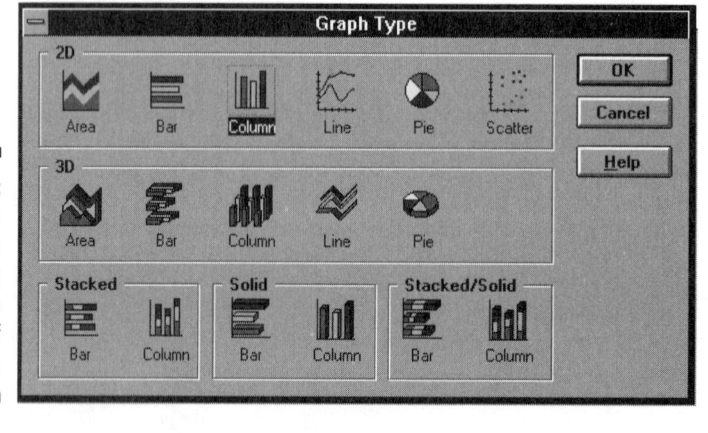

Figure 16-4: Select a graph type by clicking on the graph of your choice.

The graph types are broken into five different groups. They are:

- 2D — Flat-appearing graph styles
- 3D — Three-dimensional graph styles
- Stacked — Composite proportional graph styles
- Solid — Single-value 3D bar and column graphs
- Stacked/Solid — Combination of Stacked and Solid graph types.

Click the graph type of your choice and then click the OK button, or double-click the picture of the graph to automatically select it. You will be returned to the Graph dialog with a picture of the graph as it is currently configured and the appropriate options selectable.

To change the graph type it is not necessary to re-create the DataWindow. Click the Type... button to change graph types.

Alcohol-free bar graphs

Bar graphs are used to show single variables, displaying a value plotted with a horizontal, solid, colored bar. Each value is an independent value. If more than one value is shown, the bar is normally a different color or cross-hatch style. A good example might be the United States' population broken down by states. Each state would be listed down the left side of the graph, while each population bar would extend horizontally to the population value it represents.

Figure 16-5 shows what a 2D bar graph looks like. You see that one characteristic of a bar graph is that the bars are horizontal. This is useful when there are quite a few items with text names to graph. If they were graphed in a column graph where the bars are vertical, the text names might not fit along the bottom axis of the graph.

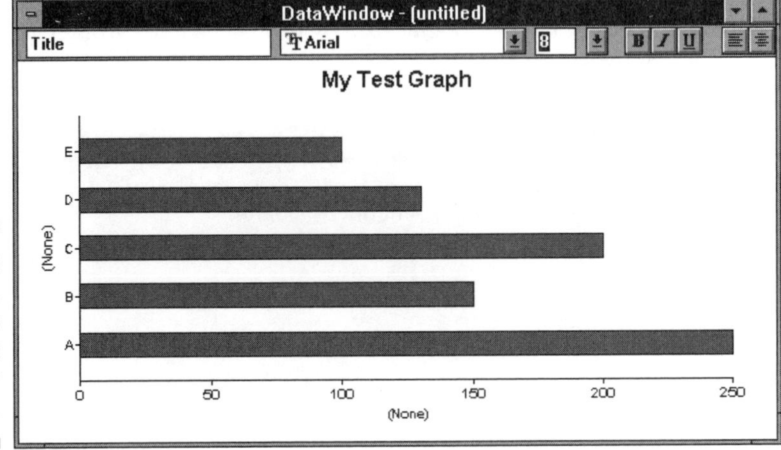

Figure 16-5: Bar none, this is the most popular graph.

Call 'em and they'll come for the column graph

Column graphs are similar to bar graphs, but the solid bars representing the value amount are vertical rather than horizontal.

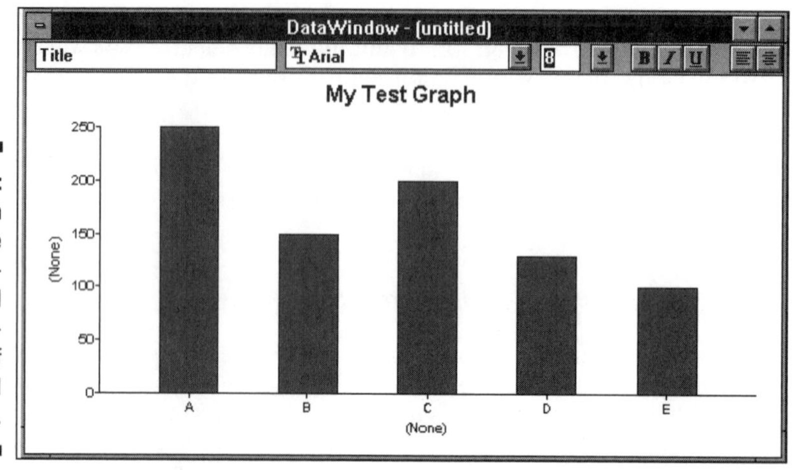

Figure 16-6: Column graphs are easy-to-read representations of plotted values.

By far one of the most widely used graph types, the Column graph displays values in a simple and straight-up manner. (Figure 16-6)

Line up for the line graph

Line graphs are used to show changes in values. There are both dependent and independent variables in a line graph. Line graphs represent how a particular value or values have changed by drawing a line through each point plotted on the graph.

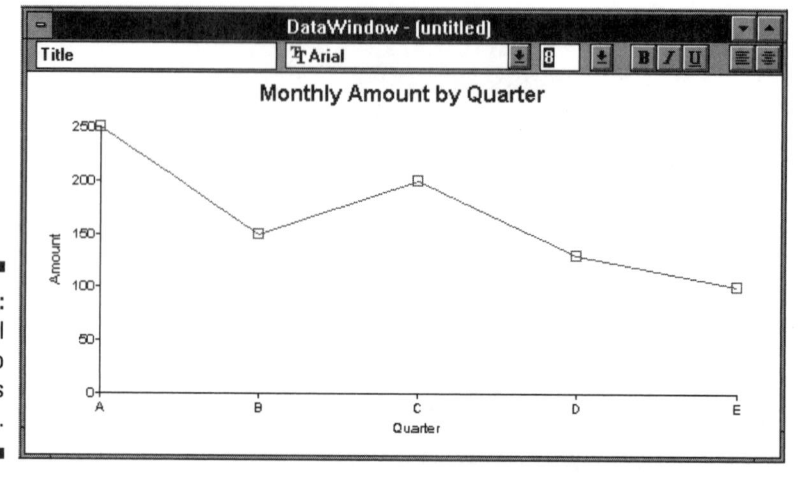

Figure 16-7: People will line up to see this graph.

It's pretty easy to see from the graph in Figure 16-7 that amounts by quarter are steadily shrinking. Putting this graph on the employee bulletin board would say everything you would want to say.

Nice area graphs

Area graphs have similarities to column graphs and line graphs. The area graph plots two variables (as in a line graph) and the value is displayed with a solid area of color beneath the line.

The graph in Figure 16-8 is a 3D area graph. Even though it says exactly the same thing as the line graph, it has more impact. It says, NOT GOOD! In fact, we can really make it say that.

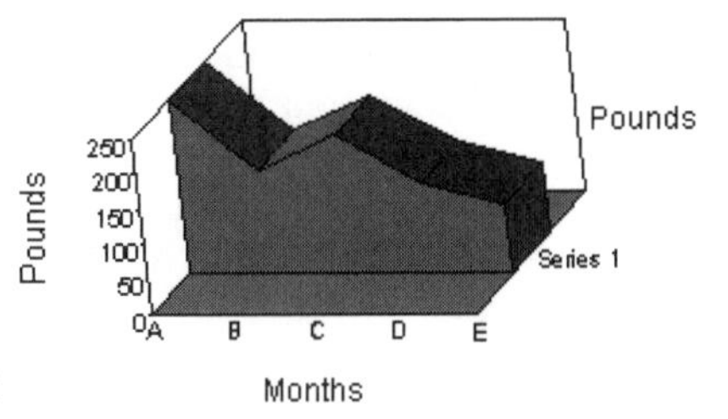

Figure 16-8: 3D graphs add a sense of realism to the information being displayed.

Even though a picture is worth a thousand words, it takes a few extra words to get the point across. You can annotate your graph by adding text objects. Select the text icon from the PainterBar and add text wherever you think it's needed. You can also select objects from the Objects menu to add even more impact. Figure 16-9 Shows our 3D area graph with some better news. ■

No one will throw your pie graph

Pie graphs are used to show proportional relationships. For example, in a budget, the office rent is shown as a certain percentage of the entire overall budget. A pie graph adds up all the values you are graphing and then determines what percentage of the whole each value represents.

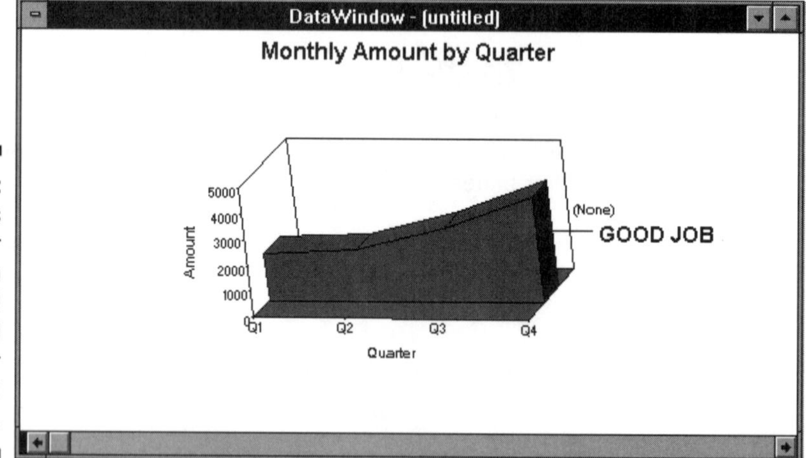

Figure 16-9: Annotations on your graph can add additional impact or personal messages.

It's easy to remember that pie graphs show proportions (Figure 16-10). Just remember that eating too much pie will change *your* proportions.

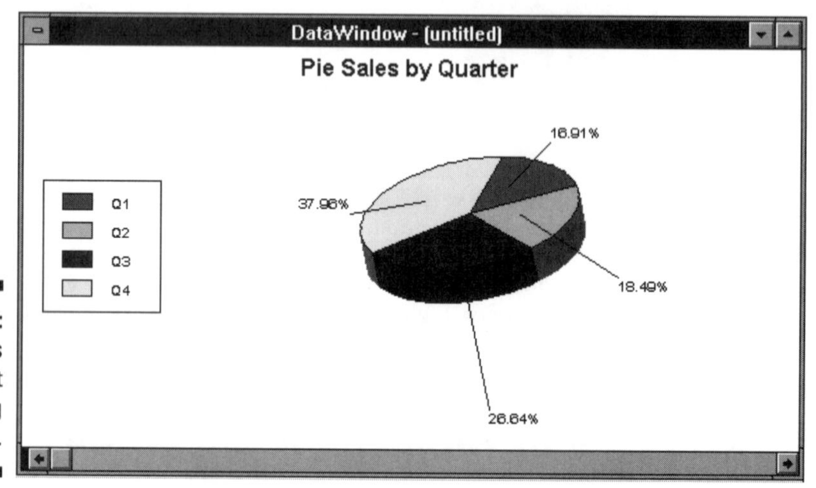

Figure 16-10: Pie graphs are good at showing proportions.

Don't try to show too many data points on a pie graph. The information becomes too small to analyze, the labels run together, and your point can get lost.

Scatter graphs everywhere

Scatter graphs are used to show singular data points in relation to other data points. Generally this type of graph is used to see trends in large groups. Linear regressions are normally run through scatter graphs to plot the linear trend in the data. Scatter graphs that show a trend will show its data points forming an oblong or cigar-shaped pattern. Data that apparently shows no trend appears more evenly distributed or distributed in random clumps.

You can see from the graph in Figure 16-11 that trends are visible from individually plotted points. This graph would have more meaning and impact if it had more points — it is a good example of choosing the wrong graph for the job. Figure 16-8 shows the same information with much more impact. Yet, if there were hundreds or thousands of data points, an area graph would probably not show trends as well as a scatter graph would.

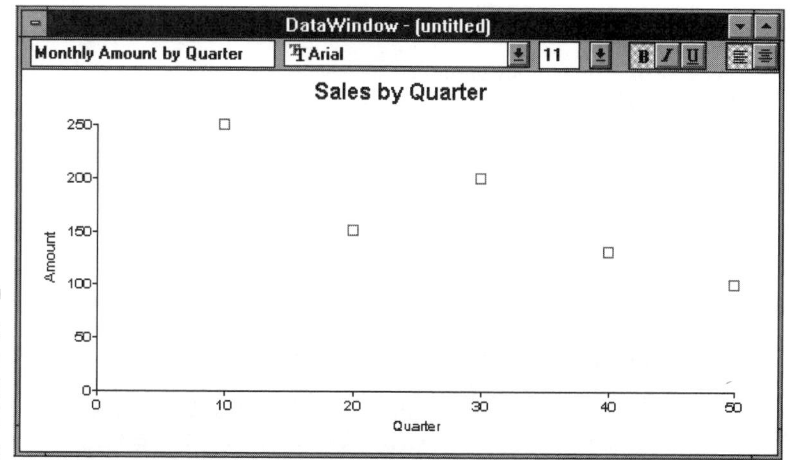

Figure 16-11: Scatter graphs point out trends.

2D or not 2D

Sometimes KISS (keep it simple, stupid) is a good rule to follow when presenting complex information. Certainly, three-dimensional graphs look slick, but sometimes the impact of a simple two-dimensional graph is just what the doctor ordered.

Once the data has been defined for a graph, it is fairly simple to move between 2D and 3D graphs. Look beyond the excitement of seeing the data "jump off the page" in 3D and answer the question, which format gets the point across?

Remember that graphs are an important way to communicate data. They're not supposed to be simply art. You don't want crowds of people standing around the monitor arguing in highbrow tones about your use of white space as a vehicle for realism, and your use of columns to represent mankind's reach to a higher understanding. You want them to say, "Hmm, looks like sales are rising and costs are dropping, but salaries are staying the same."

You can see from Figures 16-12 and 16-13 that sometimes fancy doesn't say things quite as well as plain and to the point. Don't overdo your use of 3D.

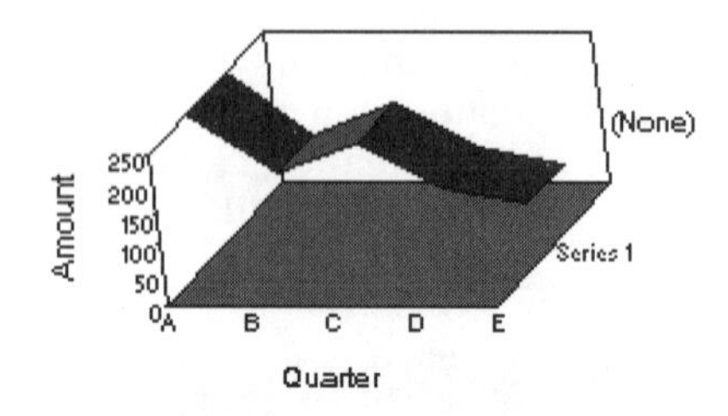

Figure 16-12: 3D graphs are pretty, but sometimes it takes an in-your-face 2D graph to really make the point.

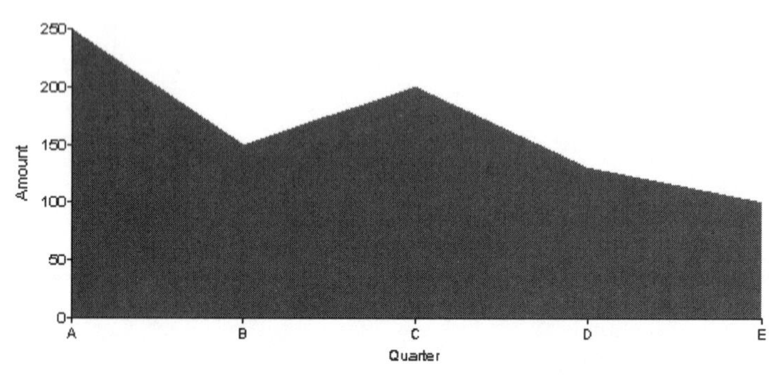

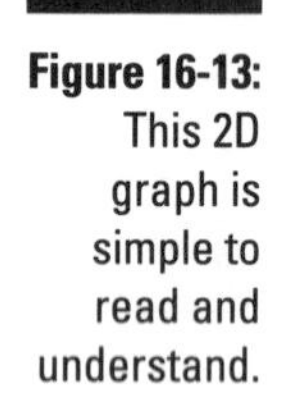

Figure 16-13: This 2D graph is simple to read and understand.

3D, the virtual reality graph

Sometimes you need a graph that will reach out off the page, grab you by the collar and say, "Look, profits are dropping and the short little column in the corner is your job going away!" The impact and style of a 3D graph can do just that. Information that may have seemed flat and lifeless can now appear to rise right from the monitor or printed page.

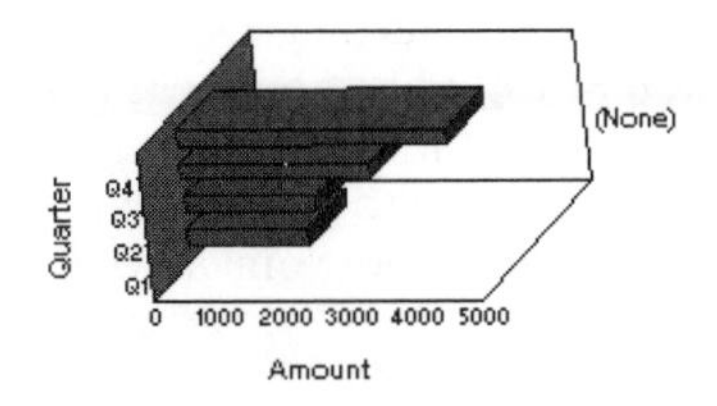

Figure 16-14: This 3D bar graph reaches out to the viewer with its message.

It's important to experiment with both the data and the graph style to get just the right image. Figure 16-14 shows values that seem to be growing like a tree. If this is the image you are trying to show, then this is the right graph.

When you select a 3D graph type, there are a number of customizing features available that you can't get in a 2D graph. These are:

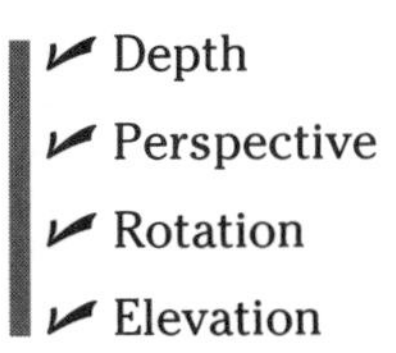

- Depth
- Perspective
- Rotation
- Elevation

Depth is an attribute that determines what ratio the depth of the 3D graph is to its width. This makes the graph appear skinnier or fatter. *Perspective* determines how far from the front of the window the image seems to be. This has the physical effect of making the graph appear larger or smaller. *Rotation* determines how much the graph is rotated from left to right. Often, the angle from which we view a graph makes a difference in how we perceive it. Rotate it to look at it a little more from one side or the other. *Elevation* allows you to change the viewer's elevation. The elevation can be changed from a bird's-eye view to a worm's-eye view.

In some 3D graphs, such as the 3D column and bar graphs, changing the elevation or rotation prevents you from seeing the values represented clearly. It's like trying to determine the height of the Empire State Building while sitting in a helicopter hovering over its roof.

The deck is stacked

The stacked graph type has all the advantages of either a bar or column graph and a pie graph. Each column or bar shows two or more values as a percentage of the whole value in the bar or column. Here's an example of how that might be used: Let's say you have measured growth patterns in different children. Each child's overall height would be shown as a 3D column. Now, within each column you break that height into three components— upper body, torso, and legs. You will now be able to see not only the height differences among the children, but the body proportions as well.

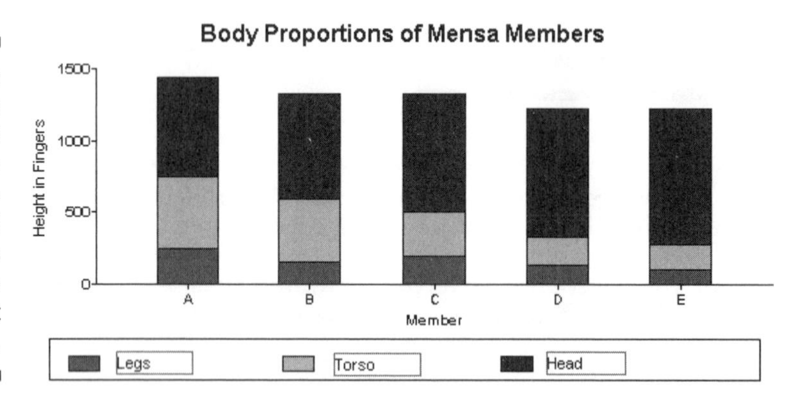

Figure 16-15: This stacked graph shows proportional differences between the different columns.

We heard that Mensa members have a good sense of humor. Figure 16-15 shows the results of a fictional research experiment. You can see how easy it is to show proportional differences with this type of graph.

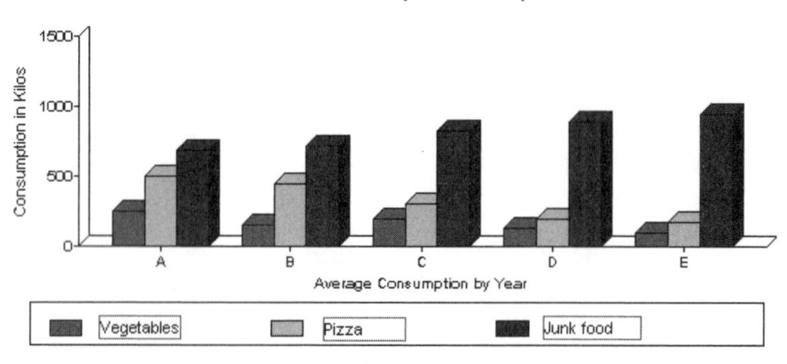

Figure 16-16: Solid graphs give a 3D effect to column and bar graphs.

Solid fun

The solid bar and column graphs show each bar or column in 3D. The graph itself is 2D. When you have only one series of values being plotted, this can sometimes be the simplest graph to read, as shown in Figure 16-16. It isn't quite 3D, yet has 2D simplicity.

Combining the stacked and solid graphs

You have seen how a stacked graph represents proportions within different bars or columns. You have also seen how giving these bars or columns some 3D shape, as in the solid graph, gives it impact without losing simplicity. With the stacked/solid graph you can combine these two features into a 3D bar or column graph that shows proportions, as in Figure 16-17.

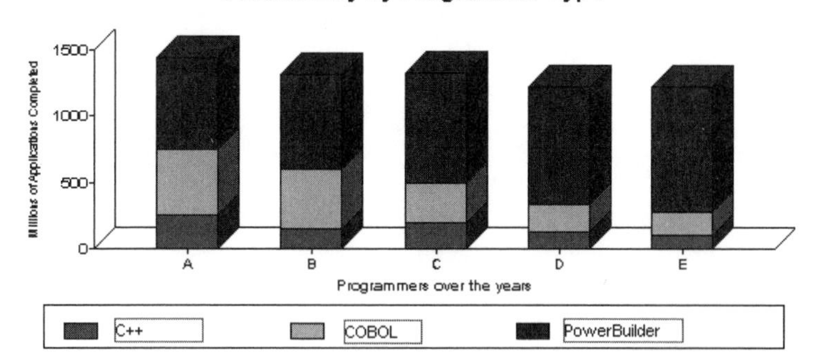

Figure 16-17: Proportions really stand out when you use the stacked/ solid graph type.

Summary

Graphs are the visual aids that will make your applications more memorable. The images that graphs create have the power to speak to people of all sizes and shapes. They add new dimensions, new understanding, and a better life for all. The next chapter will help you learn to use DataWindows as powerful data-entry tools.

Chapter 17

Using DataWindows for Data Entry

In This Chapter

- Creating data-entry windows with a DataWindow
- Preparing a window for DataWindow data entry
- Setting up edit styles in a DataWindow definition

In Chapter 9 you learned how to create data-entry windows using controls such as the SingleLineEdit, ListBox, and CheckBox. Using data-entry controls like these is the most flexible way to handle data entry in your application. The reason they're so flexible, however, is that you do all the data manipulation yourself using PowerScript.

With this approach, if you want something displayed in a data-entry control, you have to put it there explicitly. To get data out of a control, you have to write PowerScript code. And to access the database you have to write SQL commands. Most data-entry screens do all three of these things. The process normally goes something like this:

1. Data is retrieved from the database.
2. Data is displayed in controls.
3. Data is edited by the user.
4. Data is read out of the controls.
5. Data is stored back to the database.

Doing all of this yourself using PowerScript is excellent if you need total control over everything. It is said that absolute power corrupts absolutely. Well, in this case, it may not corrupt, but it does require a lot of extra, often unnecessary work.

Data Entry in a DataWindow Is Easier than Pi

There's a faster way of handling that five-step process that will almost always give you enough flexibility. DataWindows can be used to build complete data-entry screens. Each DataWindow column can be configured to make data entry simple and intuitive. Data validation occurs automatically according to validation rules that you define, and, with the help of event scripts, you can exercise a great deal of control over the behavior of a DataWindow.

There are three ways to use a DataWindow for data entry:

- Retrieve data from the database into the DataWindow control, allow the user to edit or add to the data, then update the database with the user's changes.
- Leave the DataWindow control empty, but give the user a way to add new data; when the user is finished entering data, update the database.
- Allow the user to add and edit data in a DataWindow control, then extract and process the data using PowerScript.

This chapter focuses on the first two data-entry options. These two options leverage DataWindow technology to simplify the development of database applications. The third option uses a DataWindow control as a normal data-entry control. This can be desirable, but, as you know, creates a lot of extra work.

Preparing for data entry in a DataWindow definition

There are a few tricks to setting up a DataWindow definition for use in database data entry. First, you can't use the external data source. Second, only a few of the DataWindow presentation styles can be used. They are:

- Freeform
- Grid
- Group
- N-up
- Tabular

Third, only DataWindow columns that are in the tab order can be edited by the user. Columns with zero in the tab order are display-only — the user can't edit their contents.

To change the tab order of DataWindow columns, choose Tab Order from the Design menu in the DataWindow Painter. When red numbers appear above each column, change a column's number to change that column's position in the tab order. Choose Tab Order from the Design menu again to leave Tab Order mode. ■

Finally, though a DataWindow can retrieve data from many tables, it can update only one of them. Choose Update... from the Rows menu to open the window shown in Figure 17-1. The Allow Updates checkbox must be checked in order for the DataWindow to update a database table. Select the table to update using the Table to Update: drop-down list box. This is the default unless there are multiple tables joined in the Select statement.

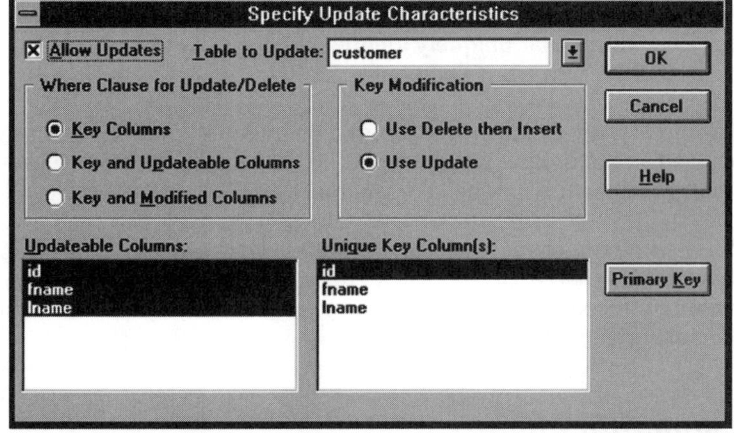

Figure 17-1: Specify update characteristics of a DataWindow definition in this window.

Two more update settings must be specified before the update characteristics are complete:

- Which columns to update
- How the table determines which rows to modify

Once you're set these, click the OK button to accept the update characteristics for the DataWindow definition.

Selecting the columns to update

The Updateable Columns: list box displays every column in the DataWindow definition. Click on the columns that you want to update. If the data source definition for the DataWindow includes multiple tables, then you should select only columns that are in the table to be updated.

Identifying a unique key

DataWindows are very smart. Most of them could probably qualify for membership in Mensa. When a DataWindow updates a database table, it doesn't waste time updating information that hasn't changed. Instead, it keeps track of modified and new rows, and sends only these rows to the database — one at a time.

However, a simple "here's the changed row, Mr. Table," isn't enough. The DataWindow must also tell the table how to locate the original row. This is done through the use of a unique key. A unique key is a column or a combination of columns that uniquely identifies the row. Set the unique key by selecting from the Unique Key Column(s): list box.

If a primary key exists on the table to be updated, then the primary key can be used as the unique key. Click on the Primary Key button to use the table's primary key as the unique key column.

When using the primary key as the unique key column isn't an option, select the columns that, together, will identify a single, unique row. When in doubt, use all of the columns as a unique key. This will always work, but it's slower than using a true unique key.

Managing change

In a network database environment, it's common for several people to attempt to change the same rows at nearly the same time. The Where clause for Update/Delete radio buttons allows you to specify how sensitive the DataWindow is to possible changes in the database table.

The Key Columns setting tells the DataWindow that a row should be updated only if nobody else has changed the values in the original row's key columns. This is the minimum verification level. The drawback to this level of verification is obvious — somebody else could have changed values in the row's other columns without changing the key columns. This level of verification doesn't detect those changes, so the new changes overwrite changes made by somebody else. If that somebody else happens to be your boss, you'll probably have an educational encounter in which you gain a deeper understanding of your boss's desire for quality and teamwork. You might even enjoy it.

To avoid this situation, choose one of the other radio buttons. The Key and Updateable Columns setting checks for changes in all of the updateable columns as well as the key columns. Key and Modified Columns checks for changes in any modified column as well as the key columns. With all three settings, if changes are detected, the update fails.

The other set of radio buttons, Key Modification, determines how changes should be made when a key column is altered. The Use Delete then Insert option will first delete the row containing the old key, then insert a row for the new key. This can sometimes have unexpected results, particularly if you're good at creating strange circumstances that your database is unable to handle. If you encounter a problem, try changing to Use Update.

Key modification is tricky business. Primary keys exist so that foreign keys will have something at which to point. If a primary key changes or gets deleted, and foreign key rows that point to the old primary key row still exist, you'll have what's known as a *mess*. To avoid this situation, set foreign keys to have one of three possible reactions to the deletion of a primary key row:

- RESTRICT — Override the attempt to delete the primary key row
- CASCADE — Delete any foreign key rows that used to depend on the primary key row
- SET NULL — Set the dependent columns to NULL

Preparing for data entry in a window

Now that your DataWindow definition is ready to be used for data entry, you need to add a few things to the window containing the DataWindow control. Start the Window Painter and open the data-entry window. If you haven't added a DataWindow control yet, do so now and attach the DataWindow definition that was prepared for data entry.

The DataWindow needs to be assigned a transaction object before rows can be retrieved or updated. Transaction objects allow the DataWindow to access the database.

Use the SetTransObject(SQLCA) function in the window's open event script to start a new database transaction for the DataWindow control.

The DataWindow control must be told when to retrieve data from the database. Use the Retrieve( ) function in the place that makes the most sense for your data-entry window. Most of the time you'll probably add a Retrieve( ) to the window's open event script immediately following SetTransObject(SQLCA). If you want the DataWindow control to be empty when the user begins entering data, skip this step.

Give the user a way to update the database with the changes he's made in the DataWindow control. A CommandButton or a menu option works well. Use the Update( ) function to tell the DataWindow control to update the database.

Once the DataWindow control performs an update, Commit; finalizes the changes made to the database. To cancel the changes, use the Rollback; command. Changes to the database are not finalized until the Commit command is issued. This allows the user to back out of the changes and roll them back with the Rollback; command. You will want to strategize about the best places to commit changes to the database. If you don't issue Commits often enough, too many changes could be backed out, which forces the user to re-enter information that probably shouldn't have been rolled back. Committing too often does not allow the user enough of a cushion for backing out of changes later in the editing process.

Finally, you'll probably want to give the user a way to add and delete rows in the DataWindow control. Create a couple of CommandButtons, or a few menu options, or some other user interface element if you prefer. One of these elements will delete the current row, the other will add a new row to the end of the DataWindow control.

Use the following script to delete the current row, where *DataWindowName* is the name of your DataWindow control. DeleteRow( ) deletes the row passed as a parameter, and GetRow( ) returns the current row.

```
DataWindowName.DeleteRow(DataWindowName.GetRow())
```

Use the following script to add a new row to the end of the DataWindow control. After adding a new row using the function InsertRow(0), this script forces the DataWindow control to scroll to the new row using the ScrollToRow( ) function. This simply makes sure that the new row will be visible within the DataWindow so that the user can edit it easily. The InsertRow(0) function returns the number of the new row.

```
dw_test.ScrollToRow(dw_test.InsertRow(0))
```

Figure 17-2 shows a sample window that uses a DataWindow for data entry. All of the controls described above are present on the window in the form of CommandButtons.

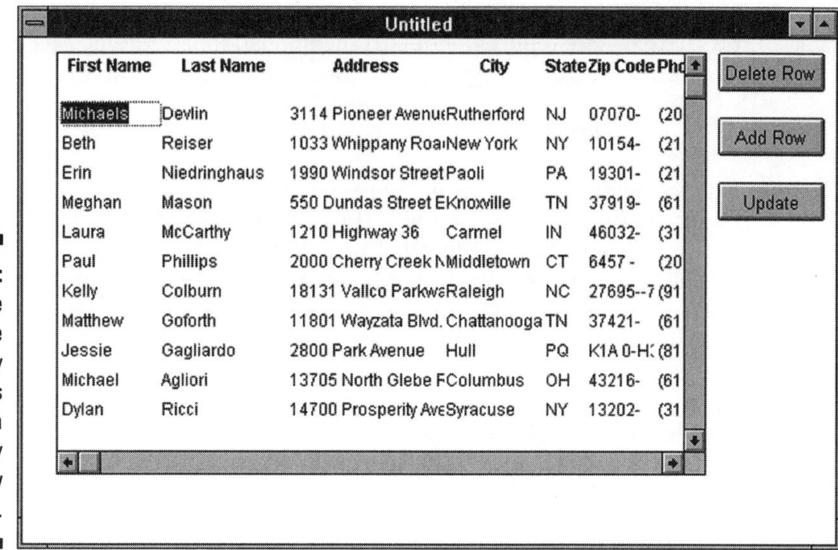

Figure 17-2: Create complete data-entry windows using a data-entry DataWindow and controls.

If the table being updated in the DataWindow control contains a primary key, then a unique key value must be placed in the primary key column for all rows added to the DataWindow control. Since the user of your application normally doesn't know about primary keys, you must write a script to do this automatically when a new row is added; you can't rely on the user to type it in. In fact, the user should normally never see the key columns in a DataWindow — only the columns that the user can modify should be visible.

Write a function that searches the existing primary key values and returns the next available value. This can be done easily if your primary key column is a numeric data type. Use the following script, where *PrimaryKeyColumnName* is the name of the primary key column, and *TableName* is the name of the table containing the primary key:

```
long lMaxKeyValue

Select max(PrimaryKeyColumnName) into :lMaxKeyValue from TableName;
lMaxKeyValue = lMaxKeyValue + 1

return(lMaxKeyValue)
```

Call this function when you need to find out what the next available primary key value is for the table. For more on using SQL in PowerScript, see Chapter 20.

Store the next available primary key value in the primary key column for all new rows. Use the SetItem( ) function to accomplish this. SetItem( ) accepts three parameters, the *row* and *column* to store a value in, and the *value* to store:

```
DataWindowName.SetItem(row,column,value)
```

Call the function that returns the next available primary key value and store primary key values in each new DataWindow row right before the Update( ) function is used. This minimizes the chance that two users on the network will call the next available key function at the same time and try to use the same key values for their new rows. ■

Adding Controls to a DataWindow Definition

By default, each column in a DataWindow definition uses the edit style defined in the extended attributes section of the database table definition. The edit style of each DataWindow column can be changed to allow the user to edit the contents of a column using a different user interface control. The controls available are:

- CheckBox
- DropDownDataWindow
- DropDownListBox
- Edit
- Edit Mask
- RadioButtons

If a different edit style isn't specified in the table definition, the default edit style is Edit. Edit is essentially a SingleLineEdit-style control.

Changing the edit style of a column

To change the edit style of a column, start the DataWindow Painter and click on the column with the right mouse button. Choose Edit Styles from the popup menu, then choose the edit style you want from the next popup menu.

Choosing CheckBox brings up the window shown in Figure 17-3. This window allows you to choose from one of the predefined CheckBox edit formats or to create your own.

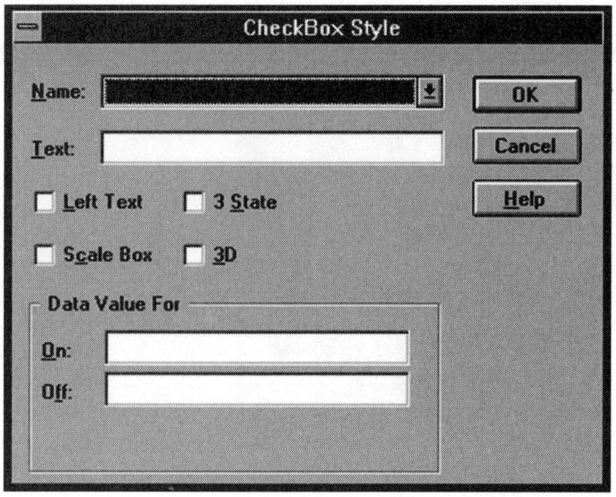

Figure 17-3: Configure the format of your CheckBox edit style using this window.

To choose from one of the predefined CheckBox formats, click on the Name: drop-down list box and select from the list. The other fields fill in automatically with the formatting instructions appropriate to the CheckBox format you select. If you don't want to use a predefined format, then leave the Name: list box blank and configure a new format yourself.

Choosing DropDownDataWindow brings up the window shown in Figure 17-4, which allows you to select the DataWindow that you want to drop down. From here, pick the column you want to display and the column from which you want to obtain a data value when the user selects from the DropDownDataWindow. You can also choose from predefined DropDownDataWindow edit styles.

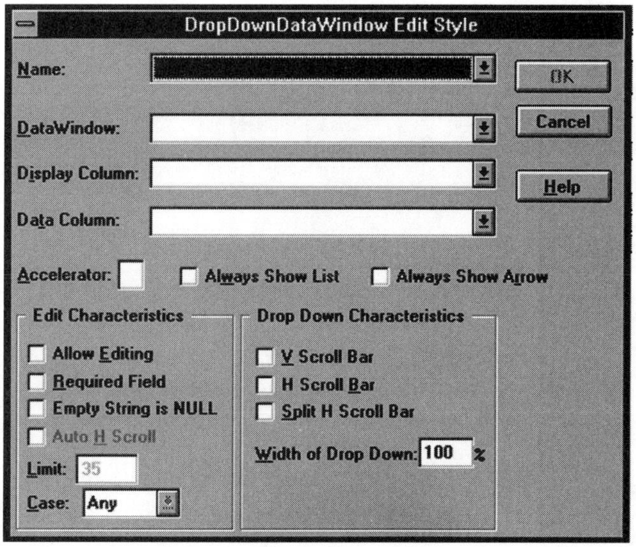

Figure 17-4: Set up the DropDown-DataWindow edit style through this window.

Choosing DropDownListBox brings up the window shown in Figure 17-5. This window allows you to choose from predefined DropDownListBox edit styles or to define your own.

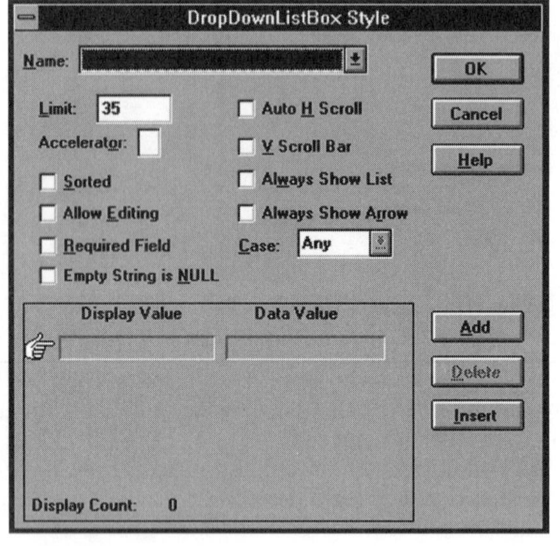

Figure 17-5: Choose a DropDown-ListBox style or create a new one using this window.

Choosing Edit brings up the window shown in Figure 17-6. This window allows you to choose from predefined Edit styles or to configure a new one.

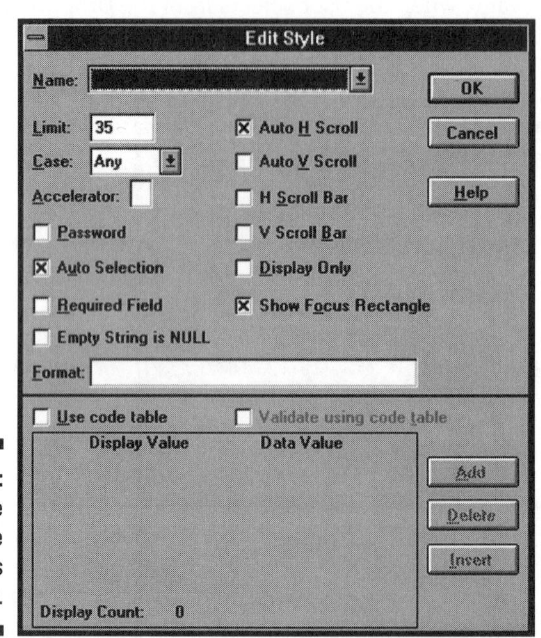

Figure 17-6: Configure an Edit style from this window.

Choosing Edit Mask brings up the window shown in Figure 17-7, which allows you to choose from predefined Edit Mask edit styles or create a new one.

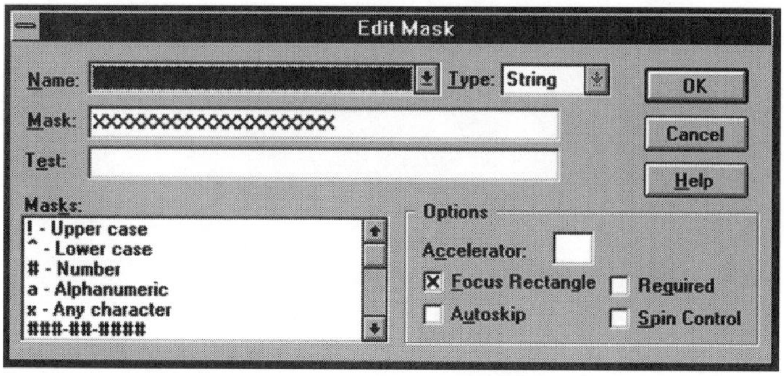

Figure 17-7: Use this window to setup an Edit Mask edit style.

Selecting RadioButtons brings up the window shown in Figure 17-8.

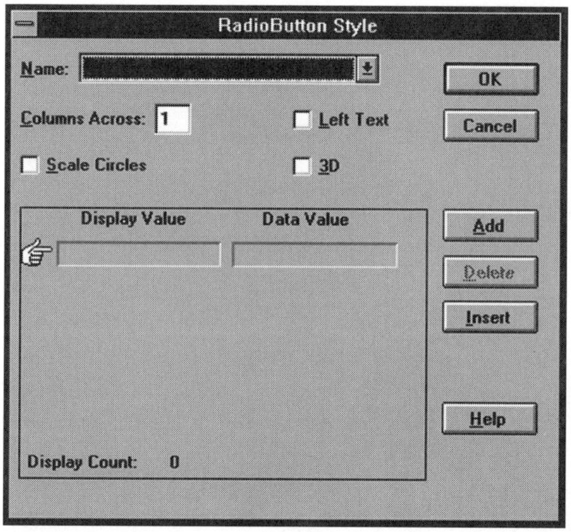

Figure 17-8: Choose or edit a RadioButton edit style using this window.

DataWindows are the fastest way to build complete data-entry screens. Using a DataWindow definition and a DataWindow control, creating a data-entry screen is a simple matter of defining what it should look like and how it should behave. Then, instructions such as retrieve data or update the database can be sent to the DataWindow using PowerScript.

Part V

Quality Assurance and Building the EXE

"I SAAIID WHAT COMPANY DO YOU REPRESENT?"

In This Part...

Imagine what it's like to see your new home being built. Every day you go out to the lot and see something new taking shape. First, you wander around the foundation thinking, "The kitchen's here and the living room's here." Then, as if by magic, the studded walls go up and it starts looking like a house. Then the roof, the siding, the windows, the stucco, and then finally, after all the fixtures are in, the finishers come in to take this exciting shell and make it a home.

That's what this part is all about. It shows you how to take your application from an exciting shell to a finished product. Part of this process involves testing and verifying the application — using the PowerBuilder tools to tweak and debug the application. Then, finally, you create the executable file. You will learn some of the tricks for keeping your executable file sizes small without sacrificing functionality. Then comes the fun part — distributing your application to the users.

Chapter 18

Using the Quality PowerTools

In This Chapter

- Using Debug to find bugs
- Telling Debug where to stop and show off
- Viewing variables in a Watch window

This chapter is about Debug. This tool is so much more than a find-it-and-fix-it debugging tool that it seems inappropriate to call it *Debug*. It's actually an excellent quality-assurance tool. Use it to do the following:

- Test program flow — Make sure all of your program components are being called correctly. See events as they are triggered and the PowerScript code as it executes.
- Test and verify data — You can validate formulas and algorithms. Actually watch the information flow through your program.
- Experiment — You can change variable values and expressions while the program is running.
- Find problem areas and bugs — With your ability to see behind the scenes, you can spot problems and fix them quickly.

This chapter will show you how to watch your program running, stop it when you want, change values on-the-fly, and how to make the best use of the Debug tool.

Unbuggering Your Application

It's not for certain, but it's possible that there are two things that can go wrong for every line of code you write. Following that bit of made-up wisdom, for a 1,000-line program there are 2,000 possible bugs. This is a bit exaggerated, but only slightly.

The Debug tool allows you to:

- Display and change the values of Global, Shared, Local and Instance variables
- Choose certain variables to watch
- Display and change the attributes and values of all your application's windows, controls, and user objects
- Walk through program execution one step at a time or run full speed, stopping at designated stop points

These features allow you to find problems in an application that isn't running correctly, or test and verify a program that's ready for delivery.

It's a good idea to use Debug as a quality-assurance tool. This lets you find problems that may exist in the application before the user does. Sometimes, everything can appear to be running correctly and then a small glitch can cause unseen disaster. Think how devastating it would be if your application made tiny little math errors every once in a while.

Remember this basic fact. If you fix a problem before an application ships, you're a hero. If you have to fix it afterwards, you're a zero. Don't let your users be your quality-assurance team. They don't have the very excellent Debug tool you have. ■

Debugging

PowerBuilder has its own first level of defense against bugs — your PowerScript code. Whenever you exit the PowerScript Painter, PowerBuilder checks your work. It looks for obvious syntax errors and undefined variables. It points out where the problem exists and gives you an idea of what the problem is.

Even with all the obvious errors corrected, more subtle problems can arise. Most of these problems have to do with program flow and data manipulation. When verifying program flow, it's important to make sure that:

- Events happen when you think they should and event scripts execute successfully
- Branching statements branch in expected directions
- Menu choices produce the correct results
- User defined functions run when called

When looking for data problems, the task becomes a little trickier. You then have to:

- Look for algorithm and formula errors
- Find mistakes in database queries or updates
- Check validation routines and data-entry values
- Look at variable lifetimes (scope) and make sure they exist when you want them and go away when you don't

Starting Debug

Start Debug by clicking the Debug icon in the PowerBar. It's the "No Bugs" icon. When the Select Script dialog appears, as in Figure 18-1, your very first task is choosing the script you want to debug.

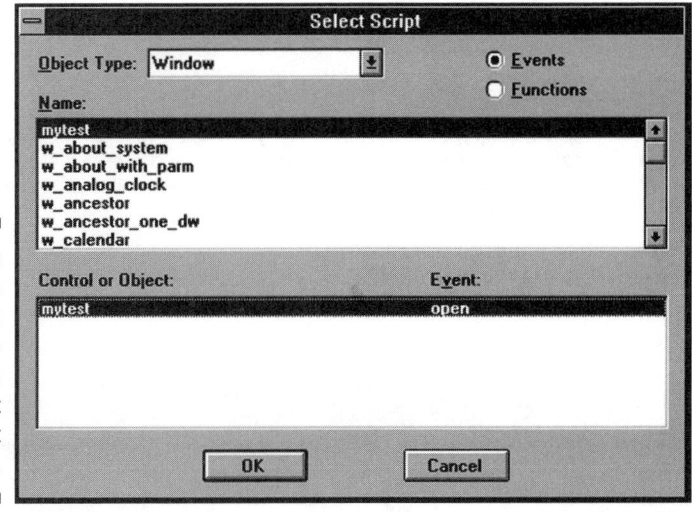

Figure 18-1: Select the script you want to debug from the Select Script dialog.

Notice the Object Type: list box in Figure 18-1. Clicking this allows you to select from a list of object types. The following object types can have PowerScript in an event:

- Application object
- Window
- Menu
- User Object
- User Defined Function

Selecting from the list causes the Name: list box to display the application's objects that are of the selected type. Figure 18-1 shows a list of windows because that's which object type is currently selected.

The list box at the bottom of the dialog shows the Control or Object name and any events that have PowerScript programs. Figure 18-1 shows that the window mytest has PowerScript in its open event. Selecting this event says that this is the script for which you would like to begin running Debug.

While you are running Debug, you will also see any functions or scripts called by the script you are debugging. Once an event is selected, the script will appear in Debug (see Figure 18-2).

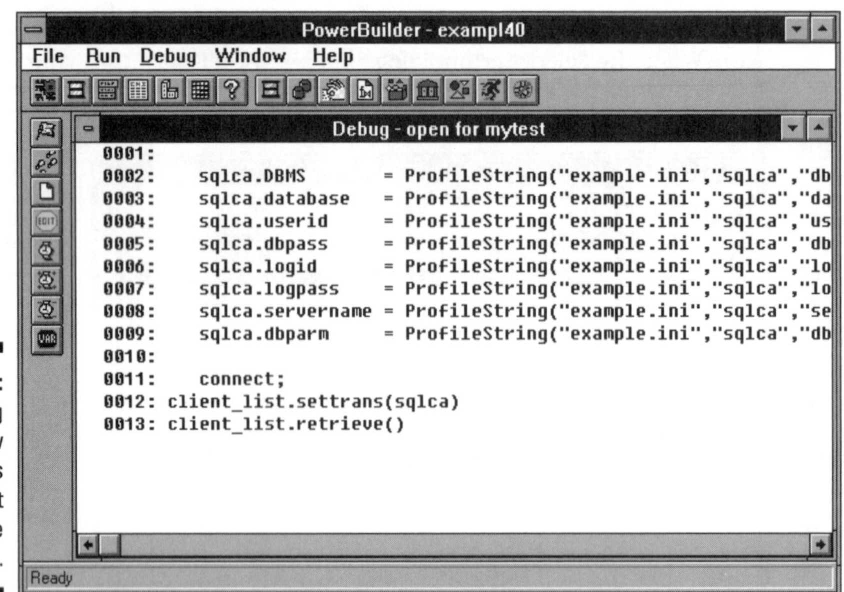

Figure 18-2: The Debug window displays your script with line numbers.

Taking a look at the Debug window

The Debug window has its own set of toolbar icons. Table 18-1 shows and describes the use of each icon.

Before you click the green GO flag, you will want to configure Debug to stop somewhere and let you take a peek. This is known as setting *stop points*. You may also want to set up *watch variables*. These are variables that you have singled out to appear in a Watch window so you can pay particular attention to them.

Table: 18-1: The Debug icons

Icon	Description
	The green flag is the GO flag, like one you might find at a racetrack. This starts the application running full speed. When the application is running this icon changes into an arrow chasing its tail.
	The footsteps are like fossil tracks found in the clay in Eastern Africa, proving that ancient humanoids walked on two feet. In Debug it means step through the program one line at a time.
	The Script icon, similar to the Script icon in the Window Painter, allows you to select a script to debug.
EDIT	The green edit sign, unlike any you may see anywhere else, allows you to edit the stop list.
	The three Watch icons allow you to show or hide the Watch window, add a watch variable to the watch list, and remove a variable from the watch list.
VAR	The VAR icon is not a special icon for Value Added Resellers. It allows you either to show or hide the Variables window.

Hey! Stop!

Running an application in Debug would be no different from clicking the Run icon if it weren't for stop points. To be able to stop the application from running so that you can view the PowerScript code behind the scenes, you have to set stop points. You can set as many stop points as you need.

Ready, set, stop!

To set a stop point, double-click the line of PowerScript code in the Debug window. A red stop sign will appear next to the line number. This lets you know that a program running in Debug mode will stop running when it reaches this point, and Debug will appear in the foreground. Your program has not been terminated — only suspended. Clicking either the Run icon (arrow chasing its tail) or single-stepping with the Step icon will continue running your program.

Placing stops within a loop can be good or bad, depending on how many times you expect the loop to continue looping. A strategy for dealing with loops is to place a stop within the loop and one directly following it. Let the program stop at the first stop point, which allows you to inspect what is happening within the loop. You can even continue through several iterations of the loop. When you have finished checking out the loop, remove the stop point within the loop and allow the program to run. It will stop again when the loop has finished and it encounters the next stop point.

Removing stop points is easy. Double-click the line with the stop point and the Stop Sign icon will disappear.

Stop points will remain in place until you either remove them or quit your PowerBuilder session. This means that you can run your application using the normal Run icon and then go back into Debug mode with all the same stop points still in place.

Changing your stop points

To edit the stop points in your program you can click the green Edit icon in the toolbar. The Edit Stops dialog will appear, as in Figure 18-3.

Figure 18-3: You get bonus points for using the Edit Stops dialog to edit your stop points.

To add a stop point using the Edit Stops dialog follow these steps:

1. Start the Edit Stops dialog by clicking the Edit icon.
2. In the Edit Stops dialog, click the Add... button. This brings up the familiar Select Script dialog.
3. Select the object type from the Object Type: list box.

4. Select the Name: of the object containing the PowerScript within which you would like to insert the stop point.
5. Select the control or object event which has the script you are interested in.
6. Double-click the line of code where you would like to place the stop point.
7. With your left hand rub your tummy and with your right, pat your head while singing your old school song (optional).

Add stop points as often as needed. The Edit Stops dialog will let you know where all the stop points in your application are.

Pulling out all the stops

You will occasionally want to remove stop points as you finish testing or debugging certain parts of your application. You can edit the stop points by selecting them in the Edit Stops dialog. Remove them by double-clicking the line with the stop point — this causes the stop point to disappear.

Removing all the stop points at once is a simple procedure. Click the Clear All button in the Edit Stops dialog. If you run your application without stop points by clicking the green GO Flag icon, the application won't stop to let you look at variables or lines of PowerScript code.

Remember that all the stop points are automatically removed when you exit PowerBuilder. You will have to add them again when you restart PowerBuilder. ■

Running a stop sign

Disabling a stop point allows you to continue through a stop point without removing it. You may want to watch your program run without stopping to test its functionality. You can then return to a previously defined set of stops by enabling them again.

To disable a stop point, do this:

1. Bring up the Edit Stops dialog by clicking the Edit icon.
2. Click the Disable button.
3. Select a stop point from the list by clicking on it. This will highlight the stop point reference in the list.
4. Click the Disable button. Notice that the lowercase letter that precedes the object name in the stop point reference changes to the letter d.

The small red stop signs in the PowerScript code change to gray when the stop point is disabled. Debug ignores all disabled stop points until they are enabled again.

Miracle cures for disabled stop points

You have seen why you might want to disable a stop point. Normally, this is a temporary condition. You will probably want to enable the stop point again. Enabling a stop point that has been disabled is very similar to disabling it. Follow these steps:

1. Bring up the Edit Stops dialog by clicking the Edit Stops icon.
2. In the list that appears, find the disabled stop that you want to re-enable. It will start with the letter d.
3. Highlight the disabled stop point by clicking on it with the left mouse button.
4. Click the Enable button. Notice that the first letter now becomes the letter e.

Any gray, disabled stop points that have been enabled return to their original red stop sign appearance. Debug will again stop your application at these points.

Watch Me

Watching your PowerScript code scroll by as your application runs may give you a thrill; it may even help you see that the program is branching where it should. Most of the time this isn't enough.

Debug allows you to single out certain variables and to watch their values in a special window. The variables that you designate to watch in this window are known as *watch variables*.

There is nothing special about watch variables except that watching them, printing their values, and dealing with these specific variables becomes easier. In a typical application, the number of variables can become huge and hard to deal with. A value that you may need to see change as the application runs may be hard to find. Setting it as a watch variable makes sure that you don't miss it.

It's a good idea to set watch variables when you are comparing more than one value, or when one value is dependent on the other. Seeing them next to one another makes this comparison easier.

The first thing you need to do to use a watch variable is to open the Variable window. Do this by clicking the VAR icon on the toolbar. The Debug window splits to allow room for the Variable window to appear. This is the window where you can view all of the application's variables and their values.

The second thing you need to do is open the Watch window. This is the area where you can view the watch variables and their values. Click the first Watch icon (the one without any plus or minus signs). The Debug window will now be split into thirds, allowing room for the Watch window.

All the Debug windows are now open and ready to accept the new watch variable. Find the variable you want to watch in the Variable window.

Some rows in the Variable window have a plus sign (+) next to them. A plus sign means that the row can expand to display several variables. Double-click on the row to expand it. Double-click on the row again to collapse it.

If you are looking for Instance variables, expand the row labeled Global Variables. Find the object that contains the instance variable, and expand the object to see the values in these variables.

Select the variable by clicking on it, highlighting it. Then click the Add Watch icon. (This is the watch with the small plus sign next to it.) The variable appears in the Watch window with any value it may have at the time.

To remove a watch variable, highlight it in the Watch window and click the Remove Watch icon (the watch with the minus signs next to it).

When you are involved in testing, one of the best things about watch variables is the ability to print their values. You can then verify that the values are correct, validating your program routines. Print them by selecting Print Watch from the Debug menu.

Sneaking in a Few Changes

A very excellent thing you can do with Debug is change the values in the variables while the program is running. This allows you to find out how your program behaves when values are changed.

Change variable values in Debug by following these easy steps:

1. Open the Variables window by clicking the VAR icon. If the Variables window is already open, clicking the VAR icon will make it go away — not a good thing to do at this time.
2. Find the variable whose value you wish to modify.
3. Double-click the variable name, opening the Modify Variable window.
4. Change the value and click the OK button.

When you continue running your application, the variable will be set to the new value.

Summary

Debug will help you find problems in your program, or verify that it is working correctly. However you use it, this tool's ability to show you program flow and the value of variables is invaluable. Don't work blind. Use this tool, and use it often.

Chapter 19

Creating the Executable Program File

In This Chapter

- Building an executable
- Freeing your application from the PowerBuilder development environment
- Using dynamic libraries and resource files
- Distributing your application to others

Until now, you've been running your application in the PowerBuilder *development environment*. Now you're ready to build an executable file so that your application can be run without PowerBuilder.

It's All in the Wrist

Creating an executable program is probably not the last step in your development process. Developers begin creating executables as soon as they have enough of an application to run by itself. Even with many ways to customize the executable file (which we will cover throughout this chapter), creating an executable program is easy.

To begin with, you create an executable program using the Application Painter.

To build an executable for your application, do the following:

1. Start the Application Painter.
2. Select Create Executable... from the File menu. The Select Executable File dialog will pop up.

3. In the Executable File dialog, either select a file name from the list or enter a new one in the File Name: box. Make sure the executable will be saved in the correct directory or folder by referring to the list at the right side of the window.
4. Click the OK button; the Create Executable dialog appears.
5. Check the executable file name and path. If you need to change it you can either type in the correct path and name or click the Change... button and use the Select Executable File dialog again.
6. Click the OK button and the executable file will be created.

These steps create an executable file. There are a few important things you have to know before you can run down the hall with your executable file screaming, "It's done! It's done!"

Getting rid of the training wheels

Before your application can talk to the database, it needs a *way* to talk to the database. PowerBuilder allows you to create a transaction object that has several parameters to take care of database communications. The default transaction object is known as SQLCA. This transaction object has to be populated with certain communication parameters before it can communicate properly with the database. These are listed in Table 19-1.

Table 19-1: Transaction object attributes

SQLCA Parameter	*Description*
SQLCA.DBMS	PowerBuilder vendor identifier
SQLCA.Database	Name of your database
SQLCA.LogId	Name of the user who will log in to the database server
SQLCA.LogPass	Password used to log in to the database server
SQLCA.ServerName	Name of the server on which the database resides
SQLCA.UserId	Name or ID of the user who will connect to the database
SQLCA.DBPass	Password used to connect to the database
SQLCA.DBPARM	Parameters passed to the database,

These values must be set within your application. A good place to set them is in the Open event of the application object. You can choose to hard-code these values in the Open event or use an initiation (.INI) file.

Using an .INI file allows you to customize your executable program for each user without having to create a separate executable file for each user. This is the recommended way of setting these attributes. ■

Create an .INI file by using the PowerBuilder Editor. You can start this by hitting Shift + F6. Add the Transaction object attributes listed in Table 19-1 followed by an equal sign and their associated values. Here is a sample .INI file that connects to the PowerBuilder sample database. The attributes are listed in the [sqlca] section of the file. This example also lists other optional parameters that can be defined at startup:

```
[sqlca]
dbms=ODBC
database=psdemodb.db
userid=dba
dbpass=sql
logid=
logpass=
servername=
DbParm=ConnectString='DSN=Powersoft Demo DB;UID=dba;PWD=sql'
```

.INI files are used on different platforms. Make sure that you convert the .INI file to the text format of the platform you are using. The return-linefeed at the end of each line is different for Windows, Mac, and UNIX. ■

To include these values in your application, use the ProfileString( ) function. This function reads the value from the .INI file and returns it to your application. ProfileString( ) has four parameters:

```
ProfileString(filename, section, key, default)
```

- For *filename,* use the name of the .INI file you have created for your application.
- The *section* is the group found in square brackets, such as [sqlca]. Don't include the brackets in the function.
- The *key* is the attribute name, such as userid or database.
- The *default* is the value that will be returned if the key is not found in the .INI file, or is included without a value; for example, logid, or logpass in the previous example's .INI file.

When you get ready to create your executable file, start the Application Painter and click the Script icon. In the Open event you should populate SQLCA or your transaction object. Use ProfileString( ) like this:

```
dbms=ProfileString("MyProfile.INI","sqlca","dbms","ODBC")
database=ProfileString("MyProfile.INI","sqlca","database",&
 "psdemodb.db")
userid=ProfileString("MyProfile.INI","sqlca","userid","dba")
dbpass=ProfileString("MyProfile.INI","sqlca","dbpass","sql")
logid=ProfileString("MyProfile.INI","sqlca","logid")
logpass=ProfileString("MyProfile.INI","sqlca","logpass")
servername=ProfileString("MyProfile.INI","sqlca","servername")
DbParm=ConnectString= ProfileString("MyProfile.INI","sqlca" &
 "ConnectString")
```

PowerBuilder provides this file for you. You can use a text editor to open the sqlca.scr file, modify it, and paste it into your code. Notice that instead of MyProfile.INI, as we used in the previous example, here we use PB.INI.

If you are distributing your executable program on different platforms, be careful not to hard-code path names. They will be different on each platform. Chapter 26 has more on cross-platform development. ■

Riding with no hands

Before you distribute your new executable file, you will probably want to assign an icon to your application. If you want to create a custom icon, there are many programs available that allow you to do this; or you can use one of the stock icons that PowerBuilder provides. To assign an icon to your application:

1. While in the Application Painter, select Application Icon... from the Edit menu.
2. Select an icon from either the Stock Icons: or the Icon Files: list in the Select Icon dialog that appears. You can also type the name and path in the Icon Name: box.

Your new custom icon will now be used with this application.

Big Programs Need Big Answers

There are still ways to customize this file by moving some of the application into *dynamic libraries* or *PBD files*. Dynamic libraries are PBLs that have been compiled as libraries and not included into the executable file (EXE). Some advantages of using dynamic libraries are:

- Smaller executable file sizes
- Saves development time by distributing dynamic libraries among other applications
- Saves memory and program load time

Dynamic libraries aren't loaded into memory until the program code contained in them is required by the executable program. By loading them into memory only when needed, the program saves memory and the time it takes to load the executable file is reduced. There is a slight loss in program efficiency, since the entire program is not in memory, but this is insignificant.

Using PBD files

The PowerBuilder Dynamic Library (PBD) is simple to create:

1. Start the Library Painter by clicking the Library icon in the PowerBar.
2. Select Build Dynamic Library... from the Utilities menu. The Build Dynamic Runtime Library dialog appears on the screen.
3. Enter the name of any *Resource files* that are to be used in your PBD files (see the next section to find out more about resource files) used in your application.
4. Select a library name from the list by clicking on one. Then click the OK button. This builds a dynamic library. The dialog box disappears when it is finished. To build another, start again with Step 2.

The new dynamic library will have the same name as the PBL file, except that it will have the extension PBD.

Using Resource files

When PowerBuilder builds an executable file, it looks to see if resources are referenced by the objects it is placing in the file. If it finds any, it copies the resources directly into the executable file. However, if a resource is referenced dynamically with a string variable, the only way the resource can be included in the executable is through a Resource file.

You may also want to include resources directly into a PBD file. PowerBuilder does not automatically do this. To include resources into a PBD file, you need to create a PowerBuilder Resource file.

A PowerBuilder Resource file, or PBR, is an ASCII file that contains the names of resources used in your application — BMP, ICO, CUR, and RLE files, for example. Creating a resource file includes these resources within the executable or dynamic library. This makes distributing your application simpler and more modular.

It takes PowerBuilder much longer to open a separate file for loading a resource than it does to load it directly from the executable. Including resources within the executable by means of a Resource file offers improved performance. The executable file is searched first for resources; if the resource is not found within the executable, PowerBuilder next searches the PBD file; if it still is not found, it searches the disk for a stand-alone file.

To build a Resource file, create an ASCII file with the PowerBuilder editor (press Shift + F6 to bring up the editor). Type in the names of the resources exactly as they appear in your PowerScript code. If you have included a path in your PowerScript code, you must also include the path with the filename when building a Resource file.

You can also include DataWindows in your PBR files. To use a DataWindow, you must include the name of the PBL file, like this:

VERYCOOL.PBL(MyDataWindow)

If the PBL file is not in the same volume or directory you must include a fully qualified path (depending on the platform you are using).

When you save your ASCII file, you must give it a PBR file name extension. You can then include this resource file in your executable.

While you are creating an executable file with the Create Executable dialog (Figure 19-1), you must include the resource file name by typing it in the Resource File Name: box at the bottom of this dialog.

Extra! Extra! Read All about It... PowerBuilder Program Eats Cincinnati!

Your PowerBuilder application is now a reality. A shiny new icon shows up on your desktop as evidence of a job well done. You click it just to watch your program load. You are flying free of the PowerBuilder development environment.

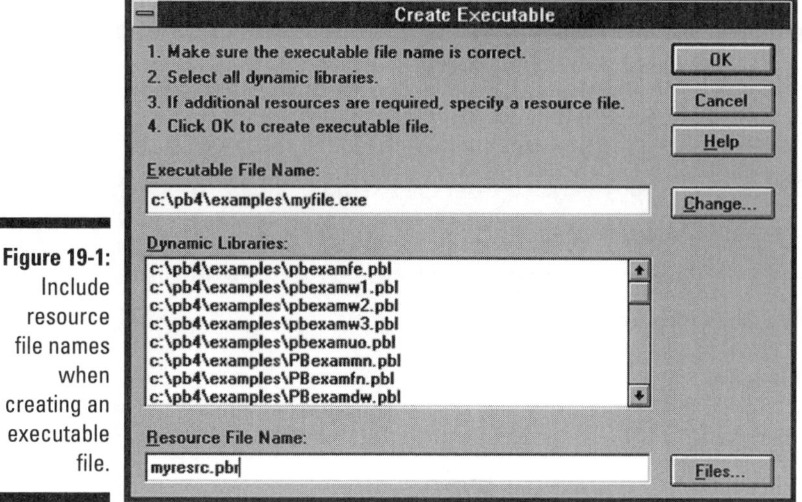

Figure 19-1: Include resource file names when creating an executable file.

You may find bugs that didn't show up in the development environment. You may have to make adjustments to path names, adjust your .INI file, tweak the database communications, or make other small adjustments to get your program running perfectly. You may decide to make the executable file larger or smaller by changing which modules are loaded into the executable and which are dynamic libraries. After building the executable a few times, you will have an application to distribute, even if it's just to the QA team for testing.

Distributing PowerBuilder executable programs

PowerBuilder applications aren't much fun if you can't share them with others. This is known as deploying your application. By the way, an application that is ready to be deployed is *not* described as being deplorable!

Your application is going to require that several files travel together:

- The executable file
- Any PBD files you've created for your application
- DLL files installed by the PowerBuilder deployment kit
- Database drivers

You can install the Deployment Kit to the user's machine from either the PowerBuilder CD-ROM or diskettes.

From CD-ROM:

1. Mount the CD-ROM and run the PowerBuilder setup program.
2. Choose the Deployment Kit from the list of installable products.
3. Select the Deployment DLLs.
4. Select the database driver required by the server your application is using.
5. Click the OK button.

From diskettes:

1. Insert Disk 1 of the Deployment diskettes into the user's diskette drive.
2. Run the PowerBuilder setup program.
3. Select the Deployment DLLs.
4. Select the database driver required by the server your application is using.
5. Click the OK button.

Sometimes you don't get all the fun of installing your application personally. If the mailman or FedEx is your application-distribution resource, you may want to use the Install Disk Builder utility included in the Advanced Developer Toolkit. This utility creates installation diskettes and a setup program for your application. This product is included with the PowerBuilder Enterprise edition. It must be purchased separately for PowerBuilder Desktop owners. ■

Packing the right files for the trip

You can refer to the *Installation and Deployment Guide* that came with PowerBuilder 4.0 for a complete list of files that must be included with your executable file. These are normally installed by the Deployment Kit. However, if you are installing your application over a network, it might be a good idea to make sure that the users obtain all the necessary files.

Now that your application is built and distributed, you get to find out how good a job you did. Don't worry, no one is perfect. You will invariably get bug reports that require you to go back and make modifications to your program. Keep good documentation of all the bugs you fix and make sure that all the users have the most current version of your program. You may consider purchasing version-control software to keep track of your application versions. Lists of compatible version-control software packages are available from PowerSoft Support.

Part VI

Doing More with PowerBuilder

"Here at MIC, leaders in OEM, it's SOP to wish a happy retirement to a great MIS like Douglas U. Hodges, or, DUH as we came to know him."

In This Part...

This part focuses on making your applications more powerful by including SQL in your PowerScript, by extending the object-oriented model, and by showing you how to create applications using an MDI interface Your applications will be more dynamic when you include SQL in your PowerScript; they can also act like virtual corporations by integrating the power of other applications.

Chapter 20

Embedded SQL

In This Chapter

- Embedding SQL in your PowerScript code
- Using embedded SQL to fill program variables
- Using cursors to select multiple rows
- Getting the results of a multi-row select

SQL, or Structured Query Language, is used to communicate from the client application to the database server program. So far, we have used DataWindows to issue the SQL commands. They have been used either to retrieve, insert, update, or delete information from a table.

This chapter shows you how to use SQL in your PowerScript without using DataWindows. This isn't to say that using DataWindows is somehow less powerful or less advanced than using SQL directly in PowerScript code; it is simply another tool. The ability to use SQL without a DataWindow allows your programs to be more flexible and efficient.

To extract information from a database into a variable using a DataWindow takes several steps:

- Set the transaction object
- Issue the retrieve function
- Get the item from the DataWindow

If there happen to be retrieval arguments, you also have to pass those to the DataWindow. The task becomes much simpler and faster if you use embedded SQL. This chapter will show you how.

Embedding SQL in Your Scripts

It doesn't matter whether you are a whiz at SQL or not; this is going to be easy. You can issue any SQL statement you want within your event scripts.

The most common types of SQL statements are Select, Update, Insert, and Delete. Other common SQL commands are the transaction SQL statements Commit and Rollback. Also, remember that SQL statements end with a semicolon. ■

The SQL Painter can be used to create the four basic SQL statements. When you have finished creating a SQL statement, you can paste the results directly into your PowerScript code.

Creating the embedded SQL statement

One of the things that makes an embedded SQL statement stand apart from the SQL used in DataWindows is that with embedded SQL, the programmer has to provide variables for the results of the query. Remember that when using DataWindows, the results of a query always have a place to go — the DataWindow. Without using a DataWindow, the results need a place to go. It's the programmer's job to provide a place for these results.

There are two basic types of query results. The first type returns selected columns in a single row from the table. The Select statement is so specific that only one row is expected as a result. For example, in the sample table named contact, there is a column called ID. This column has a unique number that identifies each contact person in the table. If you create a Select statement that queries the table for all rows in which the ID number is equal to ten, only one row will be returned.

The other possibility is that columns from several rows are returned from a query. In cases where the Select statement selects rows that aren't unique, it is possible that a query could return more than one row. For example, in the sample contact table, a Select statement could return many rows if it queries for all rows in which the last name is equal to Smith.

There are different strategies for using embedded SQL; which one to use depends on whether your Select statement is expected to return only columns from one row, or several.

Selecting a single row

When a Select statement is expected to return only one row, the first job is to create some variables for the results to end up in. An example might be in the clicked event of a button named Query.

1. Start the Script Editor in the event where you want the SQL statement to be issued. To access the PowerScript Painter in this example, double-click the control and click the Script button.
2. Create the variables as shown in the following example.

Our goal is to retrieve the first and last name from the contact table for the person whose ID number is 10. So, we will need variables for both the first and last name. The script begins by creating two string-type variables:

```
String cLName, cFname
```

The next step is to create the SQL Select statement. To make this easy, we'll use the SQL Painter:

1. Click on the SQL Painter icon (the blue SQL).
2. Click on the Select type of statement from the SQL Statement Type dialog. It is in the Non-Cursor group. This will bring up the Select Tables dialog.
3. Select the contact table from the Select Tables dialog by clicking it and then clicking on the Open button.

So far, the contact table is open in the SQL Painter. The next step is to select the first and last names where the ID is equal to 10:

4. Click on the columns first_name and last_name, which highlights them and puts their column names in the selection list across the top of the SQL Painter.
5. Click the Where tab to begin limiting the number of rows returned.
6. Click in the Column box, and from the list box that appears, select "contact"."id".
7. The Operator column has an equal sign in it by default. It's fine the way it is; so click on the Value column.
8. In the Value column, type the number 10. You will notice from the table information that the ID column is the integer type, so don't enclose the 10 in quotes.

9. Click the Into Variables icon from the toolbar or select Into Variables... from the Objects menu. The Into Variables dialog will show you a list of the columns you have selected, and allow you to put the variables you created in the Program Variable box.

   When you enter the variable names that you created to hold the results, you have to precede them with a colon. This lets PowerBuilder know that these are variable names, not column titles.

10. Enter :cFName in the Program Variable box next to the contact.first_name Selected Column. Then enter :cLName next to contact.last_name (Figure 20-1).

11. Click the OK button in the Into Variables dialog.

12. Select Return to Script Painter from the File menu. The SQL syntax will be pasted into your script.

The Select statement should look like this:

```
SELECT "contact"."first_name",
         "contact"."last_name"
    INTO :cFName,
         :cLName
    FROM "contact"
   WHERE "contact"."id" = 10   ;
```

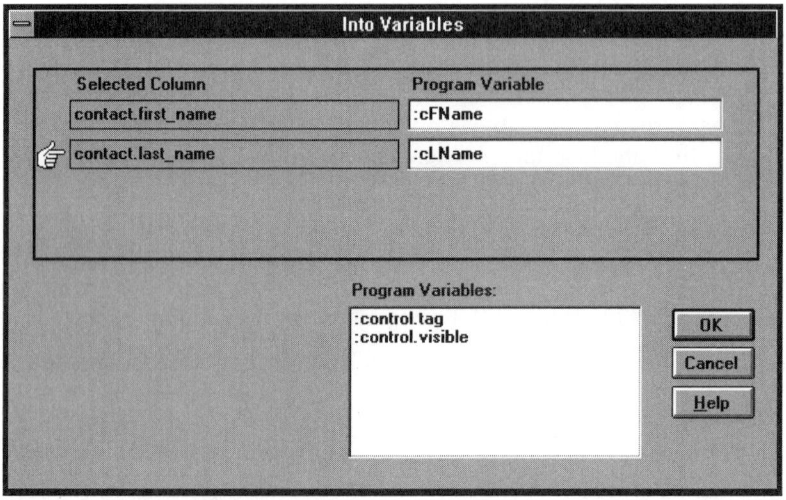

Figure 20-1: Save the results of your Select statement into Program Variables.

This Select statement is different from other Select statements you might have seen because of the Into clause. As you can see, this is where the variables you defined earlier go.

Remember to create your variables before you try to use them in your Select statement. Otherwise, you'll be gently reminded along the way that PowerBuilder doesn't know about such variables.

When this Select statement is executed, the first and last names of the selected row will be stored in your variables. You can now use them as you would any other variable. Store these values into controls for display or editing, and if you want, store them back to the database using an embedded Update command.

Setting up cursors

The term *cursor* is used to mean several things in the world of computers. It can mean:

- The blinking symbol on your screen that defines either the mouse or keyboard input position.
- A pointer to a retrieved row in a multi-row Select.
- Someone who uses swear words when referring to their computer.

The cursor used in embedded SQL contains the Select statement that will create a result set. The cursor then points to a row in the result set. It's sort of an intelligent place holder.

When you want to embed in PowerScript a Select statement that will retrieve multiple rows, you need to define a cursor. Defining a cursor is like defining certain types of variables. Wherever you can define global, shared, or instance variables, you can define a cursor.

Also like variables, cursors have scope, either global, shared, instance., or local.

To define a cursor when you are in one of the Painters, such as the Window Painter or the Menu Painter:

1. Select Declare from the menu.
2. Select either Global Variables..., Shared Variables..., or Instance Variables.... This will bring up the corresponding Declare Variables dialog.
3. In the Declare Variables dialog, you will see a Cursor icon on the right side of the dialog. Double-click this icon to start the now-familiar SQL Painter.

4. In the SQL Painter, select the tables, the columns, and criteria to create a Select statement. When you are through, click the Design icon (triangle and t-square).
5. As soon as you click the Design icon you will be prompted to enter a name. Type a name for your new cursor. Clicking OK will show the cursor you built in the Declare Variables window. Click the OK button in this window to finish saving your cursor.

Your cursor is now defined and ready to use. In some ways, it's like defining a query. You will now be able to use this cursor from your PowerScript. Where you can use it depends on the scope of the cursor — global, shared, local, or instance.

You can also declare a local variable by using the SQL Painter from the PowerScript Painter and choosing Declare in the cursor group box. This is important because many cursors are needed only momentarily, which, in that case, makes local declaration preferable. ■

You are now ready to move on to using your new cursor.

Open sez me

Issuing the *Open* command executes the Select statement that was specified when the cursor was declared. The syntax for the Open command looks like this:

```
OPEN CursorName;
```

The Select statement returns a result set that is stored in a temporary place in memory. The cursor begins pointing just before the first row. Once the cursor has been declared and opened, you need to issue another command to get the information from the result set.

Go Fetch

The command *Fetch* retrieves data from the result set held in memory. Fetch retrieves into variables one row of column values specified in the cursor. The syntax looks like this:

```
FETCH CursorName INTO Variables;
```

Fetch fills the variables that you defined with values from the result set. Because Fetch is used to get values from a result set that has more than one row, you have to process the values in the variables before you Fetch the next row.

Because you need to Fetch more than one row, Fetch is most often used in a PowerScript loop. Testing the success/failure code using the SQLCA.SQLCode attribute of the transaction object tells you if there are any more rows to be fetched. (See Table 20-1 for the success/failure codes.) Here is a PowerScript example that shows one common way to use Fetch. This can be placed in the clicked event of a CommandButton:

```
// script to declare local cursor, open cursor,
// fetch values into local variables and concatenate into a string
// until the end of the result set.
// then close the cursor and display the selected values in an mle.

String cFName, cLName, display

DECLARE mycursor CURSOR FOR
SELECT "contact"."first_name",
       "contact"."last_name"
FROM "contact"
WHERE "contact"."id" > 10
using SQLCA ;

open mycursor;
IF SQLCA.SQLCode < 0 THEN
  Messagebox("database error","open of mycursor failed")
  return
END IF

FETCH mycursor INTO :cfname, :clname;

IF SQLCA.SQLCode = 0 THEN
  DO UNTIL SQLCA.SQLCode = 100
        display = display + cfname + " " + clname + "~r~n"
     FETCH mycursor INTO :cfname, :clname;
  LOOP
END IF

close mycursor;

mle_1.text = display
```

In this example we have created two string variables to hold the results retrieved by Fetch. The integer variable iResult holds the success/failure code returned by all SQL commands.

Fetch is issued in a DO loop. If the result is zero, or success, the variables are processed (whatever you need to do with the results). Then, once iResult is not zero, the loop quits, and you know that all rows have been fetched.

Table 20-1: SQL success/failure codes as found in SQLCA.SQLCode

Result	*Description*
0	Success
100	Result set empty or end of cursor result set
-1	Error

If your SQL statement returns -1 (Error) you can use the SQLDBCode( ) or SQLErrText( ) PowerScript functions to give you an idea of what went wrong.

Summary

No matter how easy DataWindows are to use, there will be times when it makes more sense to embed SQL directly in your PowerScript code — to cut down on the number of steps it takes to fill variables with values from your tables, for example. You're now an expert at using Select Into to retrieve a single row, and at using cursors and Fetch to get multiple rows of data.

The next chapter will take you into the future of programming. It introduces the ability to share information with other applications, which will allow you to create versatile and powerful applications.

Chapter 21

Talking to Other Applications

In This Chapter

- Exchanging data between applications
- Including documents from other applications

Pretend you've just started what you hope will be a five-star restaurant. You're now interviewing prospective employees and you have three applicants for head chef — your sister-in-law's cousin Fred, who was a cook in the navy twenty-three years ago, but hasn't forgotten a thing; a guy with an unusual name, Wolfgang Puck, who says he's done this sort of thing before; and Marie, who has waited tables at the Gas and Choke Diner for years and knows more about food and indigestion than anyone you've ever met. Who do you hire?

If you hire Fred, you make the family happy. If you hire Marie, you get someone with a personal Alka Seltzer distributorship. You give them all a try and decide that Wolfgang just might be best for the job. What you'd really like is to hire all three so that you could utilize each person's unique talents.

Cooking with PowerBuilder

So what does hiring a chef have to do with PowerBuilder programming? Here's the same story with a different twist: You've just come from a planning meeting where you were in the hot seat. The department heads have decided what they want to see in the new Management Information System you are supposed to develop. Throughout the meeting you pretended to have a cold so you could cover your gasps and whimpers with your handkerchief. In short, the accounting department wants a spreadsheet, the art department wants a drawing tool, the marketing department wants a desktop-publishing system, the sales department wants a database system with ad hoc query capability, the board of directors wants graphs and reports, and the shipping department wants a drag-and-drop interface so they won't have to retrain their employees.

You ponder this impossible task while sitting in the last sunshine you expect to see for months (and not because you live in Alaska). It's July, but you call your family to wish them Happy Holidays in case you're too busy in December. Your teenage daughter starts telling you that while she was cruising the Net she found the PowerBuilder Newsgroup comp.soft-sys.powerbuilder and learned about something called OLE and DDE, which allows you to use documents from other applications right in the PowerBuilder application. It's music to your ears; you can incorporate the strengths of other applications in your PowerBuilder application. "The right tool for the right job!" you scream. Your daughter thinks you've gone nuts and hangs up. You rush to your *PowerBuilder 4.0 Programming for Dummies* book and start ripping through Chapter 21. It's a life saver; you get to spend the holidays with your family after all.

If you read this far in the chapter and you are using a Macintosh or a UNIX machine, be warned! The tools described in this chapter are generally meant to be used in a Windows environment. You can use DDE between PowerBuilder applications no matter what platform you are using, however. ■

Exchanging Glances

Don't reinvent the wheel! (Unless you improve it, of course.) ■

That's the theme of this chapter. If there are programs on the market that do the job and have the capability to exchange data, why not use them? Many Windows programs have a feature called *DDE*, or *Dynamic Data Exchange*. This is the ability to move information between two separate programs running under Windows, for example:

- Update your spreadsheet with information from your database by sending it through DDE.
- Create custom letters in your favorite word processor by sending macro commands and information from your application.

Rather than spend weeks trying to turn a DataWindow into a fully functional spreadsheet application or labor long nights attempting to make a MultiLineEdit appear like a word processor, use the real thing.

Exchanging data with other applications

Your PowerBuilder application has the ability to operate as both a *DDE client* and a *DDE server*.

- DDE clients send commands and requests for data to an external program operating as a DDE server.
- DDE servers respond to commands and provide data to an external program operating as a DDE client.

You need to consult the documentation of the external program before designing your DDE link from your application. You need to find out if the other application can act as either a DDE client, DDE server, or both. If it has DDE capability, you should be able to find information about establishing a DDE link.

Once your PowerBuilder application has established a link with the external application, they will be able to share data, execute commands remotely, and be notified of any error conditions in either application.

The client is always right

To have your application act as a DDE client, you must write the PowerScript code to establish a DDE connection to the external DDE server. There are three kinds of DDE links; please excuse the obvious "Goldilocks" reference:

- A cold link allows a single DDE request or command to be sent.
- A hot link (we just can't bring ourselves to make fun of this) allows the DDE client to be notified of any changes to data in the DDE server.
- A warm link opens a DDE channel and allows multiple command requests and data requests to be sent.

The ExecRemote( ), SetRemote( ), and GetRemote( ) functions send commands and data-exchange requests. You can use them in either cold or warm links. These are the only functions that will establish a temporary cold link. PowerBuilder's On-line Help can provide you with the syntax for these functions. Here is how they are used:

- ExecRemote( ) sends a request to a DDE server to perform a command or macro function.
- SetRemote( ) requests that a DDE server application set a cell or variable to the value passed in this function. This is an example of the client sharing data with the server.
- GetRemote( ) requests data from a DDE server.

A DDE channel does not need to be open to use these functions. However, if a warm channel is open, you must use the correct format for these functions.

To establish a warm link to a DDE server application, use the PowerScript function OpenChannel( ). Here is the syntax for the OpenChannel( ) function:

```
OpenChannel(DDEServer, TopicName, WindowHandle)
```

- *DDEServer* is the DDE name of the server application, as found in the Windows Regedit program.
- *TopicName* is either the name of the open document in the server application or "System" to send commands when there is no document open.
- *WindowHandle* is an optional parameter that specifies which window you want to act as the DDE client when more than one window is open.

You should read your Windows documentation about the Regedit program. Most Windows programs are registered with this application. DDE uses the Regedit database to map the DDE name of the application to the correct Windows application and determine if the application is DDE-capable. Be aware that Regedit is not always correct. You should become familiar with this program so that you can verify the accuracy of its database.

When a warm channel is open, you can send requests to the DDE server to perform tasks or provide data. One advantage of establishing a link is that if the server application is not running, DDE will attempt to start the application before starting the link. When you are through exchanging data, you can close the link with the CloseChannel( ) function.

A hot link should be established when the two applications share data on a regular basis. When a hot link is established, the server triggers the HotLinkAlarm event in the client whenever data in the server has changed. This signals the client that it needs to activate its GetDataDDE( ) function to get the new data, and then, using the GetDataDDEOrigin( ) function, figure out where the data came from. Your application can then acknowledge receipt of the data with the RespondRemote( ) function.

Starting and stopping a DDE hot link is done by using the StartHotLink( ) and StopHotLink( ) functions. Due to rigid health laws, EatHotLink( ) is not a valid DDE function.

Ask not what your DDE server can do for you. Or, how to make your PowerBuilder application act like a jelly donut.

Having your application act as a DDE server is like making it the victim in a game of dodgeball. Its sole purpose is to respond. For this reason, it has five different events (listed in Table 21-1) that notify it that a client program is ordering it around.

Table 21-1: DDE server events

Event	*Description*
RemoteExec	Notification that a DDE client has sent a command.
RemoteHotLinkStart	A request by a DDE client to start a hot link.
RemoteHotLinkStop	"It's over between us. End the hot link," said the DDE client.
RemoteRequest	"Could I have some more data, sir?" said the little DDE client.
RemoteSend	Notification that the DDE client sent data.

We started this section with the events instead of the functions because DDE servers tend to respond to events rather than initiate them. This is true except in the case of a hot link in which the DDE server sends data to the client that triggers the HotLinkAlarm in the client application.

Functions such as StartServerDDE( ) and StopServerDDE( ) start and stop your DDE–server-capable PowerBuilder application acting as a DDE server. There are DDE functions to get data and commands from a client:

- GetCommandDDE( ) gets the command sent by a DDE client.
- GetCommandDDEOrigin( ) figures out the origin of a command sent by a DDE client application.
- GetDataDDE( ) puts data sent by a DDE client into a string variable.
- GetDataDDEOrigin( ) determines where the data sent to the server originated.
- RespondRemote( ) lets the DDE client know that the information sent was satisfactory.
- SetDataDDE( ) sends data to the DDE client. This can happen because of a request or a change in data in the server. In a hot link, this triggers the alarm in the client.

It's a good idea to capture the return value of all the DDE functions; each returns an integer based on its success or failure. Each function has a different return value; refer to the function reference for each one. For example, the GetDataDDE( ) function returns a 1 if it was successful and a -1 if it failed due to some error. ■

Sure, the ability to exchange data using DDE is great. But wouldn't it be even better if you could use the external application's document right in your application? Use OLE and you can do just that!

Somebody Else's Documents

OLE, or Object Linking and Embedding, is a feature that allows Windows programs to share data and program functionality. OLE is a way to include documents from other applications (external application files) directly into your application, instead of just sharing data behind the scenes, as in DDE. You can actually use the external application within your PowerBuilder application to view and modify the shared document.

PowerBuilder gives your application the ability to act as an *OLE container* for documents of an *OLE server* application. Unlike its DDE capabilities, PowerBuilder applications cannot be OLE servers; but being a container application is exciting enough.

To avoid confusion, you should know that there are two versions of OLE provided by Microsoft, version 1.0 and version 2.0. For OLE in a DataWindow, which is explained later, you can use only OLE 1.0. For OLE control objects in your windows, you can use OLE 2.0, which has the added ability to create *compound documents*. These are documents that are made up of documents from multiple OLE-capable applications. ■

Using documents from other applications

A document is a file created by an OLE server application. For example, a picture created in Microsoft Paint and saved as a .BMP file is considered a document. Paint is an OLE server application. Microsoft Excel is a spreadsheet application that is also an OLE server. Excel spreadsheets can be *linked* to your PowerBuilder application, or *embedded* within it (see Figure 21-1). Documents that are linked are not actually stored with your application; only a link to the OLE document is stored. Any changes made to the document are reflected in your application. Be careful though — if a linked document is moved, the container application can no longer access the document.

This is a good reason to embed the document. Embedding stores a document with your application instead of leaving it just hanging around for anyone to move, tamper with, or erase. If you are using OLE in a DataWindow column, the data is stored in a BLOB field in a table. If you are using OLE 2.0 in a control on a window, you can link or embed the document at development time or while your application is executing.

You can use OLE embedding in a DataWindow only if your database supports BLOB (binary large object) fields. You can either refer to the documentation for your database or try to create a BLOB field in the Database Painter to find out whether or not your database can handle a BLOB. ■

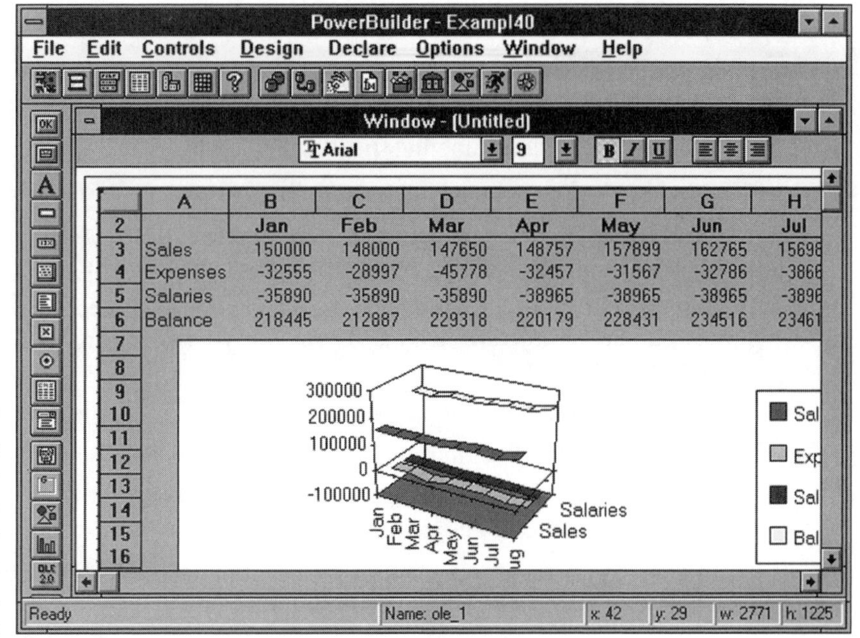

Figure 21-1: Let your PowerBuilder application Excel.

Using OLE with DataWindows

Using an OLE column in a DataWindow allows you to scroll between many different linked or embedded objects. For example, you might have employee pictures stored in BMP files. You can view their mug shots as you scroll through employee records in a DataWindow. In this case, the Windows Paint program would be the server application.

To be able to use object linking and embedding in a DataWindow, your database table must contain a BLOB column. This is where either the link or the entire document is stored. Chapter 3 has more information on setting column types in a table.

If you are creating a table to hold BLOBs:

- The table must contain at least two columns — the BLOB and a column that can be used as a key.
- The Binary column must allow Nulls so that you can have rows that do not have OLE objects.
- The actual column type depends on the DBMS you are using. The Watcom database uses the Long Binary type. ■

To create a DataWindow that has an OLE column, do the following:

1. Start the DataWindow Painter by clicking the DataWindow icon in the PowerBar.
2. Select the table containing the BLOB column as the DataSource.
3. Select the key column, but not the BLOB (it will be added later).
4. From the Objects menu, select OLE Database BLOB, then click on the DataWindow where you want the OLE object to appear; see Figure 21-2.
5. In the Database Binary/Text Large Object dialog you can enter several optional parameters, such as a name for your OLE object, client class, and client name.
6. Select the table containing the BLOB from the Table: list box.
7. Select the BLOB column from the Large Binary/Text Columns: list box.
8. You can change the Key Clause: to have PowerBuilder select which rows containing BLOBs appear in the DataWindow.
9. This step depends on whether you want to access the same file each time, or want to be able to open different files.

   If you want to access the same file, enter the name of that file in the File template: box.

   If you want to access the server application without specifying a file, select an application from the OLE Class: drop-down list box.
10. If you want the description of the current row to appear in the DataWindow title, you should enter a string expression in the ClientName Expression: box.

Your BLOB object will probably be invisible when you run your DataWindow; the OLE server won't be activated until you click on the BLOB column. To make it simple to find this column, place a graphic or DataWindow drawing object behind the BLOB object. ■

Your DataWindow is ready to run. When you run your application you will be able to insert OLE documents in the OLE column by double-clicking the column and starting the server application.

Using OLE 2.0 objects in your windows

You can place an OLE 2.0 control on your window without using a DataWindow. Here's how:

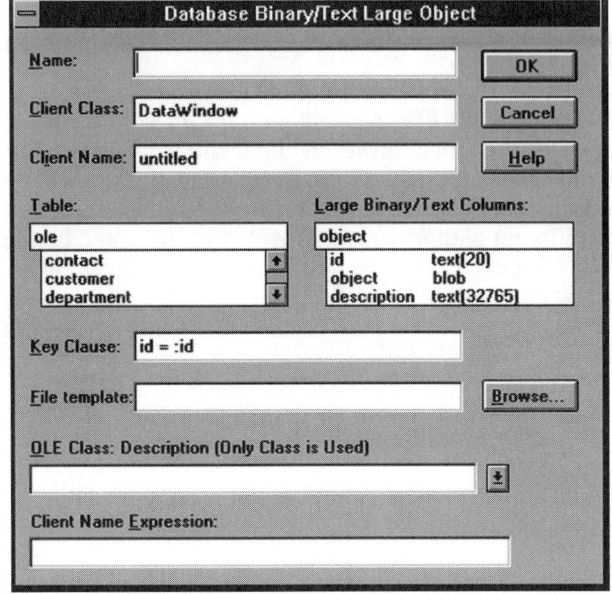

Figure 21-2: Set up your OLE column with the Database Binary/Text Large Object dialog.

1. From the Window Painter, click the OLE 2.0 icon and then place this control on your window.
2. An Insert Object dialog will immediately pop onto the screen. Specify either just the server application or a particular document you would like to appear all the time:

   To specify a server application you can select a server and file type from the Object Type: list box. The server application will start and begin creating a new file.

   To open a particular file each time, click the Create from File: radio button. Then, enter the complete path and filename of the document in the File: box. If you want to embed only a link to that file, make sure you check the Link: checkbox.
3. When you have finished defining either the server application or the document, click the OK button; your server application now becomes active. If you have specified a specific document, it begins to load.

You can specify the OLE object at a later time. To skip specifying either the server application or document, click the Cancel button. ■

4. If necessary, resize your OLE control to allow enough room to view your OLE document.

Summary

DDE and OLE features have made it possible for you to create applications that are not bound by the limits of PowerBuilder, time, or your ability. With external applications, you can build powerful applications by including programs that specialize in certain tasks like word processing or graphics creation. More and more, as applications become more open, they will communicate with each other on different platforms, in different languages, and in different operating systems. DDE and OLE are the beginning to a very exciting way of developing applications.

Chapter 22

Programming with User Objects

In This Chapter

- Creating and using new user interface controls
- Defining custom classes
- Building and destroying objects using classes (didn't the pharaohs do this in Egypt?)

There are two ways to enhance your PowerBuilder applications with User Objects:

- Build new visual objects, such as user interface controls, and use them on your windows.
- Create new non-visual objects, or *class types*, and use them to create User Objects in your PowerScript code.

Do the following to create a new User Object:

1. Click on the User Object icon in the PowerBar (the one that looks like children's building blocks).
2. When the Select User Object window appears, click on the New button.

The New User Object window appears on the screen, allowing you to choose the type of User Object to create (see Figure 22-1).

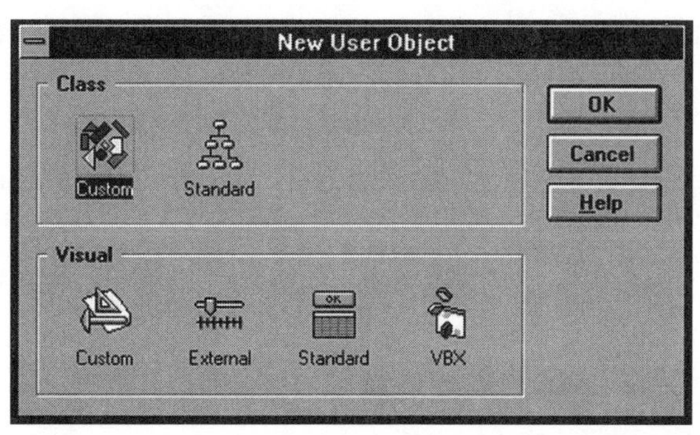

Figure 22-1: Select the type of User Object you want to create in the New User Object window.

To create a new class type, click on one of the icons in the Class box. To create a new visual object, click on one of the icons in the Visual box. When you've selected the type of User Object to create, click the OK button to continue.

Creating New Controls with User Objects

There are four types of visual User Objects:

- Custom
- External
- Standard
- VBX

They're all the same, only they're different. If you want to use an existing Visual Basic (VBX) control in your PowerBuilder application, choose the VBX type. The Select VBX Control window shown in Figure 22-2 allows you to choose a VBX control to use as a VBX User Object.

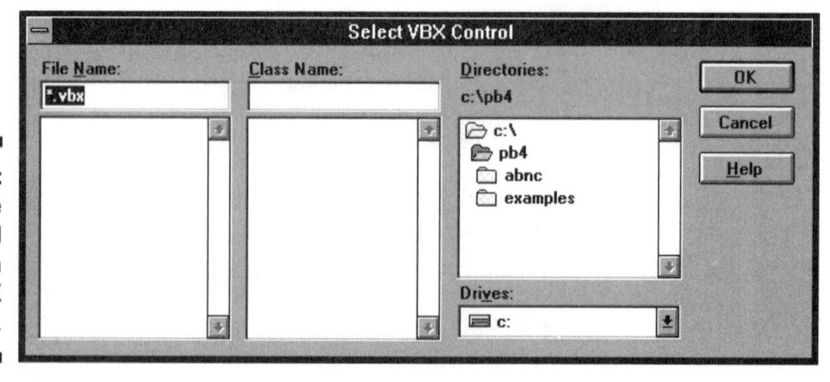

Figure 22-2: Select the VBX control to use in your VBX User Object.

To use an external control, choose the External type. The Select Custom Control DLL window shown in Figure 22-3 allows you to select the DLL containing the external control.

You can't use just any external or VBX control in your PowerBuilder application; controls created and sold by others often require a special license to use them in your programs. If you try to use a control that you don't have a license for, a message like the one shown in Figure 22-4 appears.

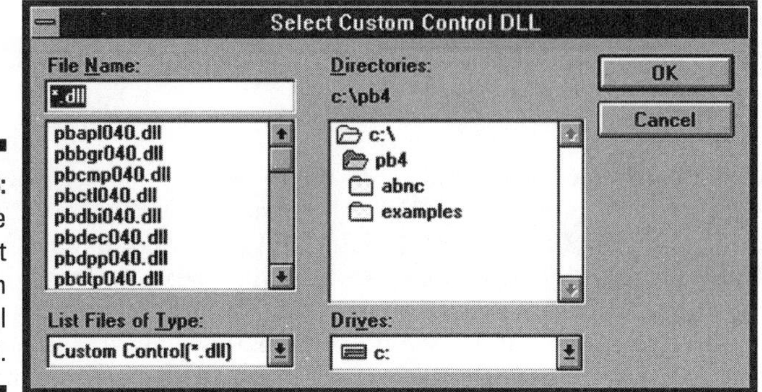

Figure 22-3: Select the DLL that contains an external control.

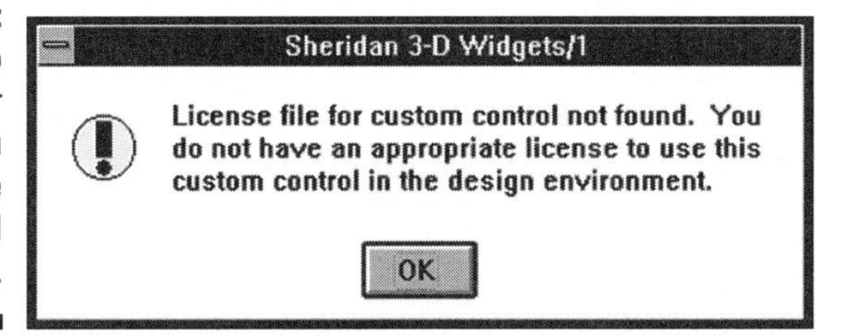

Figure 22-4: Click OK to accept your fate — you can't use unlicensed controls.

To build a User Object using a standard PowerBuilder control, choose the Standard type. The Select Standard Visual Type window shown in Figure 22-5 allows you to choose a standard PowerBuilder control for your User Object.

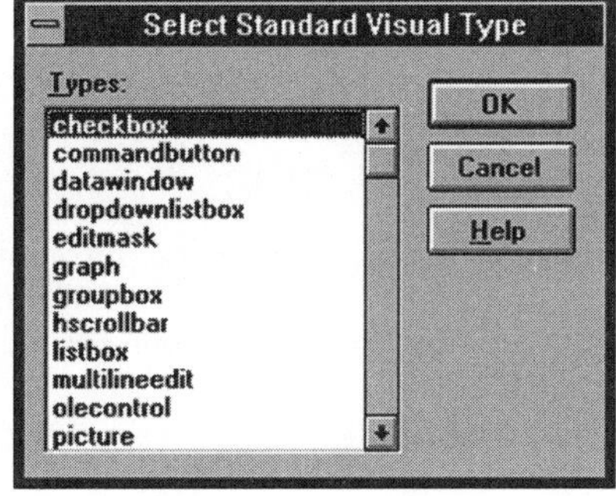

Figure 22-5: Select the standard visual object to use for your User Object.

When you create a Standard Visual User Object, you usually add event scripts, change attributes, and declare object variables and functions. For example, you might create a Standard Visual User Object using the Command-Button control and do the following:

- Change the text attribute to the word Cancel.
- Create a clicked event script containing the function call: CLOSE(parent).
- Save the new User Object as cb_cancel.

Now you have a generic Cancel button that can be used on any window. When the user clicks the Cancel button, the script CLOSE(parent) closes the window containing the Cancel button. This isn't a very complex example of a Standard Visual User Object. You may decide that creating Cancel buttons for each of your windows is simple enough that you don't want to create a User Object of this sort. That is a valid decision; however, imagine that you are creating a PowerBuilder application that has twelve windows and each window contains a Cancel CommandButton. You decide that typing the word "Cancel" and entering the event script "CLOSE(parent)" twelve times is no big deal, so you don't create a Standard Visual User Object for the Cancel buttons.

Now imagine that the users of your application start complaining about your Cancel buttons. They say that they're losing data and wasting time because they keep clicking on the Cancel button accidentally, and the window closes instantly without giving them a chance to abort. You think: "Go play a few video games. Develop some hand-eye coordination so you won't click on the Cancel button by mistake." However, you certainly can't say this to your users. So you're forced to make a change to your program; you need all twelve Cancel buttons, when clicked, to display a message box that asks users if they're really, very sure that they want to cancel. If a user clicks the No button, the window doesn't close. If you had created a Standard Visual User Object for the Cancel CommandButtons, you could simply modify the clicked event script in your User Object to look like this:

```
IF MessageBox("Cancel","Are You Sure?",StopSign!,YesNo!) = 1 THEN
     CLOSE(parent)
END IF
```

Then, each of the twelve Cancel buttons would be changed automatically and you'd be done. Since you didn't create a User Object, you have to modify each of the twelve Cancel buttons. Now *you* start complaining.

A Custom Visual User Object lets you combine many PowerBuilder controls and User Objects to create a new User Object.

Once you select the type of User Object you want to create and click on the OK button, the User Object Painter opens.The User Object Painter, shown in Figure 22-6, closely resembles the Window Painter. It also closely resembles our great-aunt Sally. In fact, the PainterBar in the User Object Painter is exactly the same as the PainterBar in the Window Painter. The PainterBar can be used only when creating Custom type User Objects. When creating User Objects of other types, the PainterBar is disabled.

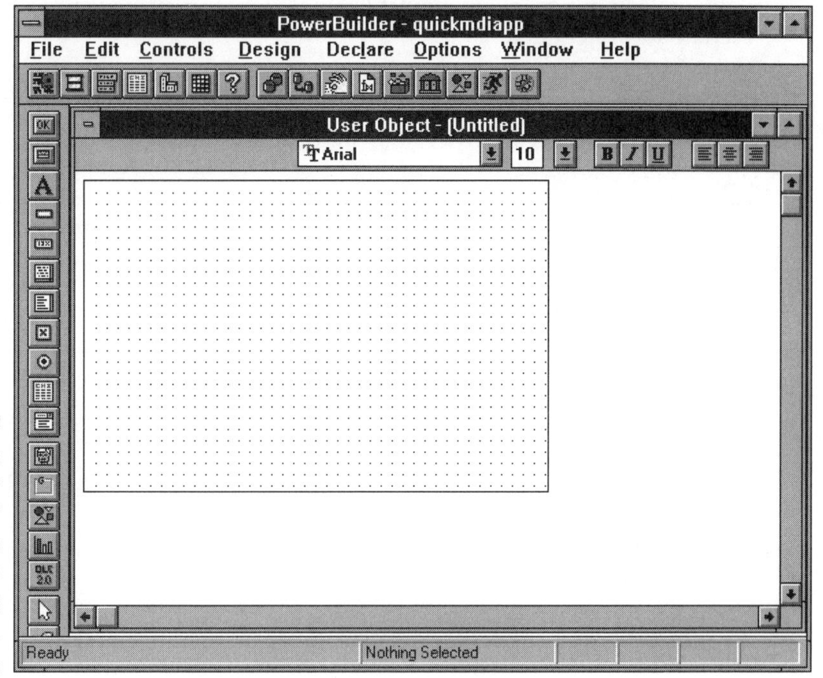

Figure 22-6: Create User Objects of all types using the User Object Painter.

When you create a VBX, External, or Standard type Visual User Object the User Object Painter displays the new control, allowing you to:

- Modify the control's attributes, just as you do in the Window Painter (click with the right mouse button and choose the attribute to modify, or double-click to open the Name... window)
- Modify event scripts for the control, just as you do in the Window Painter (click with the right mouse button and choose Script... or double-click then click on the Script button)
- Declare shared or instance variables, User Object functions, or User Object structures by choosing from the Declare menu, as you do when declaring these things in a window.

Building Custom Visual User Objects in the User Object Painter

Create Custom Visual User Objects exactly the same way that you create a window. Two things you will most likely do when creating a new Custom Visual User Object are:

- Add controls to the Custom Visual User Object using the PainterBar.
- Add PowerScript to the events in the controls.

Think of a Custom Visual User Object as a window that is used like a control. You might create a Custom Visual User Object that contains several related controls. For example, a DataWindow control often needs CommandButtons to do things like add rows, perform a Retrieve( ) to fill the DataWindow control with data, or perform an Update( ) to send data back to the database. A Custom Visual User Object is perfect in these situations because it allows you to treat the DataWindow control and its associated CommandButtons as a single unit. Do the following to create this type of User Object:

1. Click on the User Object Painter in the PowerBar.
2. Click on the New button to create a new User Object.
3. Click on the Custom icon in the Visual section of the New User Object window.
4. Click on the OK button.
5. Click on the DataWindow icon in the User Object PainterBar; then click on the User Object to add a DataWindow control.
6. Double-click on the DataWindow control and choose a DataWindow definition to attach, then click OK. Change the Name: field to dw_test and click OK. If you want the DataWindow control to perform a Retrieve( ) as soon as it appears on the screen, add the following code to the constructor event script:

   ```
   SetTransObject(sqlca)
   Retrieve( )
   ```

7. Now click on the CommandButton icon and place a few buttons on the User Object. Modify the Text attribute and clicked event script for each CommandButton. For example, set the Text attribute in one of the CommandButtons to Add Row and place the following script in the clicked event:

   ```
   dw_test.InsertRow(0)
   ```

8. Choose Save from the File menu when you're done creating the User Object. Give the User Object a name and add some comments in the Comments: section so you'll remember what this User Object does.

When you place this Custom Visual User Object on a window or on another Custom Visual User Object, it will provide both the DataWindow control and its associated CommandButtons in one fell swoop.

Placing a Visual User Object on a window or Custom User Object

To place a Visual User Object on a window or on a Custom Visual User Object, click on the User Object icon in the PainterBar. Next, select the User Object from the Select User Object window, as shown in Figure 22-7.

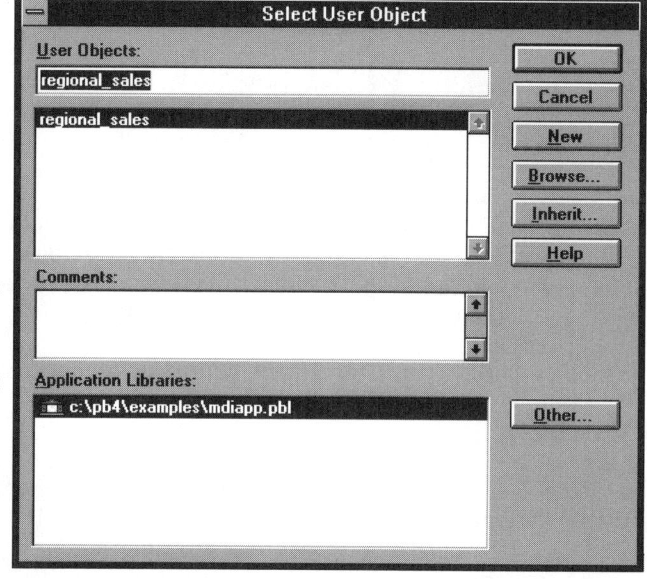

Figure 22-7: Select the User Object to place from the Select User Object window.

Now click on the window or Custom User Object in the location you want a Visual User Object to appear.

Creating User Objects that Can't See

Non-Visual User Objects are used only in PowerScript code. They don't have a visual component, so you can't place them in windows or on Custom Visual User Objects. Non-Visual User Objects are also known as *classes*. There are two types of Class User Objects:

- Standard
- Custom

Standard Class User Objects are created from one of PowerBuilder's built-in class types. When you create a new Standard Class User Object, the window shown in Figure 22-8 allows you to choose a standard class type for your new User Object.

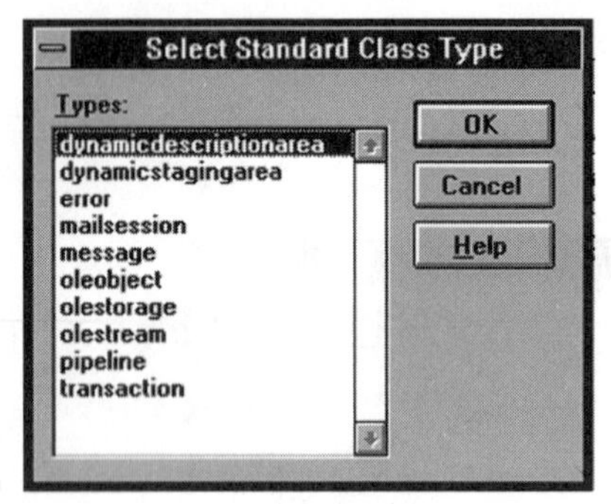

Figure 22-8: Select a standard class type for your User Object.

When you create a Standard Class User Object, your User Object begins with all of the abilities built into the class you select. Instance variables, User Object structures and functions, and event scripts that you create are all added to the class to create your Standard Class User Object.

When you create a Custom Class User Object, your User Object starts from nothing. You have to give it variables, structures, functions, and scripts in order for it to be useful.

Custom Non-Visual User Objects are the most important component in an object-based application. Teaching object-based or object-oriented development is beyond the scope of this book, but here are a few hints:

- Custom Non-Visual User Objects allow you to create new classes, which can be used from anywhere within your PowerBuilder application.
- You can create instance variables for your new classes using any class type in PowerBuilder, including DataWindows, windows, and other custom classes.
- Use the CREATE and DESTROY commands to create and destroy instances of class types.
- Buy and read a book on Object-Oriented Analysis and Design.

- Even if you have no idea what this means right now — never, ever, ever violate the principles of encapsulation in your PowerBuilder application if you can possibly help it; find a way even if it means a little more coding. (Doesn't this make you hunger for our next, more advanced book on PowerBuilder?) ■

Using Non-Visual User Objects in PowerScript code

To use a Non-Visual User Object in PowerScript code, you must first declare a variable for the object. For example, if your Non-Visual User Object is named EmployeeClass, use the following to declare an EmployeeClass variable:

```
EmployeeClass VariableName
```

where *VariableName* is the name of the variable to create.

Next, use the CREATE command to create a new Non-Visual User Object, and store the new User Object in *VariableName*, like this:

```
VariableName = CREATE EmployeeClass
```

Now *VariableName* contains a Non-Visual User Object. To call functions in the User Object, use the following syntax:

```
VariableName.FunctionName()
```

where *FunctionName* is the name of the User Object function you want to call.

Destroying Non-Visual User Objects

Once a Non-Visual User Object has been created with the CREATE command, it will stick around taking up memory until it's destroyed. To destroy a Non-Visual User Object, use the DESTROY command along with the name of the variable in which you created the User Object. For example:

```
DESTROY VariableName
```

User Objects represent a very powerful and flexible approach to designing the pieces of your application. While Non-Visual User Objects are a bit advanced, normal Visual User Objects are useful in most applications.

Summary

User Objects greatly enhance your ability to program effectively. Almost every PowerBuilder application benefits from the use of User Objects. When deciding whether or not to use User Objects in your application, consider the possibility that changes may be required in the future. It's always easier to change a User Object than it is to change many individual objects. The PowerBuilder User Object is one of the best implementations of object-oriented principles available in an application-development tool; avoid using them at your own risk.

"YOU KNOW THAT GUY WHO BOUGHT ALL THAT SOFTWARE? HIS CHECK HAS A WARRANTY THAT SAYS IT'S TENDERED AS IS AND HAS NO FITNESS FOR ANY PARTICULAR PURPOSE INCLUDING, BUT NOT LIMITED TO, CASHING."

Chapter 23

Creating MDI Applications

In This Chapter

- Letting PowerBuilder lay the foundation for your MDI application
- Using menus in an MDI application
- Giving help in case your users haven't got a clue

Multiple Document Interface, or MDI for short, is an application style in which multiple document windows, called *sheets*, can be opened within an *MDI Frame*. Often, the sheets in an MDI Frame are similar, as in a spreadsheet application or a word processor where the user can work with many documents at once. There are several benefits to MDI-style applications, as the following sections illustrate.

A Quick MDI Application

There are two ways to create an MDI application using PowerBuilder:

- Create the application from scratch.
- Build on a PowerBuilder MDI application template.

To learn MDI application development, build your first few MDI applications using an MDI application template. An MDI application template contains the basic windows, menus, and scripts required in most MDI applications. To create an MDI application template, do the following:

1. Start the Application Painter.
2. Choose New... from the File menu to create a new PowerBuilder application.

3. Select an application library, and give the new application a name using the dialog boxes that appear on the screen.
4. When asked if you would like PowerBuilder to generate an Application template, click Yes.

PowerBuilder generates an MDI application template and displays it in the Application Painter (see Figure 23-1).

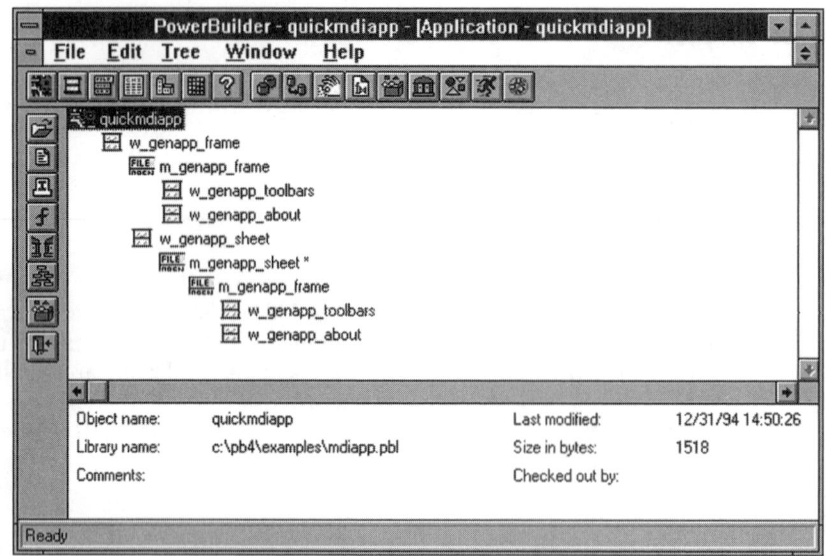

Figure 23-1: Use the Application Painter to generate an MDI application template.

Now run the application to see what PowerBuilder did for you. Click on the Run icon in the PowerBar or choose Run from the File menu. A fully functional, though useless, MDI application appears on the screen, as shown in Figure 23-2.

The window titled Frame is an *MDI Frame* window. In MDI applications, each document opens within an MDI Frame. The MDI Frame has a *client area*, which is like the stage for a play, where documents are displayed and managed. Look for the window named w_genapp_frame in Figure 23-1; this is the MDI Frame window you now see on the screen.

The window titled Sheet:1 is a document within the MDI Frame. Documents within an MDI Frame are called *sheets*. Think of them as sheets of writing paper. Just as you can write on only one sheet of paper at a time, only one MDI sheet can be the *active sheet*. In Figure 23-2, the sheet titled Sheet:1 is the active sheet. It was created from the window named w_genapp_sheet, which you saw in Figure 23-1.

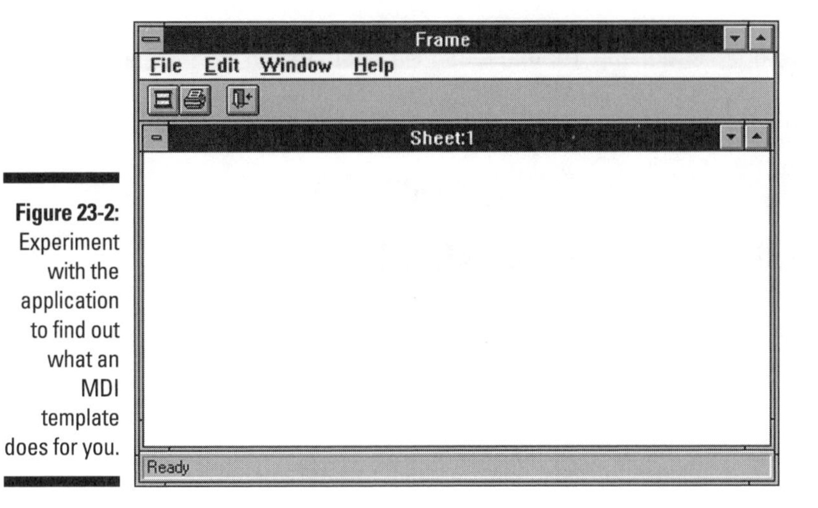

Figure 23-2: Experiment with the application to find out what an MDI template does for you.

Each sheet can have its own menu. The MDI Frame window displays the menu for the active sheet. If the active sheet doesn't have a menu, the MDI Frame window displays its own menu. The menu displayed on the MDI Frame in Figure 23-2 is the menu for Sheet:1, m_genapp_sheet. An MDI Frame window can also display a toolbar; on this sheet's toolbar there are three icons — one to create a new sheet, one to print, and one to exit the application.

To see what happens when multiple sheets are open, choose New from the File menu to open a new sheet. The menu stays the same because both sheets use the same menu, m_genapp_sheet. Notice that Sheet:2 appears on top of Sheet:1; this is the *layered* sheet display. To see both sheets at once, choose Cascade from the Window menu. Your screen now looks like Figure 23-3 as the MDI Frame window cascades Sheet:1 and Sheet:2. You can also tile the sheets by choosing Tile Vertical or Tile Horizontal from the Window menu.

To switch between open sheets, choose from the list of sheets in the Window menu. This list is automatically updated each time a new sheet is created. You can also click on a sheet to make it the active sheet. Click on Sheet:1 now to make it the active sheet. Now choose Close from the File menu. Sheet:1 closes because it was the active sheet when close was selected.

Choose Close again to close Sheet:2. Now your screen shows an empty MDI Frame window. Notice that the menu has changed. The MDI Frame is no longer displaying the menu for a sheet; there aren't any sheets left! Instead, the MDI Frame's own menu, m_genapp_frame, is displayed.

An MDI application isn't limited to displaying sheets. Popup windows and response windows can also be part of an MDI application. There are two response windows in this quick MDI application — w_genapp_about and w_genapp_toolbars. To open w_genapp_about, choose About... from the Help menu. To open w_genapp_toolbars, choose Toolbars... from the File menu.

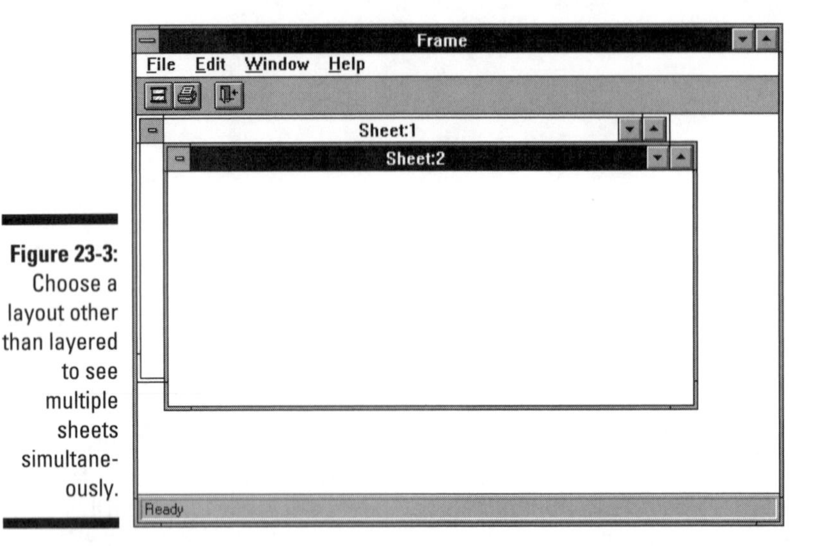

Figure 23-3: Choose a layout other than layered to see multiple sheets simultaneously.

You may have noticed that messages appear in a special message bar at the bottom of the MDI Frame window. This message bar is called *MicroHelp*. It's called MicroHelp because of its size. Coincidentally, a poorly written MicroHelp message is little help, too; and that was a *microjoke*.

When you're done perusing this MDI application, click on the Exit icon. This takes you back to the Application Painter in PowerBuilder.

Who framed Roger Rabbit?

The MDI Frame window did, of course! To find out how a frame works, open w_genapp_frame in the Window Painter.

To open the Window Painter for w_genapp_frame from the Application Painter, click on the window's name and then choose Go To Painter from the Tree menu. ■

This MDI Frame window is an MDI Frame with MicroHelp window style. To see the settings, double-click on the window.

Opening and closing sheets in the MDI Frame window is accomplished through the use of window functions on the MDI Frame. Choose Window Functions... from the Declare menu to access these functions. Two of the window functions, wf_newsheet and wf_closesheet, handle opening and closing sheets.

The wf_closesheet function contains the following code to close the active sheet:

```
window   lw_Sheet

     /* Close active sheet */
     lw_Sheet = this.GetActiveSheet ()
     if IsValid (lw_Sheet) then
          Close (lw_Sheet)
     end if
```

The first line in this function creates a reference variable of type window, called lw_Sheet. Next, lw_Sheet is set to reference the active sheet using GetActiveSheet( ) to return the active sheet in the MDI Frame.

The empty window object lw_Sheet isn't truly a window object. It's a *pointer* to a window object. Before it can be used as a window object, it must point to a real window object. Setting lw_Sheet equal to the return value of GetActive-Sheet( ) accomplishes this.

Next, lw_Sheet is tested with the IsValid( ) function to make sure it's a valid window object. If there's no active sheet when GetActiveSheet( ) is used, it returns an invalid value. If lw_Sheet is a valid sheet, then the Close( ) function is used to close it.

The wf_newsheet function contains the following code to create a new sheet in the MDI Frame:

```
w_genapp_sheet lw_Sheet

     /* Enable printing */
     wf_enableprint (true)

     /* Open a new instance of a sheet */
     return OpenSheet (lw_Sheet, this, 3, layered!)
```

The first line in this function creates a reference variable of type w_genapp_sheet, called lw_Sheet.

This is different from the first line in the wf_closesheet function, in which an empty window object is created. Remember that the sheets in this MDI application are all w_genapp_sheet windows. This means that the function Get-ActiveSheet( ) returns a w_genapp_sheet window when it's used in the wf_closesheet function. Why can the w_genapp_sheet window returned by

GetActiveSheet( ) be stored in the empty window object lw_Sheet? The answer is that it can't be; not entirely, at least.

The w_genapp_sheet window definition builds on the basic window definition. This means that the *window* and *w_genapp_sheet* window types have something in common; they both have all of the attributes and abilities built into a window object. Since w_genapp_sheet windows perform the same close operation as normal windows, an object of either type can be used when sending a close instruction to a w_genapp_sheet window. ■

Next, the MDI Frame window function wf_enableprint is called to enable the Print menu option. Finally, a new sheet is opened and the function is completed with the following:

```
return OpenSheet (lw_Sheet, this, 3, layered!)
```

Four parameters are passed to the OpenSheet( ) function:

- *lw_Sheet* is a w_genapp_sheet object, telling OpenSheet( ) to create a new sheet using the w_genapp_sheet window definition.
- *this* is a special identifier that refers to the object it's used in; in this case, the object referred to by *this* is the MDI Frame window.
- *3* is the position of the menu item to which the name of the new sheet should be appended.
- *layered!* tells OpenSheet( ) to layer the new sheet on top of any existing sheets.

The w_genapp_frame window also has several event scripts. A script in the open event creates a new sheet and a script in the enableprint event enables or disables the Print option in the menu. To close the Window Painter and return to the Application Painter, choose Close from the File menu.

Uncovering MDI sheets

Open the Window Painter for w_genapp_sheet by clicking on the window's name in the Application Painter and choosing Go To Painter from the Tree menu. The w_genapp_sheet window is very simple. There are no window functions and only two events have event scripts — open and close.

Even though almost any type of window, with the exception of the MDI Frame, can be used, it's best to use the Main Type window. Double-click on the w_genapp_sheet window to open the Window Style window. Notice that the Window Type is Main, and that the menu attached to this window is m_genapp_sheet.

That's all there is to this MDI sheet window; with any luck, more exciting things will happen in your sheets.

Creating Menus for an MDI Application

Create menus for an MDI application the same way that you do for a regular application — use the Menu Painter. The menu attached to the MDI Frame window becomes your MDI Frame menu. Access the Menu Painter for the MDI Frame menu m_genapp_frame by clicking on the menu's name in the Application Painter and choosing Go To Painter from the Tree menu.

Two menu bar options appear on the MDI Frame menu, File and Help. Click on the &New menu item in the File menu, then click on the Script icon in the PainterBar. This opens the PowerScript Painter, which shows the following code for the clicked event:

```
/* Create a new sheet */
w_genapp_frame.wf_newsheet ()
```

As you can see, this menu item calls the wf_newsheet( ) function on the MDI Frame window w_genapp_frame. Other menu items in m_genapp_frame contain similar scripts.

Adding a toolbar to an MDI application

In the m_genapp_frame menu, the New menu item contains a toolbar equivalent. The Toolbar Item: section of the Menu Painter shows a Window icon when you click on the New menu item. Click the Change... button if you want to change the Toolbar icon.

You can control whether or not a toolbar displays in your MDI application with PowerScript code. To hide the toolbar, use the following:

```
MDIFrameWindow.ToolbarVisible = FALSE
```

MDIFrameWindow is the name of your MDI Frame window, coincidentally enough. To show the toolbar again, set ToolbarVisible to TRUE instead of FALSE. ■

A toolbar appears by default in your MDI application if any of the menu items contain Toolbar Item: icons. If none of the items in a menu contain toolbar-equivalent icons, then no toolbar is displayed.

Building on the MDI Frame menu with inheritance

The menu on your MDI Frame window is often a subset of the options found in the menu on your sheets. When this is the case, it makes sense to build the MDI Frame menu first, then inherit from it when building the menu for your sheets.

To create a new menu by inheriting from an existing one, click on the Menu Painter icon in the PowerBar, then click on the Inherit... button in the Select Menu window. When the Inherit From Menu window appears, choose the menu you want to inherit from and click the OK button. A new menu is created, inherited from the one you selected, and it's displayed in the Menu Painter.

To see an example of this type of inheritance, look at the menus m_genapp_frame and m_genapp_sheet. The sheet menu, m_genapp_sheet, is inherited from the MDI Frame menu, m_genapp_frame. The Frame menu begins with two menu bar items, File and Help. The sheet menu adds two more menu items, Edit and Window.

Figure 23-2, shown a few pages back, shows the sheet menu displayed on the screen. The menu bar items begin with File, then Edit and Window, and end with Help. When you open the sheet menu in the Menu Painter, you see that the order of the menu bar items is different from what's in Figure 23-2. This is because the Shift Over\Down checkbox is checked for the Help item on the menu bar.

Menu items added in the sheet menu display in front of menu items in the Frame menu that have the Shift Over\Down checkbox checked. This makes it possible for certain menu items to remain in the same relative position in both menus, as in the case of the Help menu item, which always displays on the right side of the menu bar.

Help! I'm Stuck in an MDI Application!

Have you ever been trapped in an MDI application, 100 miles from the nearest land, almost out of food and water, radio broken, flares gone, a computer virus in your life raft, and.... No, of course you haven't. Well, if you ever find yourself in this situation, MDI MicroHelp will give you just the hint you need to save yourself.

You've already seen how MDI MicroHelp works in an application. Now you want to know how you can display messages using MicroHelp, don't you? There are two ways:

- Enter MicroHelp messages in the Menu Painter.
- Use MicroHelp PowerScript functions.

The next two sections show how to display messages using MicroHelp.

Setting MicroHelp in an MDI menu

To change the MicroHelp message displayed for a menu item, start the Menu Painter and select the menu item. Then type a message in the MDI MicroHelp: field. The message in this field displays in the MicroHelp bar.

If a toolbar icon is defined for a menu item, the message entered in the MDI MicroHelp: field is also displayed for that toolbar icon.

Setting MicroHelp with PowerScript

There's a PowerScript function that lets you change the MicroHelp message. You can use this function in any script in your application, as long as your MDI Frame window has MicroHelp. Use the following syntax:

```
MDIFrameWindow.SetMicroHelp(helptext)
```

MDIFrameWindow is the MDI Frame window with MicroHelp; the MicroHelp message to be displayed is *helptext*.

MDI applications have several advantages over normal application styles. For example, they can display toolbars, provide MicroHelp, and automatically adjust the application menu when the user changes the active sheet. Still, there's nothing wrong with non-MDI applications. If you aren't sure whether MDI makes sense for your application, you probably don't need it.

Summary

MDI applications allow you to use some of the powerful features of a windowed graphic user interface. Even though an MDI application will run a little differently on different platforms, the basic idea of opening more than one instance of the same window, sharing menus, and organizing your application within one frame window still applies. If you still aren't clear on MDI, Microsoft Word and Excel are MDI applications. You can have multiple documents or work sheets open at the same time within the application frame window; while quickly moving between the open windows, the menu changes to reflect the settings in each window.

The next chapter will give you even more power for developing applications by showing you even more about objects and how to use them.

Part VII
The Part of Tens

"OH THOSE? THEY'RE THE SEAT-CUSHION-MOUSE. BOUNCE ONCE TO ACCESS A FILE, TWICE TO FILE AWAY— KEEPS THE HANDS FREE AND THE BUTTOCKS FIRM."

In This Part...

This part of the book gives you concise explanations of many PowerBuilder programming topics. Many of the topics covered in this part will be more useful to you if you read other parts of this book first. One way or another, this part gives you a lot of valuable tips that you won't want to miss.

You'll learn creative ways to use objects in your PowerBuilder applications. The sometimes-confusing task of optimizing your application's performance is demystified. Finally, we explore the special requirements of developing applications for use on multiple platforms.

Chapter 24

Ten Ways to Use Objects in Your Applications

In This Chapter

- Implementing practical and useful aspects of object orientation in PowerBuilder
- Creatively designing your application using objects
- Considering advanced features of OLE 2.0

You've probably been subjected to endless streams of information about the benefits of object orientation. Sooner or later those streams become a flood and you're left with well-intentioned promises. By now you know the standard promises of object orientation:

- Reusable code that can be utilized in many applications
- More reliable applications that are easily debugged
- Applications designed to change and grow so that they'll never become obsolete (this is a good goal for corporate America, too!)

Turning these promises into reality can be a daunting task. There are many reasons for this, not the least of which is that ideal object orientation requires new tools and new operating systems. In most cases, these tools and operating systems either haven't yet matured or haven't yet developed momentum in the computer industry.

Until this situation changes, and PowerSoft creates the object-oriented development tool to end all object-oriented development tools, you can implement the most practical aspects of object orientation using the "object oriented" features of PowerBuilder. These features give you a way to achieve some benefits of object orientation without losing sight of the goal: to get the job done. This chapter shows you ten ways to do just that.

Use Inheritance in Your Application

Inheritance doesn't happen by accident; well, maybe it does for *some* people. Inheritance in PowerBuilder, however, must be planned in order for it to work correctly. The first step is to create an *ancestor object.*

Ancestor objects are windows, menus, or user objects that you create because you want to use multiple objects with common elements in your application. Once you create an ancestor object, you can inherit from it to create new objects. The following example illustrates the use of inheritance.

Suppose you want four windows in your application that all have the same general layout — two DataWindows, one CheckBox, and two CommandButtons. Each of the four windows performs different processing and displays different data. You want all four windows to look similar, but don't want to go through the tedious process of creating, sizing, and positioning each control in each window.

The answer is to create a single ancestor window containing the two DataWindows, one CheckBox, and two CommandButtons. Then, inherit from the ancestor window to create each of the four windows. The process of inheriting from an ancestor object is the same for each type of object:

1. Click on the icon in the PowerBar to access the Window, Menu, or User Object Painter.
2. When the Select window appears, click on the Inherit... button.
3. Choose the ancestor object to inherit from and click on the OK button.

You aren't limited to inheriting from an "official" ancestor object. You can inherit from any window, menu, or user object. The object you inherit from is considered the ancestor object. The only difference is in the way that you think about, design, and use an object. In fact, any window you may create in PowerBuilder is actually inherited from the master of all ancestor windows, the PowerBuilder window object. ■

One of the greatest things about inheritance is that any changes you make to an ancestor object are automatically reflected in objects descended from the ancestor. In the previous example, this means that if you want to change something in all four windows, you don't actually have to make the same change in all four windows. Instead, you make the change once in the ancestor window and each of the four descendants automatically changes.

Any scripts or functions present in an ancestor object will exist in an object inherited from the ancestor. The next few sections talk about the use of scripts and functions in an ancestor object.

Sometimes your ancestors really do know what they're doing

Sometimes it's useful to call the event scripts or object functions of an ancestor in a descendant. This is a little like talking to the dead. Use the following PowerScript code to call the clicked event of the ancestor:

```
call super::clicked
```

The super keyword indicates that the event script referred to is in the object's ancestor. If an object has multiple ancestors (the object is inherited from an object that is inherited from another object), you can call the clicked event in the original ancestor object using:

```
call AncestorName::clicked
```

Where *AncestorName* is the name of the original ancestor object. To call the script of an object, such as a control, in the ancestor object, use the following:

```
call AncestorName`ObjectName::clicked
```

Where *ObjectName* is the name of the object in the ancestor. The quote separating *ObjectName* and *AncestorName* is a back-quote, not a normal single quote. For example, the following calls the clicked event of a CommandButton named cb_ok in an ancestor window named w_foowin_ancestor:

```
call w_foowin_ancestor`cb_ok::clicked
```

Calling a function in the ancestor object is much simpler: Just use the function as you normally would! For example, an ancestor object function called DrinkMe( ) can be used in a descendant object with:

```
DrinkMe()
```

When an object has multiple ancestors, use the following to refer to an ancestor other than the immediate one:

```
AncestorName::FunctionName()
```

AncestorName is the name of the ancestor; *FunctionName* is the name of the function in the ancestor.

You can't call ancestor functions in this way from scripts in the objects of a descendant. This method works only in scripts for the descendant object itself. For example, it would work in the open event of a window inherited from an ancestor, but it wouldn't work in the clicked event of a Command-Button on the descendant window.

To overcome this limitation, create a new function in the descendant that calls the ancestor function. Then call the new function in the script for the CommandButton. ■

Extending ancestor event scripts in a descendant object

Extending an event script from an ancestor object means that when the event script executes in the descendant, the original ancestor event script is executed first, followed by the event script in the ancestor. In effect, this "extends" the processing of the original event script, adding whatever processing exists in the descendant's version of the same script.

By default, all of the event scripts in an ancestor object are extended in the descendant object. To verify that a script is extended, open the PowerScript Painter for the event script and click on the Compile menu. You'll see that Extend Ancestor Script is checked in the menu.

You can extend an ancestor script by executing the event script of the descendant object first, then executing the event script of the ancestor. To do this, override the event script as described in the next section, type the new event script, then add a line like the following to call the event script in the immediate ancestor object:

```
call super::open
```
■

Overriding ancestor event scripts in a descendant object

To override an ancestor's event script in the descendant, do the following:

1. Start the PowerScript Painter for the event script.
2. Choose Override Ancestor Script from the Compile menu.
3. Type the new event script.

The event script in the descendant object now executes instead of the ancestor's event script, as it would in extend mode.

Use Objects in PowerScript Code

Objects can be used in PowerScript by creating and using object variables. An object variable is created in the same way as a normal variable, but with a variable declaration. The following example creates a new window object variable called wObject:

```
window wObject
```

When you create an object variable, you build an empty storage container. To tell the storage container which object to hold, do one of the following:

- Set the object variable equal to an existing object.
- Create a new object dynamically.

There are two ways to point the object variable to an existing object. One way is to use the equal sign (=), like this:

```
ObjectVariable = ExistingObjectName
```

ExistingObjectName is the name of an existing object that matches the type of the object variable. Another way is to set the object variable equal to the return value of a PowerScript function that returns an object reference. The following example creates a new window object variable and sets it equal to the active sheet in an MDI application:

```
window wActiveSheet
wActiveSheet = wFrameWindow.GetActiveSheet()
```

Create objects dynamically in PowerScript

The other way to tell an object variable which object to point to is to create a new object dynamically in PowerScript. To create a new object, use the CREATE command, as in the following:

```
window ObjectVariable
ObjectVariable = CREATE window
```

This example creates a new window object and places it in the window object variable ObjectVariable. When a new object is created using the CREATE command, it must be removed from memory explicitly using the DESTROY command, like this:

```
DESTROY ObjectVariable
```

ObjectVariable is the object variable containing the object to be removed from memory. If you don't destroy a created object, it will stick around in memory being a bother.

Overloading object functions

When using inheritance, it's common to have two or more objects inherited from the same ancestor. When the ancestor contains object functions, it's also common for the descendant objects to perform their own special processing with these functions, extending or overriding the ancestor's functions.

When several objects like this share the same function name, it's possible to *overload* the function in your PowerScript code. Overloading means that you have written a function in your descendant with the same name as a function in the ancestor. You can write one function call, such as:

```
ObjectName.Function()
```

PowerBuilder determines at run time whether to execute the ancestor or descendant function by matching the argument list. If they are the same, PowerBuilder executes the descendant's function. To overload a function in this way, do the following:

1. Create an ancestor object that contains an object function.
2. Inherit from the ancestor object, creating as many new objects as you need.
3. Modify the function in each descendant object according to your needs.
4. Create an ancestor object variable using something like the following where *AncestorObjectName* is the name of the ancestor object and AncestorObjectVariable is the name of the object variable:

   ```
   AncestorObjectName AncestorObjectVariable
   ```

5. Store a reference to one of the descendant objects in AncestorObject-Variable.

6. Call the function using the following, where FunctionName is the name of the function:

```
AncestorObjectVariable.FunctionName()
```

This causes the appropriate descendant function to execute based on the object stored in AncestorObjectVariable. Without function overloading, you would have to create some kind of CHOOSE CASE statement containing a function call for each type of descendant object and a way to pick which CASE branch to execute. Enough about that, it's too horrible to even think about.

Create objects that perform their own database operations

One of the most interesting ways to use objects in your applications is to create objects that perform their own database operations. Just think, you don't even have to send them to medical school, and they perform their own operations! For example, you could create an employee object (most parents expect that their children will one day become employee objects) that has a function designed to retrieve data from the database for a single employee. Another function in the employee object could update the database with changes to the employee's data.

This type of object can be created using a Custom Visual or Custom Class User Object. Add User Object functions to do the database operations; add instance variables or a DataWindow object to store the employee data when it's retrieved from the database.

To use this type of object in your application, create object variables in PowerScript code using the CREATE command. To create many object variables, use an array that is dynamically resized.

OLE 2.0 Automation

OLE 2.0 allows you to do much more than simply link or embed objects from other applications in your application. You can use PowerScript to communicate directly with the OLE 2.0 server application through *OLE 2.0 Automation*.

OLE 2.0 Automation allows you to manipulate an OLE 2.0 object in your PowerBuilder application using the commands and abilities in the OLE 2.0

server application. For example, you could use OLE 2.0 Automation to write, format, and print an entire Microsoft Word document from your Power-Builder application, all using PowerScript.

For more about OLE 2.0 Automation, see *More PowerBuilder Programming for Dummies*, coming soon. The On-line Help in PowerBuilder and the documentation also provide an overview of OLE 2.0 Automation.

Summary

There are many ways to do creative things with objects in PowerBuilder. Using the techniques described in this chapter, you can take advantage of some of the practical benefits of object orientation in your PowerBuilder applications.

Chapter 25

Ten Ways to Optimize Your Applications

In This Chapter

- Making your applications work faster by writing efficient SQL
- Adding indexes to improve database retrieval speed
- Using dynamic libraries to control memory efficiency

There are many ways to make an application run faster and better. This chapter covers only ten of the many things you can do to make things a little quicker, a little more efficient, a little slicker, or a little more elegant. This is the artistry of programming. There have been many all-nighters spent tweaking an application to get it to run just a little faster; here are ten ways to get a little more sleep!

Explaining SQL

One of the options in the SQL Painter is Explain SQL. When you select this from the Objects menu, PowerBuilder evaluates the path your SQL statement takes when executed. Seeing this explained in the SQL Statement Execution Plan dialog box helps you modify your SQL code until you find the most efficient SQL syntax.

The information displayed in the SQL Statement Execution Plan dialog box depends on which DBMS you are using. Figure 25-1 shows an example using the Watcom database.

This option is especially useful when the SQL statements involve multiple tables, indexes, and complex retrieval arguments. Refer to your DBMS manual for detailed information on how to write efficient SQL code.

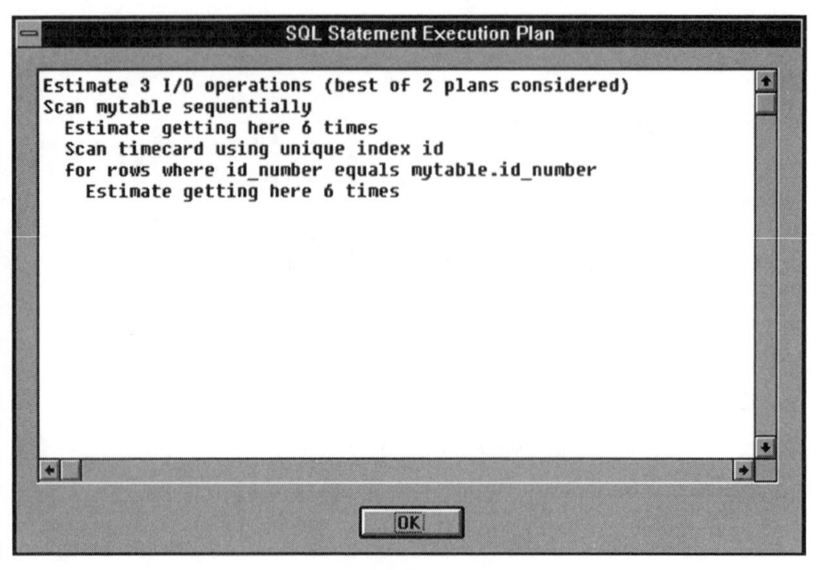
SQL Statement Execution Plan

Estimate 3 I/O operations (best of 2 plans considered)
Scan mytable sequentially
Estimate getting here 6 times
Scan timecard using unique index id
for rows where id_number equals mytable.id_number
Estimate getting here 6 times

Figure 25-1: The SQL Statement Execution Plan helps you to create more efficient SQL by showing the execution path.

What You Need Is What You Get

Sometimes when an application is running it seems like a lot of time is spent waiting for data retrieval from the database. DataWindows have a special feature that helps make short work of that problem. Selecting Retrieve Only As Needed from the Rows menu in the DataWindow Painter tells PowerBuilder to retrieve only as much information as can be displayed in the DataWindow.

As a user scrolls beyond the information currently displayed, more information is retrieved from the database. This makes scrolling a little slower, but it gives the user a much faster initial look at information in the DataWindow. Once all the rows have been retrieved, scrolling speeds up again.

The Retrieve Only As Needed feature is overridden if aggregate functions or sorting are specified in the SQL Select statement. To properly calculate aggregate functions, or to sort data, all selected rows must be retrieved first and then displayed.

There are definitely some pros and cons to using Retrieve Only As Needed mode. It's faster, but it locks the table so that others can't use it until the retrieve has been completed.

To overcome the problem of a locked database when using Retrieve Only As Needed, you can post an event to take the DataWindow out of this mode after the first screen has been retrieved and displayed. This gives the user something to look at while the retrieve finishes, which gives the appearance of speed without holding the database captive. Refer to the On-line Help for information on posting and triggering events. ■

Using Indexes

Database indexes speed access to information by an incredible amount; how much depends on the DBMS. More than any other factor, a well-indexed database can improve the speed and efficiency of your application.

PowerBuilder has the ability to add single or multi-valued indexes. Unless the DBMS documentation provides detailed information on optimizing indexes, you will have to experiment with your indexes until you find the indexing scheme that provides the best performance.

Your DBMS will decide whether to use an index during an SQL Select based on whether it believes the index will aid the query. If the index has not been designed so that the Select statement makes use of it, rows will be retrieved as though the table had no indexes.

Using Inheritance for Performance

Inheritance saves time. Don't tell that to Charles Darwin! It saves time during application development by saving you the trouble of re-creating complex objects. You can create ancestor objects and, by inheriting from them, create new objects, adding new features only as they are needed.

When you go back to an application to make modifications, you can save time and trouble by making changes in an ancestor object so that they will be reflected in all its descendants. This would be like getting a nose job and having it straighten your children's noses automatically.

Not only is inheritance a labor-saving tool, it also helps your application run more efficiently. When the application loads, only one copy of the features in the base class are loaded into memory. Objects inherited from the base class or ancestor refer to the features loaded into memory. This is like having the best kid in the class do the homework and having everybody else photocopy it. In PowerBuilder, this kind of initiative is rewarded; it's frowned upon in most other situations, though.

A performance issue to keep in mind is that the first time a window is opened, all the ancestor classes have to be loaded, slowing performance. One way around this might be to open an ancestor window invisibly when the application first starts. Another method is using the Create statement to create the window. This will keep it invisible until it is opened, and boy will it open fast.

Memory Friendly

With PowerBuilder Dynamic Libraries, PBD files, you can distribute some or all of your PowerBuilder objects rather than incorporating them into one huge executable file.

PowerBuilder Dynamic Libraries are similar to Windows DLL files. They're linked to your application only when the application is executed. This keeps the size of your executable smaller, freeing valuable computer memory.

It does take a few extra steps for PowerBuilder to call objects from a dynamic library. This slows execution down slightly, but uses memory much more efficiently in large programs. You will find that there is a good balance between performance and executable size of your application. Programs that use PBD files are more efficient for these reasons:

- Executable files are smaller; they load faster and use less memory.
- Entire PBD files are not loaded into memory; only individual objects are loaded, and only when they're needed.
- Seldom-used objects don't use valuable memory, yet are still available in the event they become needed.

Another performance tradeoff you may want to make is to include resources used in your PBD files directly in the PBD rather than in the executable. It's true that including the resource in the executable makes your program run faster, yet including the resource with the PBD in which it is used creates a self-contained PBD file that's reusable in other applications.

Remember that PowerBuilder searches for resources first in the executable file, then in PBD files, and lastly searches for external standalone resource files.

Please keep in mind that although there are many similarities between the Windows DLL files and PowerBuilder PBD files, they aren't interchangeable.

Optimizing

Using PowerBuilder's Optimize feature enables you to defragment PBLs. Most of the time you spend with this application will be in the development environment, but you need to be mindful of the running environment as well. Optimizing PBLs as you make changes to them keeps your application running fast and reduces disk-space requirements. Optimizing removes unused space in the PBL and rejoins fragmented elements, which creates a more compact file.

Optimizing does not at all affect the objects stored in them. It does not make changes to or recompile objects. It only corrects the internal fragmentation that occurs over time as you edit objects in a PBL.

It's a good idea to optimize your PBL files at least once a week during application development.

To optimize a PBL, follow these steps:

1. Start the Library Painter by clicking the Library icon in the PowerBar.
2. Select a PBL by clicking on the PBL name or its Library icon.
3. Click the Optimize icon.

Your PBL is now optimized and ready for use. This procedure is not necessary prior to creating an executable file. Optimizing provides efficiency in the development environment only.

Charting a Better Course

Organizing libraries is a way to produce greater efficiency in your application. Here are a couple of ways to organize them for better efficiency:

- Group objects that work together into the same PBL.
- Use only one PBL in small applications.
- Create PBLs that contain all of your ancestor objects.

A common way to organize objects into PBL files is to put all the window objects in one PBL, the menus and structures in the same PBL as the application object, and the DataWindows in another PBL. This works for small applications but presents a loss of efficiency in larger applications.

Another way to add efficiency to your application is that when creating an executable, you arrange library entries so that libraries with the most frequently used objects come first. Normally, in this arrangement, PBLs containing ancestor objects would come last; these objects are not referred to heavily and are therefore used infrequently.

Finding a Path to Success

System-search paths, such as your DOS, Windows, or UNIX path, can increase efficiency. Specify directories or files that will be used the most frequently early in the path. This enables your computer to find files without searching through directory after directory. You can refer to the documentation for your operating system to learn more about specifying paths and how file searches are implemented on your particular platform.

Getting Inside External Functions

PowerBuilder creates an efficient executable program. The applications run fairly quickly, but there may be times when fast isn't fast enough. If you've ever been on the way to a hospital with someone about to give birth, you know what we mean. Using external functions written in lower-level languages such as C can give your programs all the benefits of PowerBuilder along with the flexibility of running compact, efficiently written functions that are written with only one process in mind.

If you are using the C or C++ language to write your external functions, you can also purchase embedded-SQL products. You can query the database right from your external function, process your query, and return a value much more quickly than you can using PowerBuilder's SQL query ability.

Keeping It Small

Tuning your application for the greatest efficiency is normally an experimentation process in which two factors weigh in the balance. Our final suggestion for optimizing your application involves a balancing act between PowerBuilder Library size and the total number of PowerBuilder Libraries.

It's a good idea to keep the size of your PBL below 800K in size. Maintaining libraries below this size helps your application run more efficiently. And, as you saw earlier in this chapter, how information is grouped into libraries and the total number of libraries also affects performance. You will have to experiment to find the balance between these factors that gives optimum performance.

One last word about size: The executable file shouldn't exceed about 1.2 to 1.5 MB. Use the PowerBuilder Dynamic Libraries to keep the size of the executable below this range. ■

Summary

Experimentation and balancing all of the performance factors will help you develop a fast and efficient application. There are many more factors than the ones listed in this chapter. Just learning how to optimize SQL is a science all its own. This is an endeavor well worth your time. While optimizing your SQL code, you should learn how your DBMS handles indexes. Indexes and good SQL go hand-in-hand. Good application development takes patience; but you shouldn't waste that patience waiting for your program to finish processing.

Chapter 26

Ten Tips on Building Cross-Platform Applications

In This Chapter

- Preparing for cross-platform differences
- Getting your application to run on other platforms
- Planning cross-platform database connections

PowerBuilder supports development of applications on the Windows, Windows NT, Macintosh, and UNIX platforms. You can move the applications between platforms with little or no changes needed. There are a few things to watch out for, though, and this chapter gives you ten good tips.

INIs and Outees of Cross-Platform Development

.INI files, or text files used for initializing applications, are used on all the supported platforms. Be aware of the following when using them.

To Win or not to Win, but never to lose

If you are developing your application in Windows on a PC, don't refer to the WIN.INI file. This is the Windows initialization file and is not used in UNIX or on the Macintosh.

The end of the line

When using .INI files on different platforms, make sure that you convert the .INI file to the text format of the platform you are using. The return-linefeed at the end of each line is different among Windows, Mac, and UNIX.

There are utilities to move text files between DOS and UNIX and back again. These come standard with most flavors of UNIX and are available as shareware for the Windows/DOS platform. These are called:

- DOS2UNIX to move text files from DOS to UNIX format.
- UNIX2DOS to move text files from UNIX to DOS format.

The UNIX .INI file

The WindU file found in UNIX is the equivalent of WIN.INI; one is supplied with PowerBuilder for UNIX.

Staying on the Path

Path names are handled differently on all three platforms:

- In DOS/Windows, path names often begin with a drive letter, such as C:.
- In DOS/Windows, directories in the path are separated with a backslash (\).
- On the Macintosh, the drive name is a text name.
- Macintosh folder names are separated by a colon (:).
- In humans the stomachs and back ends are separated by a colon.
- In UNIX, there are no drive names; drives are tied together in the directory hierarchy.
- In UNIX, the directories are separated by a forward slash (/).

Here is an example of the difference between the .INI filename for Windows, the Mac, and UNIX.

Windows: C:\MYPROFILE.INI

Mac: Hard Disk:PowerBuilder:PROFILE.INI

UNIX: /bin/APPS/PB/WindU

When creating path names for UNIX, it is important to be aware that UNIX is case-sensitive. Notice in the previous example that some of the directory names are uppercase. If these are not typed exactly as they are found in the UNIX directory hierarchy, UNIX won't find your files. ■

Delivering the Executable

Go ahead and write your PowerBuilder application on the platform you like best. You will be able to compile and run it on all the other supported platforms. However, when it comes time to create the executable, it must be created on the platform on which you intend to deploy the application.

Move your PowerBuilder libraries to the platform where you want the application to run and build a new executable with the Application Painter.

If you're using the PowerBuilder dynamic libraries (PBDs), you can share them across platforms. Since only PowerBuilder reads these files, no changes need to be made to them as they move across different platforms.

Mapping Window Types

The Windows environment is rich with window types. If you are going to run your Windows-developed application on a Macintosh, it's a good idea to know how your windows will map to the Macintosh desktop. Table 26-1 maps Windows and Macintosh window types.

It's a good idea to contact PowerSoft's on-line support for more information on window mappings and other cross-platform anomalies. Ask them about Xwindow mappings. ■

Table 26-1: Window mappings between Windows and Macintosh

Windows	*Macintosh*
MDI Frame Window	Mac Desktop
Main or Child Window	Window
Popup window	Modeless dialog
Response window	Modal dialog

The story of MDI and the Mac desktop

Since all Macintosh windows share the master window, you can move a window outside of its parent window and the window will not be clipped at the edge of the parent window.

Don't place controls in MDI Frame windows. Controls placed there will disappear on a Macintosh because the window background on the Macintosh is invisible.

Serving Up Cross-Platform Menus

It's always a good idea to study the different application style guides for each platform. One important difference between the different platforms' environments is the Application menu.

Menus are important because users become used to looking for similar functionality in all of their programs. This has been the greatest boon to user-friendliness ever. Unfortunately, the time hasn't come for these standards to cross platforms yet. Here is one example:

The Quit menu selection on the Macintosh corresponds to the Exit menu selection in a Windows application. And although Xwindow (UNIX) applications have drop-down menus similar to the other windowing environments, to quit or exit an application in Xwindows, you normally select Quit from the application's Window Control menu found in the upper-left corner of the window. Xwindows applications do have a File menu selection, but the choice to exit the application is not found there.

Mouse button behavior for menus is very different between platforms. Normally the Macintosh mouse button and the PC's left mouse button are used to make menu selections in those environments. Xwindows makes use of both the left and right mouse buttons. The right mouse button drops a menu down, showing its selections. The left mouse button makes the selection.

Using Controls Across Platforms

Controls look and act differently on each platform; but they aren't so different that you can't prepare for those differences. Thinking ahead and taking some simple precautions will make running your application on different platforms much easier. For example, don't place controls in the bottom-right corner of a window; this is where the size box is in resizeable windows on the Macintosh. Following are some other differences to take into consideration.

The shape and size of things to come

3-D controls

3-D controls are standard in Windows and Xwindows, but not on the Macintosh. When defining control borders, accepting the default border style for PowerBuilder controls converts borders to the Macintosh default style. If you specify 3-D for your controls, they will not display correctly on the Macintosh.

Button borders

The Macintosh CommandButton border is thicker than those found on the other platforms, so you should leave more room around CommandButtons if you're going the Macintosh route. If you create your application in Windows and don't leave room for the thicker border your controls will overlap.

Tab-key behavior

Another difference among platforms is the way the Tab key behaves. In Macintosh applications, you can tab between edit controls but not to CommandButtons. Because you can't tab to them, you have to click CommandButtons with a mouse. Macintosh applications always require the use of a mouse, and therefore have no concept of focus. So for Mac applications, don't add scripts to the getfocus or losefocus events.

About using VBX controls

VBX controls, controls developed in Visual Basic, are not supported in the Macintosh and Xwindow environments.

It's a good idea to stay away from using VBX controls in your application. Developers who are used to using these controls in applications they developed in earlier versions of PowerBuilder will find that these controls don't operate the same way in version 4.0. VBX controls beyond version 1.0 are not supported, and even some 1.0 controls no longer work. It appears that support at Microsoft for VBX controls is going away in favor of a new standard.

Developing On-line Help

Table 26-2 shows the tools necessary to create and compile On-line Help on each platform.

Table 26-2: Platform-specific tools for creating on-line help

Platform	*Tool*
Windows	Any Rich Text Format editor and the Windows Help engine
Macintosh	Microsoft's cross-platform help compiler and the Mac Help engine
UNIX	Bristol Technology's HyperHelp compiler and the UNIX Help engine

Using Fonts Across Platforms

You may have to be a little more conservative in your use of fonts when developing applications that will run on more than one platform. Each windowing environment has a set of fonts developed for it. Make sure that any fonts you use map to the fonts available on other platforms.

Using Windows fonts

Windows comes with about a zillion fonts. What Windows doesn't come with, most Windows applications supply. Getting these exciting and bold fonts to map to other platforms may be a bigger chore than you want to handle. If you know your application is going to run only in the Windows environment, you can be a little more daring with your use of fonts. But if you think there is ever a chance that you may want to run this application on a Macintosh or in UNIX, be more conservative.

Fonts on a Macintosh

A good thing to know when developing applications to run on both Windows and Macintosh platforms is that Windows system fonts map to the Chicago font on the Mac.

When selecting fonts that will map to both Windows and Macintosh, try to use TrueType fonts. TrueType fonts are supported on both platforms.

UNIX and Xwindows fonts

The WindU file contains the font mappings. These sections map groups of font-name aliases to groups of font names found on almost all X servers and printers.

The WindU file supplied with the UNIX version of PowerBuilder has a set of XDISPLAY, PowerScript, and PCL font values for common Microsoft Windows font names. The default font names are:

- Arial
- Helv
- Courier New
- Times Roman
- Times New Roman
- TMS
- MS Serif
- MS Sans Serif

You can add your own font mappings to this list. Consult your PowerBuilder documentation for more help with this.

Cross-Platform Database Connectivity

The following database connectivity options are provided in the multi-platform environment:

- Sybase SQL Server
- Oracle 6.0 and 7.0, except for Windows NT, where Oracle 7 is not supported
- Watcom SQL for Windows and Macintosh, but not for UNIX

Make sure you keep checking with PowerSoft support to find out which new databases are supported across multiple platforms. Database connectivity will probably be the one thing that changes more than anything else over time.

Other Cross-Platform Thingees

- Dynamic Data Exchange (DDE) can be used across platforms only with other PowerBuilder applications. Other Macintosh and Xwindows applications are not likely to support DDE. Dynamic Data Exchange is primarily a Windows feature.
- You should either limit or not use external function calls from a DLL, as they may not behave as expected. Different platforms support these external function calls in different ways. If you are going to make external function calls, make sure you test them thoroughly on all platforms.
- Don't use the minimize feature of a window. On a Macintosh, you can't iconize a window as you can in Windows and Xwindows. PowerBuilder ignores the minimize attribute when running an application on a Macintosh.
- Don't assume a standard screen size. Design and build applications for the smallest possible screen size.
- Windows Message IDs have no meaning on other platforms. Any use of message IDs in your application will be ignored when running outside of the Windows environment.
- Macintosh and UNIX support long file names. If you intend to run your application in Windows, however, you need to use filenames that are no longer than the supported 8 characters so that they work in the DOS environment.
- Macintosh computers do not have a right mouse button. You can simulate a right–mouse-button click on a Macintosh by using Ctrl + click.

Summary

The ability to develop applications with PowerBuilder that will run on several platforms is one of the most exciting things to happen in a long time, at least since popcorn. As the Macintosh and UNIX development systems become more mature, we will see more cross-platform planning strategies than those covered in this chapter. This is truly the cutting edge. It will be up to you to keep track of what's happening by staying connected to the PowerSoft support group.

Appendix

A Look Across Platforms

The appendix gives you a look at what the PowerBuilder development environment and applications look like on the following platforms:

- Microsoft Windows
- Microsoft Windows NT
- Macintosh
- Xwindows Motif

You can refer to Chapter 26 for more information on creating applications that will run on multiple platforms.

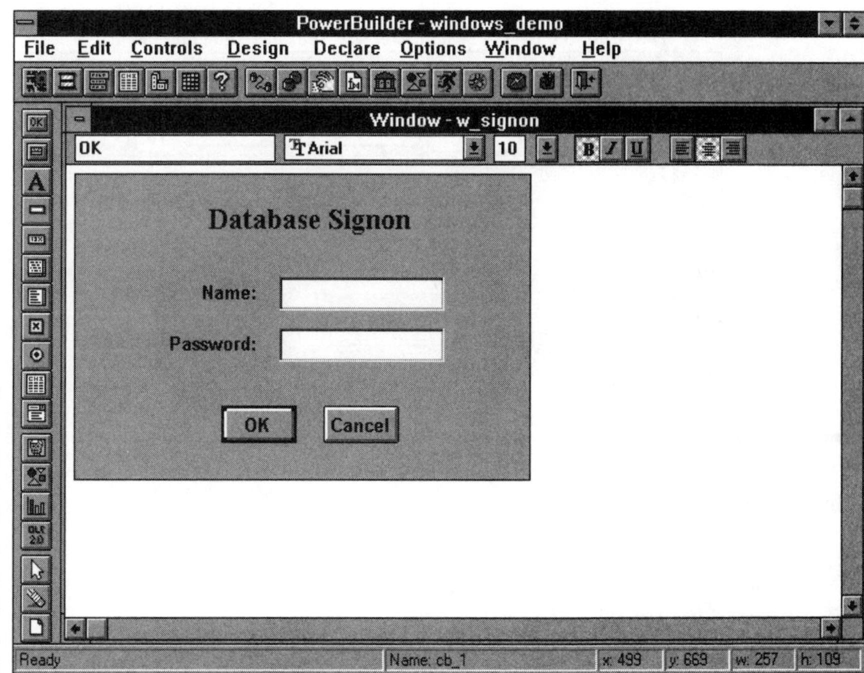

Figure A-1: This is what PowerBuilder 4.0 looks like in the Windows environment.

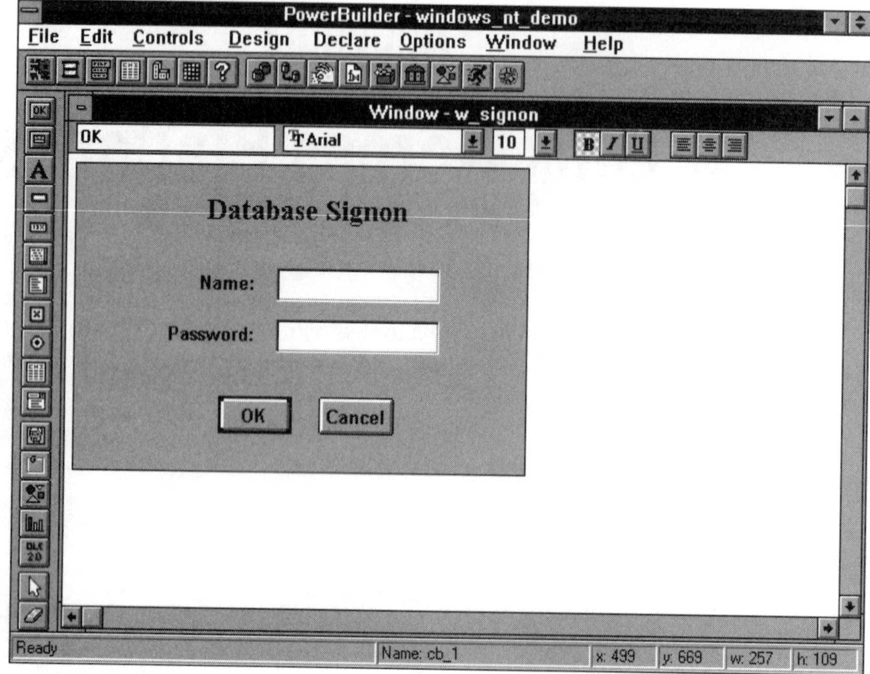

Figure A-2: This is what PowerBuilder 4.0 looks like in the Windows NT version.

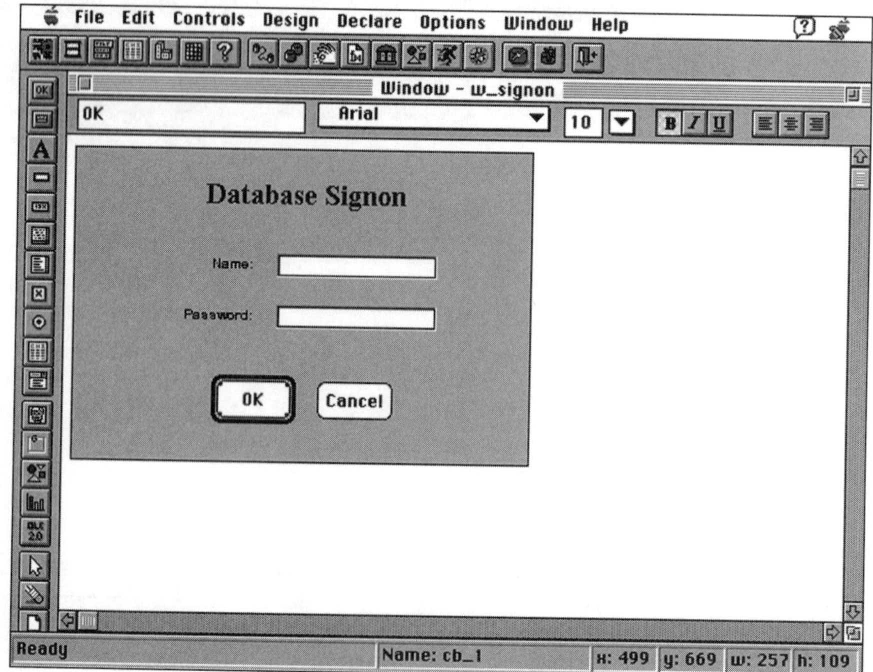

Figure A-3: This is what PowerBuilder 4.0 looks like on a Macintosh.

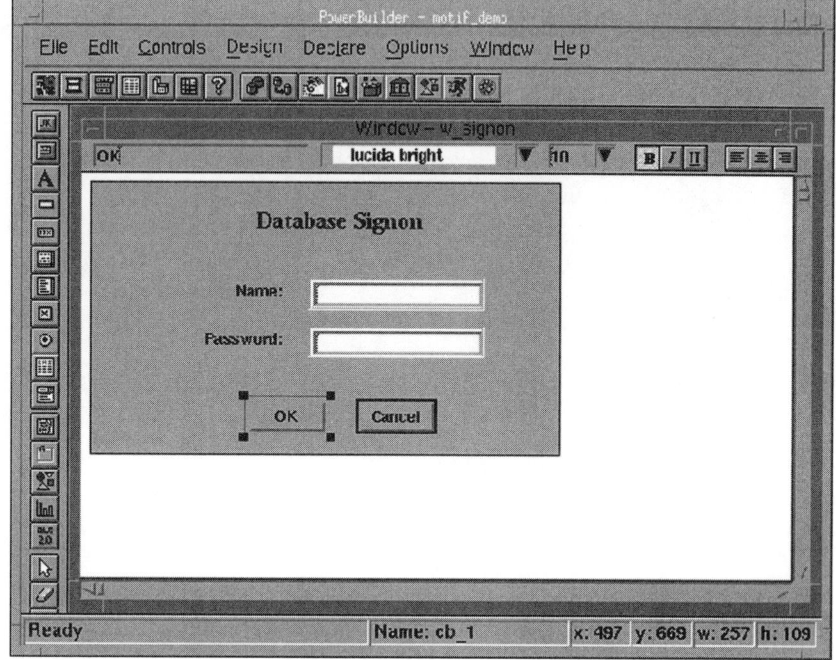

Figure A-4: This is what PowerBuilder 4.0 looks like in the Xwindows Motif environment.

Index

• E •

• F •

• G •

• H •

• I •

• J •

• K •

• L •

• M •

• N •